'Monica Hanaway sees perfectly the whole process of coa
an x-ray. She generously shares with her readers the lat
theoretical score on coaching supervision and concrete examples. The book came to me
at exactly the right time, inspiring to try new techniques in working with clients during consultations. Monica Hanaway has the talent to explain theoretically complicated notions in a comprehensive style, simultaneously keeping the highest standards of professional research.'

**Dana Rone,** *Sworn Advocate at Law, Certified Mediator,*
*Docent in Turība University, Latvia*

'I'm delighted that Monica Hanaway has followed up her *Handbook for Existential Coaching Practice* with this book aimed at supervisors. I am unaware of any other books in this field. Whilst not being didactic it gives a very clear picture of how existential coaching supervision can look. She shows this through reference to theory, practical approaches, and the use of case examples.'

**Colleen Harris,** *MVO, FRSA, MICG, Personal Brand*
*Coach, Communications Adviser, Diversity Adviser,*
*Deputy Lieutenant of Greater London, UK*

'Monica Hanaway has shown very clearly how supervision, a practice that tends to be associated with psychotherapy, works with existential coaching. I particularly liked how she compares the expectations of a psychotherapeutic supervisor and a coaching supervisor from an existential and phenomenological perspective. The readers of this book will come away with a clear understanding of existential coaching supervision, existential coaching, and existential phenomenological thinking. I see this book being of great value for experienced and less experienced supervisors of coaches and psychotherapists.'

**Diana Mitchell,** *Supervisor, Coach, Psychotherapist*

'Monica brings us closer to the supervision of coaching as a strategy that is concise and assertive, a strategy where listening, pausing, and the suspension of the judgment prevails in addressing the description of the phenomena in supervision. I appreciate the practical style Monica Hanaway has used to bring her professional life into the writing of this book. When reading it, I identified with the coach, as someone who has the challenge of live supervision to improve professional performance. Monica goes further and connects deeply with her coachee, as shown in the practical examples in the book, where paradoxes and apparent contradictions emerge, which Monica masterfully turns into sources of learning for readers. With this book, I was able to explore the rebelliousness of the existential-phenomenological approach by reading how non-directive support is given to the coachee.'

**Carlos Ignacio Gallego Soto,** *Master in Social Psychology,*
*Leadership Mentor, Business Consultant, University Adjunct*
*Associate Professor, and Associate Professor at Diálogo Existencial –*
*Existential Dialogue – Center for Studies in Existential*
*Philosophy and Phenomenology*

'Monica Hanaway has a deep understanding, knowledge, and applicability of existential tenets, in coaching and its use in supervision. Her framework in supervision is based on phenomenological investigation, that allows the supervisee to consider their work from an existential phenomenological perspective. I consider myself privileged having had the opportunity to working alongside Monica for a few years at Regents University London, where I could witness in practice, everything that she is incorporating in the present book, plus – what can be considered as essential qualities for an existential phenomenological supervisor, such as her warmth, excellent quality of listening, respect of the supervisee's silence, and her willingness to give the necessary space, in order for the work to be explored.'

**Luci Moja,** *Supervisor, Coach,*
*Psychotherapist, and Academic*

'As one of the first of its kind, this book addresses the highly pertinent issue of the place of supervision in coaching. Building on her *Handbook for Existential Coaching* the author highlights the key factors that identify an existential approach to supervision packing the book with case examples of how paradox, incertitude, and relationality can be acknowledged and held as part of the supervisory relationship.'

**John Nuttall,** *Asst. Dean and Head of School of Psychotherapy*
*and Psychology, Regent's University London, UK,*
*Certified Management Consultant*

'Existentialism offers a unique perspective, not just on coaching and supervision, but on our human experience in general. While all supervisors will be able to relate to many of the themes described in this book, Monica Hanaway once again does a superb job in linking theory to practice and placing the tangible professional challenges and dilemmas of supervision practice within a sound philosophical framework. Both novice and experienced coaching supervisors will benefit greatly from this book's concise introduction to the existential landscape and approach, its thorough exploration of how the most prominent existential thinkers can contribute to everyday issues in coaching supervision, and its practical application of the phenomenological method through the use of detailed case studies. In true existential fashion, the book grounds its existential-phenomenological approach to supervision in philosophical inquiry and sound ethics. Another important milestone on the road to anchoring coaching supervision in solid philosophical roots.'

**Yannick Jacob,** *Existential Coach (MA), Positive Psychologist (MSc),*
*Coach Trainer & Supervisor (FMR Programme Leader MSc*
*Coaching Psychology), Mediator (conflict resolution) and*
*author of* An Introduction to Existential Coaching

'It is a challenge to write a book on supervision which is consistent with the existential-phenomenological rather than a directive approach. Monica Hanaway works with the tension of acknowledging the importance of "unknowing" whilst offering clear ways to integrate the existential-phenomenological approach into supervision.'

**Mugur Mitroi,** *President of Mediation*
*Council of Romania*

'In this latest literary offering Monica Hanaway takes further critical strides to make explicit the relevance and importance of the existential approach, in this case, to the world of coaching supervision. Supervision, and especially existential supervision, remains the key personal and professional development practice for the committed coach. In this work Monica takes our understanding of existential coaching supervision from potentially some sort of mystical, dark art to a clearly articulated, accessible, and powerful practice. This is an evolution of understanding that has relevance for both newly qualified coaches and supervisors to seasoned practitioners. On a personal note, as a coaching supervisee of Monica's, I also have the privilege of being able to attest to the hugely positive impact Monica's coaching supervision has had on me over the years. She truly practises what she writes.'

**Jamie Reed,** *Team and Leadership Coach, Director of Human Leadership Ltd.*

'I value Monica's books very highly because of their intrinsic emphasis on putting theory into practice. In this book her valuable approach, concentrating on the key strengths of existentialist philosophy, including freedom of choice, agency, and responsibility, is combined with a focus on phenomenology, all of which are set in the context of coaching supervision. This latter, to me, means above all a recognition that all interactions and relationships are a process of discovery, calibration, and refinement. In this context in particular the case examples are very helpful, as is the detailed discussion of ethics and ethical codes. This useful book is therefore also highly recommended to anyone in a management role, but particularly those who supervise, motivate, and coach managers, team leaders, and supervisors.'

**Thomas Hyrkiel,** *Head of Publishing, Global Company*

'Having produced the *Handbook of Existential Coaching Practice*, Monica has filled another gap with this new and innovative book in which she provides a framework for supervisors wanting to use an existential approach in their work with coaches. Monica writes from the distinct perspective of a successful business leader, coach, mediator, psychotherapist, supervisor, lecturer. Monica passes this knowledge on in the most effective way in her new book bringing in the very special existential perspective. As someone has been supervised and trained by her, I have witnessed her expert ability to tease out the significant, introspective questions that gently challenge one to reflect upon core values or behaviours, and ways of working. I would highly recommend this book to supervisors, students, coaches, and anyone interested in knowing more about the practical use of existential ideas in coaching and supervision.'

**Marni Alexander,** *Coach and Therapist*

'Monica's extraordinary ability to listen with immense depth and creativity leads to very apposite and useful suggestions through which I can support my coaching clients. Her gift of language and expressiveness yield words of immense insight and clarity. I always learn from Monica. Her wisdom and empathy is rare and when combined with her skills and modesty makes it a privilege to have her as my supervisor. In this book she explains the theoretical basis to her existential approach to coaching supervision, following it with practical examples.'

**Sue Blum,** *Coach and Mediator*

# AN EXISTENTIAL AND PHENOMENOLOGICAL APPROACH TO COACHING SUPERVISION

As the methodology for coaching supervision has grown and developed in recent years, so too has the need for comprehensive engagement with the needs of supervisees. This ground-breaking and much-needed new book from Monica Hanaway presents a unique existential approach to coaching supervision.

This book includes an introduction to the model, with emphasis on the philosophical focus of the existential coaching approach and concepts such as uncertainty, freedom, emotions, values and beliefs, meaning, and relatedness. Hanaway offers supervisors ways of working with their supervisees on each of the key existential themes, as well as a comparison with other coaching supervision models.

This book describes how a supervisor can bring an existential approach into their work, both with existential coaches and with those working in different modalities who are interested in adding to their portfolio of service. It will be of immense value to academics and students of coaching psychology.

**Monica Hanaway** is an executive and leadership coach, business consultant, mediator, psychotherapist, and trainer. She has authored *The Existential Leader, An Existential Approach to Leadership Challenges, Handbook of Existential Coaching Practice*, and *Psychologically Informed Mediation*. She is passionate in her mission to bring existential thought beyond the academic arena into the business and wider world, believing it is an approach which has a lot to offer to these uncertain times.

# AN EXISTENTIAL AND PHENOMENOLOGICAL APPROACH TO COACHING SUPERVISION

*Monica Hanaway*

LONDON AND NEW YORK

First published 2022
by Routledge
2 Park Square, Milton Park, Abingdon, Oxon OX14 4RN

and by Routledge
605 Third Avenue, New York, NY 10158

*Routledge is an imprint of the Taylor & Francis Group, an informa business*

*British Library Cataloguing-in-Publication Data*
A catalogue record for this book is available from the British Library

*Library of Congress Cataloging-in-Publication Data*
Names: Hanaway, Monica, author.
Title: An existential and phenomenological approach
to coaching supervision/Monica Hanaway.
Description: New York: Routledge, 2021. |
Includes bibliographical references and index.
Identifiers: LCCN 2021013212 (print) |
LCCN 2021013213 (ebook) |
ISBN 9780367673369 (hardback) | ISBN 9780367673376 (paperback) |
ISBN 9781003130895 (ebook)
Subjects: LCSH: Personal coaching. | Supervision. |
Existential psychology. | Existential phenomenology.
Classification: LCC BF637.P36 H34 2021 (print) |
LCC BF637.P36 (ebook) | DDC 158.3–dc23
LC record available at https://lccn.loc.gov/2021013212
LC ebook record available at https://lccn.loc.gov/2021013213

ISBN: 978-0-367-67336-9 (hbk)
ISBN: 978-0-367-67337-6 (pbk)
ISBN: 978-1-003-13089-5 (ebk)

Typeset in Bembo
by Deanta Global Publishing Services, Chennai, India

To celebrate

the safe arrival into this uncertain world of

Orson Rex Hanaway-Oakley

8th December 2020

Welcome to the family, little guy

# CONTENTS

# ACKNOWLEDGMENTS

With thanks to my family for their encouragement during the writing of this book.

I also wish to thank those supervisees and clients who continue to inspire me with their commitment and their work, some of whom agreed to me drawing on their experience and material in this book.

# INTRODUCTION

In late 2019, Tatiana Bachkirova and David Clutterbuck invited me to contribute a chapter on existential coaching supervision for the second edition of their book, *Coaching & Mentoring Supervision* (1st edition, McGraw Hill, 2011). During my research for that chapter, it became clear that very little has been published on this approach. This isn't too surprising as coaching, although now very popular, is still a relatively new profession and there are very few coaches who describe themselves as existential coaches. Even within the wider coaching field supervision, although highly recommended, is not yet mandatory across the profession, in the way it is for psychotherapists.

In writing the Bachkirova and Clutterbuck chapter, with the limitations inherent in writing for a large edited book, I soon realised that there was so much more I would like to explore and share about bringing an existential approach to coaching supervision. Consequently, I undertook further research and began expanding the chapter for my own interest. Gradually this personal interest has grown into this book.

To set existential coaching supervision in context I believe it is necessary to start by considering what we understand by supervision through looking to the experience in those professions which aim to support, develop, and 'treat' others. The nature and style of supervision in these professions has a lot of commonality but also some key differences, including the different philosophical beliefs about the role of supervision and the differences between psychotherapy supervision and coaching supervision.

In addition to looking at individual face-to-face supervision I have included short sections on e-supervision and group supervision. The former is becoming increasingly common in Covid-restricted times and group supervision is commonly offered on training courses with many graduates choosing to continue with group supervision, often peer-led.

From the consideration of supervision in general, I move on to focus on what is understood by the existential. Some readers may already be well versed in the philosophical background to the approach and how it is currently being applied in psychotherapy, leadership development, and coaching. For others, the concepts may be new or have been restricted to an academic or literary interest. In order to understand how a supervisor may bring an existential approach into their work with a supervisee, the key themes of existentialism also need to be understood, so I devote a chapter to giving a brief overview of these themes. These existential themes include

1

the importance of relatedness, time and temporality, authenticity and trust, uncertainty, freedom and responsibility, meaning-making, values and beliefs, and the paradoxical nature of existence.

This is followed by a chapter outlining the use of phenomenological investigation, drawing on the writings of Husserl, Heidegger, and others. I explain how this practical approach can be used in coaching and coaching supervision. This includes the use of 'bracketing' as an aid to avoiding any assumptions, prejudices, or beliefs which make it more difficult for the supervisee to attend to the worldview of the client and the supervisor to attend to that of the supervisee. Once assumptions are removed then supervision can focus on the supervisee's work with their client through the use of the existential givens.

In Part Three I draw on the theoretical material introduced in Parts One and Two and set them firmly within the context of coaching supervision, exploring the challenges the approach poses for supervisor and supervisee. I outline some practical ways of using the approach.

An important aspect of the work of a supervisor is to ensure that the supervisee is acting ethically and so a separate chapter is given to looking at the ethical aspects of coaching from an existential viewpoint. This section identifies those ethical requirements which are shared between different professional coaching bodies and notes that those who provide coaching within an organisational setting may have a number of different ethical responsibilities (to client, coach, supervisor, organisation, profession body, and the world) which present the possibility of being in tension with one another. The latter part of the chapter focuses on the existential perspective on ethics which calls for consideration of the question 'why be ethical?' This is addressed via reference to a number of existential thinkers including de Beauvoir, Sartre, Kierkegaard, etc. The author returns to the existential concerns considered earlier in the book, identifying the main ethical issues contained in each.

In Part Four, I aim to describe how the approach is used in a very practical way through offering some case examples. Each example covers a small part of a coaching contract which shows particular elements of the existential approach.

The existential approach is relevant whether the supervisor is working with a coach who defines their work as existential or a coach coming from a different modality who wants to understand more about the approach and use their understanding to add to their coaching offer.

# PART ONE

- *The meaning and role of supervision in professionals concerned with the support, development, and treatment of others*
- *The current position of coaching supervision*

PART ONE

# 1

# THE MEANING AND ROLE OF SUPERVISION IN PROFESSIONALS CONCERNED WITH THE SUPPORT, DEVELOPMENT, AND TREATMENT OF OTHERS

The verb to 'supervise' has its origins in the Latin 'supervidere'. In business it is usually linked with hierarchy and it sits within a management function. The word comprises of two parts: 'super' meaning 'over' or 'from above', and 'videre' meaning 'to see'. In supervising something you are generally overseeing a project, or the people working on it; this may include assessing what needs to be done, assigning the work, and making sure it gets done to a certain standard. In business it is focused on the needs of the organisation.

Within a broader definition of its meaning its importance has long been recognised in professions that provide interpersonal support and development, such as psychotherapy, social work, psychology, and mental health services where staff can be under both personal and professional pressure. In these professions, supervision needs to straddle aspects of both the professional and personal needs of the supervisee. Although it remains focused on the professional, it recognises that the key tools for those working in these professions are the individual's psychological resources and resilience. Supervision provides a safe place to keep those tools sharp and to ensure that the correct tool is being used for the job in hand. Thus, supervision is widely accepted as being an essential aspect of ethical and effective practice and the cornerstone of continuing professional development.

Although coaching often focuses on business issues, business is made up of people, not issues or components, and each of these individuals experience deep, rich, and diverse human dilemmas which can at times become important elements in the coaching process. So, it would be strange not to refer to the thirty years' experience, debate, and analysis which have taken place in those psychological professions where supervision was adopted much earlier than in coaching. Indeed, many practising coaches are professionally trained, and practise or have practised as counsellors or psychotherapists. Even where this is the case, it is important to remain clear about the different focus and boundaries in psychotherapy and coaching. Whybrow and Palmer (2006) suggest that even non-clinical populations contain potentially vulnerable clients, and it is essential that when coaches find themselves working with such clients, they are aware of their own personal and professional limitations. This immediately flags up the potential advantage of having a supervisor who is very clear on these boundaries and who is able to signpost the supervisee to more appropriate support if this is what the client requires. The supervisee may enable the client to access such services rather than trying to substitute for them.

Despite the need to remain conscious of these different professional foci, it is necessary to provide a brief overview of the main models of supervision. I am starting with looking to psychotherapy, with its long history of requiring clinical supervision for all therapists throughout their professional careers. There are many excellent books available which provide detailed analysis of these approaches for those wanting to know more; here I aim to just provide an outline.

The practice of clinical supervision started as a form of 'apprenticeship' in which a supervisee with minimal skill and knowledge would observe, assist, and receive feedback from a more experienced professional. It was assumed that such an experienced professional would automatically make a good supervisor. Although it may be correct to assume that the relational skills held by such a person would help them in their role as supervisor, it soon became clear that a more considered approach, which included providing training opportunities for supervisors, would provide a better experience for both supervisee and supervisor. Indeed, Falender and Shafranske (2004) noted that clinical knowledge and skills are not as easily transferrable as the master–apprentice model implied, and that observation was of little use without reflection. At the same time, the hierarchical nature of such a master–apprentice model began to be questioned and ideas developed to build models of supervision which recognised the complexity of the relationship between supervisor and supervisee, as well as that between supervisee and their client. This movement resulted in a number of different supervision models which can be briefly divided into the following categories.

## Psychoanalytical/Psychotherapy-based supervision models

The Psychoanalytic/Psychotherapy models emerged in the first phase of the development of supervision, during the 1920s. These models leaned heavily on psychotherapy/ psychoanalysis theory and held closely to the fundamental belief that supervisees learn best if they experience the qualities of therapy in the supervisory relationship (Bernard & Goodyear, 2009).

In the early days of Freudian analysis, supervision was largely informal, but in 1922 the International Psychoanalytic Society formulated a set of standards within which personal analysis of the trainee was the cornerstone. This was considered by some people to have created a tension between psychotherapy and supervision as some supervision models required the supervisor to provide both supervision and personal therapy to the supervisee. Psychotherapy-based models of supervision often feel like a natural extension of therapy itself, within which 'theoretical orientation informs the observation and selection of clinical data for discussion in supervision as well as the meanings and relevance of those data' (Falender & Shafaanske, 2004:9). The supervisor is intent on develop the supervisee as a person as well as a practitioner.

## Counselling/Psychotherapy-based supervision models

By the 1950s we see developments in supervision based on broader counselling/ psychotherapy orientations. These continued to use interventions and counselling techniques (Bernard & Goodyear, 2009) and covered a range of approaches including Psychodynamic, Person-Centred, Cognitive-Behavioural, Solution-Focused, and Narrative. The approaches were still quite therapy-focused, with supervisors focusing on elements such as defence mechanisms, transference and countertransference, affective reactions, etc.

The more psychodynamic approaches continued to draw on psychoanalytic theories and were classified by Frawley-O'Dea and Sarnat (2001) into three groups: patient-centred, supervisee-centred, and supervisory-matrix-centred.

## *Patient-centred supervision*

This focuses on the patient's presentation and behaviour, with the supervisor taking a didactic role aiming to enable the supervisee to understand and respond to the patient's material. The supervisor is considered to be analytical, detached, experienced and knowledgeable, and to hold 'considerable authority' (Frawley-O'Dea & Sarnat (2001). Due to the focus on the patient, there is little or no focus on the supervisor–supervisee relationship, and as long as both hold the same theoretical beliefs there is little space for disagreement or conflict. The authority of the supervisor can provide a feeling of safety for the supervisee, leaving them fully open to learning from the supervisor. However, should there be a disagreement the supervisee might be left feeling very vulnerable.

## *Supervisee-centred supervision*

This draws on several psychodynamic theories including self-psychology, ego psychology and object relations. It focuses more on the supervisee's experiences in their work and explores any anxieties, resistances, and problems in learning. The supervisor remains a detached authority figure but moves away from being didactic to become more experiential. The aim of the supervision is to enhance the supervisee's understanding of their own psychological processes (Haynes et al., 2003).

## *The supervisory-matrix-centred supervision approach*

This attends to the material of both the client and the supervisee and introduces the need to also examine the relationship between supervisee and supervisor. The supervisor is no longer seen as the uninvolved expert but as a participant in the supervisory relationship who must also reflect on their own personal processes and the relational themes within their relationship with the supervisee. This calls for an awareness of any parallel processes in which the supervisee's behaviour with their client parallels their interaction with the supervisor (Haynes et al., 2003).

## Developmental models of supervision

From the 1970s, supervision models moved away from counselling and psychotherapy theories and started to place more emphasis on education, and on the developmental stages of supervisees across their professional lifespan not just in the early stages of their careers, moving from 'novice' through to 'professional', 'experienced professional', and then to 'senior professional/expert'. The growing focus on reflecting on practice was a major shift in supervision. It separated supervision from counselling and historically marked the point when the focus of supervision shifted from the person of the worker to the work itself.

Developmental and social role frameworks/models began to be developed (Skovholt & Ronnestad, 1992; Carroll, 2006; Bernard & Goodyear, 2009). These were often categorised into three main groups: stage developmental models; process developmental models; and lifespan developmental models.

**Stage developmental models** describe supervisees moving through progressive stages in their professional maturity and within the supervisory relationship. The beginner is seen as highly motivated, but with only limited awareness and quite dependent on the supervisor. Over time and through the experience gained, the supervisee becomes more consistently motivated, more fully aware, less self-conscious, and more autonomous.

An example of a stage developmental model is **The Integrated Developmental Model** (IDM) developed by Cal Stoltenberg et al. (1981) which was based on Hogan's (1964) descriptions of trainee levels of development, and Hunt's (1975) application of Conceptual Systems Theory (CST) (Harvey et al., 1961) in the teaching environment. Hunt broke down the development phases into four from neophyte to master counsellor and used dimensions of interpersonal perception, identity, motivational orientation, emotionality, and cognitive structural attributes to characterise each of these levels. CST theory is concerned with the cognitive variables, referred to as CL (conceptual level). Hunt (1978:78) described CL as 'a personality characteristic that describes persons on a developmental hierarchy of increasing conceptual complexity, self-responsibility and independence'. Stoltenberg's model used these concepts to promote personal and professional growth through three development levels by closely attending to three overriding structures:

- Self and Other Awareness (Cognitive and Affective)
- Motivation
- Autonomy

These were considered under the following categories:

- Intervention Skills Competence
- Assessment Techniques
- Interpersonal Assessment
- Client Conceptualisation
- Individual Differences
- Theoretical Orientation
- Treatment Goals and Plans
- Professional Ethics

Another influential developmental supervision model is that of **Loganbill et al.** (1982) which is based on processes which are 'continually changing and recursive' (Bernard & Goodyear, 2009:94) and expressed by characteristic attitudes towards the work, the self, and the supervisor. This model dismisses any ideas of linear progression through stages, in favour of continual cycling, 'with increasing…levels of integration at each cycle' (Bernard & Goodyear, 2009:94). The model was influenced by the theories and assumptions of developmental psychology, particularly those of Margaret Mahler, Erik Erikson, and Arthur Chickering and was based on four assumptions:

- The training experience is more than the incremental build-up of skills but rather 'the integrated formulation of a therapist with an identity' (Loganbill et al., 1982:15).
- There are distinct, sequential, hierarchical, and necessary stages just as 'infants learn to crawl before they learn to walk, though the ultimate goal is not to crawl well…So, it is with the supervisee some of the stages and processes may be very painful, but it is developmentally important for the supervisee to experience them fully' (ibid:4).

- Although the stages are sequential, different learning tasks may be at different developmental levels.
- To progress one assumes 'a careful sequence of experience and reflection" (ibid:15). Development is not restricted to the life of a formal training programme but continues throughout professional life. Loganbill et al. suggested that the stage model is actually one in which a counsellor 'may cycle and recycle through these various stages at increasingly deeper levels' (ibid:17).

**Blocher's Cognitive Developmental Approach** (1983) was another approach focusing on the influence of cognitive structures on social perception and judgment, and so represents a 'constructivist' approach to human cognitive functioning (Kelly 1963; Lewin 1935; Werner 1978). Blocher used knowledge in human cognitive development (Harvey et al., 1961; Loevinger, 1976; Perry, 1968; Piaget & Inhelder, 1969), claiming that the development of the supervisee is not arranged in a series of hierarchical stages but is a more idiosyncratic process determined by their unique learning style and developmental history. The goal is to facilitate the supervisee in acquiring new, more complex, and more comprehensive schemata for understanding human interaction. Blocher (1983:28) saw supervision as 'psychological education in the fullest and most complete sense of the term. It uses psychological content in a systematic way to change the psychological functioning of the learner'.

Later models include **Skovholt and Ronnestad** (1992) who identified eight stages of counsellor/therapist development, refining it in 2003:40 to six phases:

- Phase 1: The Lay Helper Phase (pre-training phase)
- Phase 2: The Beginning Student Phase
- Phase 3: The Advanced Student Stage
- Phase 4: The Novice Professional Stage
- Phase 5: The Experienced Professional Stage
- Phase 6: The Senior Professional Stage

They also proposed 14 themes of development:

1. Professional development involves an increasing higher-order integration of the professional self and the personal self
2. The focus of functioning shifts dramatically over time from internal to external to internal
3. Continuous reflection is a prerequisite for optimal learning and professional development at all levels of experience
4. An intense commitment to learn propels the developmental process
5. The cognitive map changes: beginning practitioners rely on external expertise; seasoned practitioners rely on internal expertise
6. Professional development is a long, slow, continuous process that can also be erratic
7. Professional development is a lifelong process
8. Many beginning practitioners experience much anxiety in their professional work. Over time, anxiety is mastered by most
9. Clients serve as a major source of influence and serve as primary teachers
10. Personal life influences professional functioning and development throughout the professional lifespan
11. Interpersonal sources of influence propel professional development more than 'impersonal' sources of influence

12. New members of the field view professional elders and graduate training with strong affective reactions
13. Extensive experience with suffering contributes to heightened recognition, acceptance, and appreciation of human variability
14. For the practitioner there is a realignment from self as hero to client as hero

**Process developmental supervision models** focus on processes in the supervisee's work which 'occur within a fairly limited, discrete period' (Bernard & Goodyear, 2009:92). Within this group there are different models including:

**Reflective models of practice** which use reflection to improve practice. The focus is on an experience in the supervisee's practice which has an emotional or intellectual impact that requires deeper understanding.

**Event-based supervision** is task-focused with the supervisor and supervisee analysing how the supervisee manages discrete events in their work. The events are identified through a direct request of the supervisee, or the supervisor picking up on less direct cues.

**Task-focused developmental models** break down supervision into a series of manageable tasks. Carroll's integrative model (1996), identifies seven central tasks of clinical supervision:

- Creating the learning relationship
- Teaching
- Counselling
- Monitoring (e.g. attending to professional ethical issues)
- Evaluation
- Consultation
- Administration

Supervisors employing a developmental approach need the skills to accurately identify the supervisee's current stage and provide feedback and support which is appropriate to that stage, while at the same time facilitating progression onto the next stage (Littrell et al., 1979; Loganbill et al., 1982; Stoltenberg & Delworth, 1987). This requires supervisors to use an interactive process, often referred to as 'scaffolding' (Schunk & Zimmerman, 2003). This encourages the supervisee to use their prior knowledge and skills to facilitate new learning. As the supervisee approaches mastery at each stage, the supervisor gradually moves the scaffold to incorporate knowledge and skills from the next advanced stage. Throughout this process, not only is the supervisee exposed to new information and skills, but the interaction between supervisor and supervisee develops to foster the acquisition of advanced critical thinking skills.

Of course, it is not just the supervisee who passes through developmental stages during the supervisory relationship. The supervisor also goes through developmental stages as they develop and hone their skills and gain experience in appropriately matching the phased needs of the supervisee.

## Systems model of supervision

The systems approach to supervision (SAS) was developed as a visual road map for supervisors to consider the numerous factors that could impinge on teaching and learning by offering a common language relevant to supervisors of different theoretical perspectives and set within a visual representation of concepts that depicts their relationship to each other.

It is focused on the relationship between supervisor and supervisee and places power in both (Holloway, 1995). Holloway describes seven dimensions of supervision, all connected and clustered around the central supervisory relationship. These dimensions are: the functions of supervision, the tasks of supervision, the client, the trainee, the supervisor, and the institution. These components form a dynamic process which interrelates and influences one another.

The central aspect in SAS is the holding environment created by the supervisor which gives the supervisee the time and safety to reflect on their interpersonal behaviours, emotional reactions, and subsequent actions and so grow professionally. Interpersonal competence and emotional reflection (Forrest et al., 2008; Johnson et al., 2012) are key components in competency benchmarks for counselling psychologists (Kaslow et al., 2009). The development of the SAS model draws on positive psychology and relational cultural theory for its values and thus is very relevant to coaching.

In the SAS model, there are considered to be three essential elements that guide the understanding of the formation and quality of the supervisory relationship:

- The interpersonal structure of the relationship as described by the power (empowering rather than controlling) and engagement across the five sub roles of supervision
- The developmental phase of relationship
- The learning contract of supervision

The model acknowledges the inherent tensions for the supervisor in their dual responsibility to monitor the supervisee's competence and provide the safe trusting relationship required for the supervisee's professional growth (e.g., Baltimore, 1998; Burns & Holloway, 1990; Frawley-O'Dea, 1998; Itzhaky & Itzhaky, 1996). The supervisor has to sensitively move from expert to empowerer and navigate a number of different and sometimes conflicting roles – role model, advisor, mentor, consultant, and guide. These movements take place over the lifespan of the supervisory relationship as the supervisor and supervisee refine their understanding of each other's expectations and needs within their agreed contract and cultural background.

SAS places great importance on cultural values (gender, ethnicity, race, sexual orientation, religious beliefs, and personal values) which are embedded in the supervisor's attitudes, actions, and social and moral judgments. This is very consistent with the existential approach. In addition to these cultural aspects supervisors' views and experiences are described by five factors:

- Professional experience
- Professional role
- Theoretical orientation
- Cultural worldview
- Interpersonal style

The model also identifies five characteristics of the supervisee:

- Experience in practice
- Theoretical orientation
- Learning goals and style
- Cultural worldview
- Interpersonal style

## Cognitive-behavioural supervision (CBS)

Psychotherapy-based models did not stop being used as developmental and systems models increase in popularity. One such model is cognitive-behavioural, in which the primary goal is to teach the techniques of CBT (Cognitive-Behavioural Therapy). The supervisor draws on the observable cognitions and behaviours of the supervisee's professional identity and their reaction to the client (Haynes et al., 2003). Supervision sessions and CBT treatment have many similarities. Both are systematic, goal-directed, structured, time-limited, collaborative, person-focused, confidential, and active, with clear boundaries and a recognised power imbalance which requires ethical management. CBT emphasises mutual trust and openness, the facilitation of change, starting with strengths, development of conceptualising skills and balanced 'meaning systems'. This requires the supervisee to acquire 'self-change skills', using objective measures and actively eliciting feedback.

According to Perris (1993), CBT supervision tends to follow a relatively didactic model, focusing more on the theoretical and technical aspects. Greenwald and Young (1998) advocated a schema-focused supervision model bridging CBT and depth-oriented approaches including developmental, interpersonal, and experiential elements. This method is seen as helping organising case information and it requires case conceptualisation, developing a strategy, implementing interventions, resolving difficulties, and understanding the role of the supervisee's own schema.

As one might expect there is a structured approach to what a CB supervision session looks like. Liese and Beck (1997) and Liese and Alford (1998) suggest that each CBT supervision session should consist of:

- Checking in
- Setting the agenda
- Bridging from the previous supervision session
- Returning to enquire about previously supervised cases
- Discussing the homework set at the previous session (reading, case conceptualisation, or experiments)
- Prioritising items on the agenda
- Discussing a recorded case
- Direct instruction and guided discovery
- Using standardised supervision instruments
- Setting new relevant homework
- Summarising and eliciting feedback from the supervisee

## Person-centred supervision:

Person-centred supervision based on the work of Carl Rogers also remains popular. It is centred around the belief that the client has the capacity to resolve their own life problems without interpretation and direction (Haynes et al., 2003). In supervision it is assumed that the supervisee has the resources to effectively develop their professional skills. The supervisor is not seen as an expert but as a collaborator, working with the supervisee. The supervisor's main task is to provide a safe environment where the supervisee can be open and fully engaged (Lambers, 2000). Person-centred supervision relies heavily on the supervisor–supervisee relationship to facilitate effective learning and growth. We see echoes of the early psychoanalytic models in that the aim of person-centred supervision, whilst not being a therapy in its own right, becomes therapeutic through the supervisory relationship. Purton (2004) sees the aim of person-centred supervision as being to promote the personal and professional development of the supervisee, guiding them in using their internal power and resources. Unlike CBS any goals for supervision are defined by the supervisee, as the supervisee is considered to be 'the one who knows'. So, the goals in person centred supervision are to:

- Trust the supervisee's inner resources
- Be a trustful companion in difficult professional moments
- Create the appropriate climate for growth

Lambers (2000) suggests that the supervisor 'has no other concern or agenda than to facilitate the therapist's ability to be open to his/her experience so that (s)he can become fully present and engaged in a relationship with the client. The person-centred supervisor accepts the supervisee as a person in process and trusts the supervisee's potential for growth'.

## Feminist model of supervision (and those focused on power differentials):

More recently there has been a movement calling for supervision bringing a greater awareness and focus on some of the political aspects the therapist or coach are working with, the power dynamics that are evident in the relationship between the supervisee and their client, and those present in the supervisor–supervisee relationship, together with the philosophies which inform these approaches. Falender (2009:27) noted, 'Although most traditional definitions of supervision allude to the power differential, they typically omit attention to oppression, privilege, and social context, which are central to feminist models'.

Despite a growing interest in models centralising power dynamics, there is still little published literature on feminist supervision. As feminist discourse is acknowledged as beyond gender to include race, culture, class, sexuality, and other intersecting facets of identity (Falender, 2009; Gentile et al., 2009; Nelson et al., 2006), I am using feminist supervision here as a platform to explore an approach which is equally relevant in multi-cultural and critical psychology and indeed when working with other groups with a perceived, and or acknowledged power differential.

It could be argued that the very nature of supervision contains a power hierarchy with the belief that the supervisor dyad contains a knower and one who is yet to know. To supervise from a feminist stance invites critical reflection on this knower–known dichotomy and requires greater attention to context, subjectivity, difference, power, and mutuality. Although work on defining what makes one form of supervision feminist is still relatively new, there are researchers who have explored various tenets of the approach, (Gentile et al., 2009; Mangione et al., 2011; Nelson et al., 2006; Szymanski, 2003, Fickling&Tangen 2017, Monroig 2017, Brown 2018). Szymanski (2003:221) offered one definition of feminist supervision, describing it as 'a collaborative relationship that is characterised by mutual respect, genuine dialogue, attention to social contextual factors, and responsible action' with DSC (diversity and social context) as a core dimension.

The research emphasises the need for the supervisory relationship to be a sensitive, informed and positive one which supports and benefits the supervisee, client, and supervisor. I believe this should be the aim of all supervision, but in feminist supervision there is greater acknowledged emphasis on the analysis of power, and the disruption and exploration of oppressive narratives that might emerge. The approach aims to better understand and interrogate the experience of living a gendered life within intersectional identities and in doing so draws on a phenomenological methodology, whether consciously or not. It identifies, takes note of, and explores any toxic effects of manifest and non-conscious pervasive and systemic bias in the supervisory processes, and seeks to identify any examples in which any member of the supervision triad (client–supervisee–supervisor) is devalued or disempowered by systemic aspects of social hierarchy. The supportive context allows for tension within the competing roles of the feminist supervisor who is providing both challenge and support to be recognised, whilst retaining the aim of protecting clients, while still focusing on the supervisee (Falender, 2009).

The literature on feminist supervision highlights power analysis in the relationship as a crucial component of feminist supervision (Mangione et al., 2011; Murphy & Wright, 2005; Szymanski, 2003, 2005). Given the focus on equality of power, it is not surprising that the aim is for supervisor and supervisee to join together to think critically about dominant cultural norms in their practice and ensure the supervisee's practice upholds or subverts structural norms of systemic marginalisation, oppression, and devaluation. The approach is inherently transformative, strength-based and empowering and 'locates pathologies and challenges to competence not in vulnerable individuals – either clients or trainees – but in the rigidities and biases of the larger systems in which they struggle to exist' (Monroig, 2017).

The process of feminist supervision is aimed at developing informed empowerment in the supervisee which should be mirrored in the supervisee's work with their client. Neither supervisor nor supervisee would set out to take a leadership stance, with the supervisor being more drawn to the role of listener, with a joint setting of the supervisory agenda invited by such questions as 'what would you want me to watch for?'. In this egalitarian model the supervisee would be encouraged to take note of the cultural background, and current cultural context of the client and if the coaching encompasses any focus on competencies then cultural competencies should be acknowledged and valued. The client should be empowered to identify and live by their own values and to be aware of the consequences of living by those values for themselves and others. The coaching would equally consider what it may be like for the client not to live by those values.

Any supervisor working within a feminist model is committed to be self-reflective, and to continually monitor their own bias and distortions. They will not ignore any perceived power dynamics in the supervisee's work with clients or in their supervisory relationship. The supervisor remains consciously aware that intentionally or not, they provide a model for the supervisee and so will seek to ensure that is one of authenticity.

## Integrative supervision models

Many coaches and therapists choose to work in a more integrative way and so may look for integrative supervision. An early model IDM was described earlier but other integrative approaches are in use. As the name implies, they all draw on more than one theory and technique (Haynes et al., 2003). Haynes, Corey, and Moulton describe two main approaches to integration: technical eclecticism and theoretical integration.

Technical eclecticism tends to focus on differences, choosing from many approaches, and is a collection of techniques. This path calls for using techniques from different modalities without necessarily subscribing to the theoretical positions that developed them.

In contrast, theoretical integration refers to a conceptual or theoretical creation, not just a blending of techniques. It aims to produce a conceptual framework bringing together the best of two or more theoretical approaches.

Both approaches will usually include the aim to integrate body sense, feelings, thoughts, etc. whilst not being theory-led. The supervisee would be expected to use their felt sense of the client, together with their own personal integration of theory, plus their own exploration and self-awareness to support the client in deepening their self-knowledge through experience rather than theoretically based insight.

Foster (2011) suggested that the role of integrative supervision is to support supervisee reflection, and therefore, supervision itself becomes a piece of action research, with client, supervisee, and supervisor reflecting the process in their own way, with focus not just on the work with a particular client, but with the supervisee's personal development. This means that Integrative Supervision has, at its core, the task of understanding the client's experience through the use of the therapist's own embodied experience and those different theoretical frameworks that feel relevant. None of the theoretical frameworks are considered as 'truth' but as devices to support creativity.

This places the relationship between supervisor and supervisee at the forefront with attention being paid to body language (the supervisee and the supervisor), language both tone and choice of words. Foster (2011) believes that 'by giving ourselves up in a safe space to a bodied reverie on the client we can recall information that we didn't know we knew', it falls on the supervisor to co-create with the supervisee the safe space where such reverie is possible.

To create a safe supervisory space, it is important to consider whether supervision is always a good thing. Ellis (2001) has explored the research material on what may be considered to be 'bad' supervision. He differentiates between *bad* and *harmful* supervision. The former he considers to be ineffective supervision that does not harm or traumatise the supervisee, whilst the latter is supervision through which the supervisee suffers harm.

He gives examples of *bad* supervision as being when there is 'a serious mismatch in the supervisee's and the supervisor's personality styles and/or theoretical orientations, the supervisor's disinterest and lack of investment in supervision (e.g., chronically late, cancels supervision appointments without making up the time), ineffective or unproductive supervision, or the supervisor is not forthcoming about his or her evaluation of the supervisee's skills (especially a poor evaluation) or only offers critical evaluative feedback at the end of the term' (2010:402). He considers that *harmful* supervision occurs when the supervisor is negligent, acts inappropriately or with malice, demeans the supervisee, behaves in a discriminatory or prejudiced manner, and/ or clearly violates ethical standards. Such behaviour stems from the misuse of the supervisor's power. It is important for all supervisors to carry an awareness of the power inherent in the role of supervisor, and show respect to their supervisee, themselves, the role of supervision, and their profession.

# 2

# THE CURRENT POSITION ON COACHING SUPERVISION

Supervision is an essential part of practice for professional coaches. While supervision is not the only route in coaching to achieve CPD and reflection space, the leading bodies are now both encouraging, and increasingly requiring participation in supervision, and are recognising and accrediting individual supervisors.

Although still not compulsory, coaches are now actively encouraged to have supervision not just by coaching organisations and fellow coaches but by leading thinkers and employing organisations as '…research shows that supervision has benefits for coaches, their clients and the organisation they work for, and that effective supervision is weakened if it neglects any of these. Most importantly, it highlights that good supervision is fundamental to making sure that coaches are able to work effectively' (Arney, 2007:36).

Coaches, particularly those new to the profession may struggle to manage the demands of client issues, ethical dilemmas, and the emotional demands of the work. Supervision can be a safe place to work with all these demands. For more experienced coaches, supervision provides an opportunity to develop their skills further, and to discuss and challenge elements in their coaching practice.

Despite this growing understanding of what supervision can add, coaching supervision remains under-researched. Interest in the subject is growing, and writers such as Carrol (2006), Hawkins and Shohet (2020), Bachkirova et al (2011), Hawkins and Smith (2007, 2013), and others are continuing that research, intent on continually developing and improving what is on offer.

Despite this ongoing commitment to development, there is no agreed definition of coaching supervision. Hawkins and Smith (2007) saw supervision as providing 'a protected and disciplined space in which the coach can reflect on particular client situations and relationships, the reactivity and patterns they invoke for them' (2006:142). Bluckert, quoted in Hawkins (2007:147), agreed with this, but also considered what supervision provides in terms of monitoring and safeguarding for the client:

> Supervision sessions are a place for the coach to reflect on the work they are under-taking with another more experienced coach. It has the dual purpose of supporting

the continued learning and development of the coach, as well as giving a degree of protection to the person being coached.

Not everyone in coaching circles shares the same view of the function of supervision. Barbara Moyes writing in *International Coaching Psychology* (Vol. 4 No. 2 September, 2009) identified at least four different views. Not surprisingly, organisations employing coaches and the coaches themselves were seen to have different requirements from supervision (Hawkins, 2006). Coaches tended to place greater value on the developmental and quality assurance functions of supervision. Hawkins research showed that 88% of his sample of coaches used supervision to develop their coaching capability and 86% looked to supervision to assure the quality of their coaching. Hawkins saw this as indicating that for coaches, quality assurance was about their skills rather than client protection, with supervision providing the link between theory and practice.

The second thing a coach looked for in supervision was the facilitation of change helping them to shift when they felt stuck in their work. Such a shift can be transformational, resulting in the coach behaving differently towards the client and so enabling the client to change. Seeing a shift and change in the coach can empower and inspire their client.

Those organisations commissioning coaching are more interested in the managerial aspect of supervision. They look to supervision to protect the client, and ultimately to minimise any organisational risk regarding unethical or unprofessional practice. They want supervision to ensure that the coaching focuses on work objectives and confirming that the coach has the capability to do the work. They see the role of the supervisor as increasing the coach's understanding of both the client, and the organisational issues. Hawkins' research showed 77% of organisations also wanted supervision to monitor the quality of coaching, whereas only 50% wanted it to improve the quality and effectiveness of the coaching (Hawkins, 2006).

The fourth view, referred to by Moyles, focuses on the supportive element of individual supervision and its role in developing coaches' confidence, and dealing with any emotional demands the coaching may present. She draws on the work of Arney (2007) who took a developmental view focused on the parallel process where the supervisor–supervisee relationship can mirror the coach–client relationship, allowing the supervisor to give the supervisee personal feedback rather than any focus on skills acquisition or development.

Other views, including those of Butwell (2006), saw group supervision as being particularly valuable for discussing difficult cases and boundary issues, warning that supervisees needed to use supervision effectively by being open in what they discussed as she maintained that, 'What cannot be achieved in any other way than supervision is the opportunity to discuss a difficult case, to explore one's feelings about a client, or to bounce ideas around on how to take a "stuck" client forward, or to have advice from someone with more experience or a different point of view on subtle boundary issues' (Butwell 2006:10).

If we look to coaching organisations, we find that the EMCC (European Mentoring and Coaching Council) describe supervision as being, 'the interaction that occurs when a mentor or coach brings their coaching or mentoring work experiences to a supervisor in order to be supported and to engage in reflective dialogue and collaborative learning for the development and benefit of the mentor or coach, their clients and their organisations', and defines its purpose as being to 'enhance the wellbeing, and develop the practice of coaches and/or mentors of all levels of experience. Supervision is considered a powerful vehicle for deep learning: its benefits extend beyond the supervisee and include their clients and sponsoring organisations'. They draw on Hawkins and Smith's (2013) description of the functions of supervision:

- The Developmental Function: concerned with development of skills, understanding, and capacities of the coach/mentor
- The Resourcing Function: providing a supportive space for the coach/mentor to process the experiences they have had when working with clients
- The Qualitative Function: concerned with quality, work standards, and ethical integrity

The ICF (International Coach Federation) on their website defines Coaching Supervision as 'a collaborative learning practice to continually build the capacity of the coach through reflective dialogue for the benefit of both coaches and clients'. They consider the focus of supervision to be on the development of the coach's capacity through offering 'a richer and broader opportunity for support and development' through the creation of 'a safe environment for the coach to share their successes and failures in becoming masterful in the way they work with their clients'. They suggest that supervision can achieve these aims by:

- Reviewing the coaching agreement and any other psychological or physical contacts, both implicit and explicit
- Uncovering blind spots
- Considering ethical issues
- Ensuring the coach is 'fit for purpose' and perhaps offering accountability
- Looking at all aspects of the coach and client's environment for opportunities for growth in the system

I have already indicated that the development of coaching supervision grew out of the experience of supervision in other therapeutic professions, as outlined in the previous chapter. However, there are very distinct differences between therapy and coaching, and writers such as Butwell (2006) and Hawkins (2006), have argued that as coaching is not psychotherapy or counselling, it should not be assumed that 'we can blithely transpose one set of standards across to another arena' Butwell (2006:7). So, there is an acknowledged need for a supervisory model, or models, which specifically address(es) the needs of coaches.

However, there is a proliferation of models and standards in coaching which can make it harder to develop a coaching specific common approach to supervision (Arney, 2006). Indeed, this has also been the case in psychotherapy supervision with different modalities using different supervision models. As we have noted, coaches and the purchasing organisations may want different things from supervision. Just as there are very different coaching models and coaching clients, ranging from those seeking life coaching to those looking for a more business focus, it makes sense that there should be different supervision models to choose from. Although a coach may feel safely held and understood working with a supervisor from the same modality, there is much to be gained by stepping out of one's comfort zone and working with a supervisor whose ideas may provide more challenges. This may be something which appeals more to the experienced coach looking to broaden their portfolio of offerings.

Coaching psychologists are turning their attention to supervision 'because supervision makes good sense from both learning and quality perspectives' (Carrol 2006:4). In 2007 the Special Group in Coaching Psychology, within the British Psychological Society, produced guidelines for coaching psychology supervision. They consider the role of supervision to be to provide interactive reflection, interpretative evaluation, and an opportunity to share expertise. However, there remains a lively debate as to how far the therapeutic model is appropriate for coaching supervision.

Many supervisors still come from a therapeutic background and one of the most commonly used supervisory methods has been the seven-eyed model which was adapted by Hawkins and Smith (2006) from the Hawkins and Shohet model, originally developed for social work and psychotherapy supervision (Hawkins & Shohet, 1998). The seven 'eyes' or areas to be looked at are:

1.  **The client system:** Focusing on the client's situation, the problem they want help with, how they present themselves, their issues, and the choices that they are making. The supervisor may encourage the supervisee to reflect on:
    *   How did the client present themselves at the first session?
    *   Has this changed?
    *   How aware are they of the issues they bring and their possible choices?
    *   Are they aware of the implications involved in choices they have made or intend to make?
2.  **The supervisee/coach's interventions:** Focusing on the interventions the supervisee makes, how and why they make them, and what else they might have done. The supervisor facilitates the supervisee's reflection on the tools they use and their effectiveness with that specific client at that specific moment in time. To begin the discussion the supervisor may ask questions such as:
    *   What do you know about the client?
    *   How did the client show up in the coaching session?
    *   What issues did they present in the coaching session?
    *   Do you tend to use the same tools regardless of the client needs?
    *   What other approaches could you take?
    This helps the supervisee to reflect on the influence the client themselves has on the work. The client may bring recurring themes or show a repeated behaviour pattern worthy of exploration.
3.  **The relationship between the supervisee/coach and their client:** Focusing on neither the supervisee nor their client but on the conscious and unconscious interactions between the two to enable the supervisee to develop a better understanding of the dynamics of the coaching relationship. The supervisee needs to learn to take a step back and critically examine their working relationship with the client. This includes the contract or agreements which have been made; the client's needs and expectations of coaching; the supervisee's needs and expectations of the client and any assumptions that are made on either side. Questions which may facilitate such discussion could include:
    *   What is the relationship like between the supervisee and the client?
    *   What are the client's expectations of the supervisee's work with them?
    *   How does this match the supervisee's expectations?
    *   How explicit have these needs and expectations been made?
    *   How much work is the supervisee putting in compared to how much work the client is putting in?
    *   What is the energy like in the relationship?
    *   Where might any tension lie?
4.  **The supervisee/coach:** Focusing on the supervisee's own experience as a tool for registering what is happening beneath the surface. This allows the supervisee to analyse what they notice about themselves, including anything the client triggers for them in terms of how they present themselves, or the material they bring. This can uncover a wealth of

information about the supervisee, any unconscious biases or prejudices they may bring, and issues they may feel less skilled to work with. Such material may stem from the similarity in client material to something the coach has personally experienced, or reminders of a particular person they know or have known. Noticing and acknowledging this can help the supervisee to self-manage, or even decide that this is an area they are not comfortable to work with. Questions which may help in the reflection may include:

- What reactions did the supervisee have to the client or the topic brought?
- What changes in energy or bodily sensations did the supervisee notice when working with the client?
- Did the client remind the supervisee of anyone? If so,
  - Why do they remind the supervisee of this person?
  - What differences are there between the client and this person?

5. **The parallel process:** Focusing on the parallel processes that appear between the supervisory relationship of the supervisee and the supervisor, and in the session between the supervisee and their client. There may be further parallel processes playing out in the wider context i.e. behaviours showing up in the relationship with their client which reflect behaviours showing up in the wider client organisation. The supervisor may sense that the supervisee wants the supervisor to provide them with the answers to their questions. A parallel process may be playing out in which the client is looking to the supervisee to provide them with the answers. The supervisor may suggest the supervisee considers:

- Are there any echoes in the supervisee/supervisor relationship which the supervisee sees in their work with their client?
- Is the client behaving in a way which reflects the organisational cultural norms?

6. **The coaching supervisor's self-reflection:** Focusing on the supervisor's 'here and now' experience with the supervisee, and how this can be used to shed light on the supervisee/ client relationship. This level of supervisory work requires a strong relationship between supervisee and supervisor. Any feedback given by the supervisor should be without judgement for the supervisee to decide whether to explore or not. Questions which may help this process may include:

- What emotions and physical reactions is my supervisor having during my supervision session?
- What does this tell me?
- What here and now embodied experiences do I notice?

7. **The wider context:** focusing on the wider organisational, social, cultural, ethical, and contractual context within which the supervision is taking place. By considering the broader context it may be easier to understand the reasons why the client does not behave in the way the coach wants or expects them to. The client's behaviour may be a reflection of the culture in the organisation, or their peer group and the degree with which they are willing to go along with or challenge that culture. It may be useful for the supervisor to ask questions such as:

- How is the culture of the client's organisation reflected in the work I am doing with this client?
- How is the client's home, work, or social environment reflected in the coaching?

Although coaching supervision still draws on psychological and social work theories and models such as the one above which has added in an organisational element making it more relevant to coaching, it also looks to other professions such as sport (Gallwey, 1979), leadership (Lee, 2003), and business (Whitmore, 2003). Lane (2006) argues that not only must these be looked to with care but believes that there needs to be use of a range of models to meet the wide needs that arise in coaching. The different areas in which we find coaching operating may call for different skill sets, and this may define what is required in supervision. If the primary aim is to achieve change for the organisation, then those commissioning coaching supervision require supervisors with a broader knowledge base than social work or psychotherapy; for example, if they want the coaching to cover strategic and leadership elements, they may choose a supervisor with experience in these areas. Hawkins' research (2006) showed that coaches working in business organisations wanted their supervisors to have business knowledge, understand organisational dynamics, and be able to think in a systemic way. They placed intrapersonal knowledge and psychological background much further down their list of requirements. Hawkins (2007) warned that the danger of using a coach from a therapeutic background was that organisational systems may be reduced to individual pathology with the coach seeking to rescue the client from the 'bad' organisation, a service the organisation was paying for. I agree that an understanding of organisational dynamics is vital, but I feel Hawkins shows little understanding of many contemporary psychotherapy approaches in which the individual is not seen as detached from their context, be that family, social, or professional. One would hope that since the early 2000s the business world's greater emphasis on emotional intelligence may have changed thinking somewhat, placing relational considerations higher in business requirements. However, knowledge of the organisational dynamics, which are inevitably intrapersonal, is important to the client, coach, and supervisor.

Butwell and Lane's questioning of borrowing from other professions resulted in the creation of what Hawkins (2006:3) refers to as three 'rather limited' approaches to supervision.

- The first is 'psychological case work' – focusing on understanding the coaching client and how to work with them. This is limiting in that it is not possible to change the client, as the client is not present during supervision. Adopting this approach can be construed as the supervisor vicariously coaching the client, and thereby disempowering the supervisee.
- The second approach is 'coaching the coach', where the focus is on the coach rather than on what is going on between coach and client.
- The third is managerial supervision, where the supervisor focuses on fixing problems.

Hawkins (2006:3) believed that until coaching develops its own models and theories of supervision, 'the practice will be constrained and coaching supervision will continue to be dressed in borrowed clothes'. He saw a major limitation in the therapeutic model with its predominant focus on the client. He considered this as appropriate for disciplines like counselling and psychotherapy, which he perhaps misguidedly saw as individually based, whereas he argued that coaching has a much broader set of 'masters' – coach, client, and organisation. It would seem strange to disregard models and methods that work in therapeutic disciplines because they do not originate in coaching, but consideration has to be given to the training needs of coaches and supervisors, particularly those working in more organisational settings. As coaches we encourage our clients to look to all their reflected experience, personal and professional to enhance their learning and the same should be found in supervision.

More recently supervision models have been developed by practicing coaches. Some use Hawkins and Smith as a starting point whilst offering new aspects. Turner is an example of this. In 1996 he introduced a model which he entitled, 'the three worlds, four territories model'. He further developed this model into its current incarnation (Bachkirova et al., 2011:41–55) in which he distinguishes between what the coach experienced in the coaching session itself, their 'here and now' experience in the supervision session, and what the coaching client experienced in the coaching session, in addition to what was going on back in their life outside the session. He goes on to also make finer distinctions about the individual players' experiences. He aims for the model to 'help the supervisor bring the coaching session live into the supervision session, raise the coach's awareness, and so enable the coach to have new options in their coaching' (Bachkirova et al., 2011:41). All aspects are brought into awareness either directly because 'they are happening in the moment or indirectly because they have been evoked through the memory, imagination and intuition of the supervisee and supervisor' (Bachkirova et al., 2011:42). So, the three 'worlds' referred to are those of – the coaching client, the coaching session, and the supervision session, with the supervisor attending to four territories: Insight, Readiness, Authentic Vision, and Skilful Action:

**Insight** refers to seeing what is and what could be in the individual's world, and is concerned with sensing and perceiving, including insight into any preconceptions, prejudices, projections, and assumptions which may be held.

**Readiness** is concerned with attending to what may constrain or enable responses to the world and includes meaning systems, personal history, habitual thoughts, etc.

**Authentic Vision** is concerned with clarifying the difference that the individual wants to make to their way of being.

**Skilful Action** is concerned with transforming vision into action.

Supervisors would focus on the coach as they are in the supervision session and link it to other worlds using the model to frame questions aimed at helping coaches explore the worlds and territories. Through learning from supervision they would be enabled to create and interlink the three worlds, bringing 'a whole network of conscious and unconscious knowledge, feelings, imaginings, perceptions, needs, desires and intuitions about what happened in the coaching and back in the coachee's world into the supervision session' (Bachkirova et al., 2011:44).

Having looked at what coaching supervision consists of I wish to look briefly at some of the current ways it is delivered.

## e-supervision

I am writing this book at the time of the Covid pandemic and hoping that by the time it is published we may be out and through the other side of this challenging period. During lockdown it has proved impossible to coach or supervise face-to-face. Personally, this has been a great loss to me. I enjoy sharing the same physical space with a client or supervisee and believe that the embodied shared experience offers more than working in a virtual way. However, many coaches, including myself, were already used to working with clients and supervisees who we never met in the flesh. It is often the case that clients and supervisees do not live in the same country. When coaching for large global companies it is possible to have the opportunity to meet in person for the chemistry session in the client's own country and perhaps hold the first and last session of a coaching contract face-to-face, with the other sessions taking place by phone or through online video platforms. There are also some coaches and supervisors who work via email or real-time messaging, although these are ways of working which do not appeal to me so I can offer little experienced knowledge of them. For those wanting to know more about the benefits and challenges in these approaches they will find more information in Clutterbuck and Hussain (2010). As coaches are so used to working remotely with their clients it is not unusual for them to receive their supervision remotely too. Even though this is the case it is recognised even by those most experienced and skilled in the technologies that the developments should be driven by the users. Li and Bernoff (2008:18) remind us to, 'concentrate on the relationships, not the technologies'.

E-supervision may contribute well to the green agenda with less cost, reduced travel, and time saved, and it opens up the opportunity to work with people wherever they are based. It makes it easier to take CPD opportunities to areas of the world where the profession is less established. This can be very positive if a supervisee is looking to be supervised by someone with specific experience or a less common approach. For example, there are very few existential coaching supervisors out there, so finding one who is local may be problematic for the supervisee.

Hay (in Bachkirova et al., 2011:242) suggests that e-supervision has significant benefits in the quality of the supervision. She believes that it provides more opportunity for the 'supervisee and supervisor to stay in the present rather than experience the full impact of transference and/ or counter transference'. She considers it a benefit that the supervisory encounter is likely to be less emotional with the supervisee staying more grounded and better able 'to continue thinking and talking even when experiencing emotive insights'. She believes this makes it less likely for the supervisor to feel the need to rescue the supervisee. As you will gather throughout this book, existential supervisors and coaches value emotional expression as tools to their work, as emotions are always connected to things, and staying with and exploring these emotions can help deepen understanding. Because someone is emotional does not mean that a supervisor will wish to rescue them, instead they may see it as a real opportunity to learn more about the supervisee's way of being-in-the-world and the values which have been threatened in order for them to feel emotional. Personally, I believe that to remove this aspect from supervision would prove very negative. In addition to providing the opportunity to model working with emotions as a supervisor, I would much prefer to experience my supervisee's authentic reactions than to experience a supervisee playing the good coach in the way Sartre's waiter in *Being and Nothingness* (1958:59) performed his waiting duties, something which Sartre considered to be 'bad faith'. I shall say more of this later when looking at some existential coaching supervision concerns.

Warren Linger, in his 2020 YouTube presentation, based on Palmer and Turner's *The Heart of Supervision* (2018) also sees positives in virtual supervision, believing it encourages us to 'adapt to different cultural norms' and 'focus on professional norms'. I am unsure how this is the case, as I would expect supervisors working face-to-face to also focus on these things and that having access to seeing fully the body of the supervisee may be better placed to see any signs of unease caused by incorrect cultural assumptions. He uses video recordings of supervisees' sessions in his supervision work and it is easier to access and discuss these when already working online. He suggests that working online makes it easier for the supervisee to select and share extracts from videoed coaching sessions with their supervisor and that recording the supervision sessions gives the supervisee increased opportunity to reflect on the session. Like Hay, he feels that working at a distance reduces the supervisor's temptation to rescue the supervisee, and so increases their autonomy.

Although it undoubtedly has its benefits it also presents challenges. I have noticed, and others have mentioned to me, that if supervision is by phone there may be a temptation to multitask, checking emails on your phone, adding to your to-do list, or even watering your plants or dusting areas you suddenly notice may need a clean! It is less easy to get away with these actions if using video, but that in itself presents other issues. During lockdown many of my coaching and supervision sessions have taken place via video with people who are working from home, often with their partners working away just as intensely in another room, or even the corner of the same room. Added to this has been the challenge of their children being around when normally they would be at school. They may be requiring entertaining or home schooling. A bonus is that the coach or supervisor can see the reality of the challenges of working at this time and a supervisor can help the supervisee set realistic expectations for themselves and their clients. Linger also noted potential disadvantages, focusing on potential damage to the relationship dynamic between supervisor and supervisee as the kinaesthetic connection may be modified or filtered through the technology. He suggests that mindfulness is easier in the virtual world although this has not been my experience.

Hay (in Bachkirova et al., 2011:240) sees 'the difference between face-to-face and e-supervision as a difference in environment and dynamics rather than a difference in context or approach', arguing that function and process remain the same. To some extent this is true but may discount less conventional supervision models which may draw on gestalt, embodiment, drama, or art in their approach to supervision. Linger (2020) points out the increased need for e-supervision requires for high-level listening skills when the supervisor is not present in the same room with the supervisee, especially the meaning the words represent. He suggests the supervisor must hold a heightened awareness of tone of voice, any hesitations, sighs, laughter, what is not being said, and 'the music behind the words'. I see as important to attend to these whether working virtually or face-to-face. It is worth noting that some supervisors may not even be working with the spoken word but be offering supervision via online messaging, therefore relying solely on the written word.

On a practical level it is important to check that whatever virtual platform is being used it can offer the necessary security and confidentiality. Some platforms are not very stable and easily hacked. The limitations of the screen can also make it harder to maintain confidentiality. Often the screen is full of the person we are speaking to and we cannot see if there are other people in the room or whether doors or windows are open, etc. Equally, the supervisee cannot see what may be surrounding the supervisor. Having said that, coaching is less concerned about confidentiality than therapy and it is not uncommon for coaching sessions to take place in public places such as cafes or in offices which are not soundproofed.

## Group supervision

The pandemic has made it difficult to meet face-to-face, and one supervision approach which has suffered is group supervision. Of course, it is still possible to do this via virtual platforms and the same pluses and minuses exist as described above. However, I can personally vouch for how exhausting I find running these types of groups virtually. They remain popular with coaches wanting to meet as an international group to share different cultural experiences and for those wanting to work with a very popular or knowledgeable supervisor with little time available to offer one-to-one supervision.

There has been very little research or writing on group supervision for coaches. The Association for Coaching (2005) suggested 'There are many ways of providing group supervision' ranging from a similar format to the Group: 'The supervisor, acting as leader, will take responsibility for apportioning time' to: 'The coaches allocate supervision time between themselves using the supervisor as a technical resource' (Butwell, 2006:43). Some take the form of peer supervision which Pinder (Bachkirova et al., 2011:197) suggests has the 'advantage of there being parity between the participants, potentially mirroring the equality the coach has with their client'. She identifies other positives including that it is free and developmental. However, it also presents challenges with all participants being equally responsible to hold security and safety and come to agreement about issues such as timings, venue, level of commitment to attend, structure of the group, e.g. will there be a rota to present cases or can anyone give a presentation at a group? She suggests that peer supervision is more suitable for those later in their career and so requiring less leadership: 'to introduce this too early in the coach's development may be close to an existential approach to supervision where there is faith in the coach's abilities to see their own answers...' (Walsh & McElwain, 2002).

Inskipp and Proctor (1995) identified four different models of group supervision: authoritative, participative, cooperative, and peer. In the first, authoritative, each person in turn works with the supervisor as the others observe. In the participative model the supervisor, whilst holding overall responsibility, seeks to develop all participants into co-supervisors. The role of the supervisor in the cooperative model is to support the group to develop its own system and supervisory skills. Finally, the peer model relies on shared responsibility.

Pinder (Bachkirova et al., 2011:199–200) describes three further models: Gordon Law, Fan, and Devils and Angels. In the first a supervisee relates a story/problem to the group, after which each group member asks them a question which remains unanswered. Each group member then formulates a hypothesis regarding the reason why the participant posed that question. The hypothesis is then related to the supervisee who goes through each question and hypothesis saying which they found most or least useful and why. In the Fan model, all members of the group are given specific tasks to supervise, e.g. aspects of an issue, themes, or modes of a certain model, e.g. the seven-eye model. Finally, in Devils and Angels, a participant presents an issue and what their next step will be and what thoughts and feelings will accompany it. The group can then ask any clarifying questions, followed by acting as devil's advocate by stating any concerns or doubts they may have about the proposed action. The presenter takes from these comments whatever fits and disregards the rest. The group then takes the role as 'angel's advocate', giving positive feedback to which the presenter responds and then plans future action.

Whatever the nature of group supervision its advantage is that it provides access to the combined knowledge of the group itself, and the knowledge and skills of an experienced supervisor who facilitates the session. This allows for the opportunity to compare approaches, views, and experiences. Some groups will seek to bring together a group of like-minded coaches, perhaps all offering the same approach or working in the same sector. Others will work hard to bring together a diverse group with a variety of experience levels, working in different settings, and aiming to recruit coaches of different gender, age, culture, and race.

The supervisor has to work to ensure the group is a safe one for all its members. Everyone must feel able to 'ask the stupid question' and not to worry they may be discriminated against for any reason. Pinder (Bachkirova et al., 2011:199–200) reminds us that, 'coaches are operating in a competitive market, the anxiety and destructive possibilities of this can be exacerbated'. Issues of confidentiality are widened as the group is made up of individuals all with their own networks. Proctor (2008) speaks of the supervisor as group manager, identifying who is taking control and who may be missing out. Any competitiveness also needs to be managed. As with all groups, participants and/or facilitator need to be alert to other group issues such as parallel process, pairing, flight, freeze or flight plus issues of gender, race, or other areas of potential discrimination (Bion, 1961). Such group dynamics are recognised as important by writers as diverse as Carl Rogers (1951), Mumford (1993), and Freud (1964), all of whom agree that groups provide benefits, such as identity, challenge, support, and learning.

## Conclusion to Part One

I clearly draw on my experience of existential and phenomenological psychotherapy in my practice as a coach and supervisor, in addition to my own business experience, life learnings, professional development, and coaching knowledge. Later I hope to further challenge Hawkins' view that a therapeutic approach is focused on the individual, outside of the context in which they exist. Indeed, the existential model, both in therapy and coaching is essentially relational and calls for the client to be considered as a being-in-the-world-with-others and requires that the person and their needs be looked as through the prism of all the existential dimensions they inhabit – the social, the personal and psychological, the physical and environmental, and spiritual.

Part One has not been intended to provide a comprehensive analysis of the current state of coaching supervision or the historical precedents it draws on, but merely to provide a framework of understanding in order to explore an existential-phenomenological approach to supervision. For those new to existential concepts, I start the second part of this book by offering a brief overview of existential thinking which is relevant for coaching. I then move on to introduce the current understanding of existential coaching. Moving on, in Part Three I look to show how these concepts influence the supervisor who wishes to incorporate an existential approach into their supervisory practice. In the final section I offer some brief examples of existential coaching supervision in action.

# PART TWO

- *The main themes of existential thinking*
- *Phenomenological investigation*
- *The existentially informed coaching approach*
- *An existential perspective on ethical issues*

PART TWO

# 3

# THE MAIN THEMES OF EXISTENTIALISM

Many people are familiar with Sartre's existential statement (1943) that existence precedes essence. This reverses the more traditional philosophical view that the essence or the nature of a thing is more fundamental and immutable than its mere fact of being, its existence. This can leave us with the fundamental question – what then does it mean to be human? Making sense of our human existence and making decisions about how to 'be' forms the heart of the existential task.

For the existentialist, there is no general definition or understanding of what it means to be human. Instead, the meaning evolves through the very act of existing. This means we define and engineer our existence. So, it could be said that existence is 'self-making-in-a-situation' (Fackenheim 1961:37). Heidegger (1962:69) described this in the phrase 'the "essence" of Dasein lies in its existence'. Heidegger uses the German word *Dasein*, which literally means 'being there' or 'presence', to describe the human being. Sartre's understanding of this gave rise to his famous statement that 'existence precedes essence' (2007:22) explaining, 'We mean that man first exists: he materialises in the world, encounters himself, and only afterward defines himself. If man as existentialists conceive of him cannot be defined, it is because to begin with he is nothing. He will not be anything until later, and then he will be what he makes of himself' (ibid). Heidegger and Sartre were not totally aligned on their understanding, but both place the task of self-making with the individual.

Our self evolves and interrelates with our context. In existential terms, I am nothing else but my own conscious existence. It is in light of this idea that key existential notions such as relatedness, time, temporality and transcendence, uncertainty, alienation, freedom and responsibility, values and authenticity are understood. The fact that as a human I must live with these existential givens forms the central challenge of my existence. They are not obstacles to be overcome but are fundamental aspects of my existence in the world and how I find meaning in my existence.

Existential thought is concerned with the whole concept of 'being', and what this means to our lived experience in a given time and place. This emphasis is evidenced in part through the titles of some key 'existential' writings such as Heidegger's *Being and Time* and Sartre's *Being and Nothingness*. I have placed existential in inverted commas here, as not all writers who are identified as existential would define themselves in this way.

Heidegger focuses attention on our Being-in-the-world and the undeniable fact that we are Being-towards-death. Although our understanding and experience of our existence is unique and ours alone we are, however, not alone in this lived existence as other people impact positively or negatively on our life project. Heidegger refers to this as Being-with. If the human being is a being-in-the-world-with-others, then the world itself is part of the fundamental constitution of what it means to be human. A human being is more than a free-floating self or ego; for Heidegger each human creates, and therefore is their own world. The world is part and parcel of our being and of the fabric of our existence. *Dasein* is not a subject distinct from the world of objects but is an experience of openness where one's being and that of the world are not generally distinguished. Heidegger distinguishes between authentic (owned), and inauthentic (disowned) ways of being and so calls for open authentic reflection on how we are living our lives. This quest for truth and transparency is an important requirement in coaching and in supervision.

Indeed, some researchers (van Deuzen & Young 2009:8) identify the beginnings of existential supervision in Heidegger's Zollikon (1959–1969) supervisory seminars with Medard Boss and his students. The seminars focused on Heidegger's ontology and phenomenology in relation to medicine, psychology, psychiatry, and psychotherapy. Heidegger challenged the participants to develop a new understanding of being, claiming that 'all objectifying representations of a capsule-like psyche, subject, person, ego or consciousness in psychology and psychopathology must be abandoned in favour of a new understanding' (Heidegger 2001:4). This new understanding calls for a more phenomenological approach, less grounded in causational theories, which is equally valid in coaching.

Sartre is concerned with the distinction between unconscious being (*en-soi*, being-in-itself) and conscious being (*pour-soi*, being-for-itself). Being-in-itself is concrete, lacks the ability to change, and is unaware of itself. Being-for-itself is conscious of its own consciousness but is also incomplete. For Sartre, this undefined, non-determined nature is what defines being human. Since the for-itself lacks a predetermined essence, it is forced to create itself from nothingness. For Sartre, nothingness is the defining characteristic of the for-itself. A stone is a stone and lacks the ability to change or create its being. Humans, on the other hand, make themselves by acting in the world. Instead of simply being, as the object-in-itself does, a person as an object-for-itself, must actuate its own being. Herein lies one of the major challenges of human existence. It calls for reflected responsible action rather than unreflected passivity.

We are all on a temporal journey between birth/conception (depending on individual beliefs) to the moment of our death (which as with the conception/birth debate can raise disagreements about quite when 'death' occurs, but I am taking it as being the time of lasting cessation of circulatory, respiratory, and brain functions resulting in loss of connectedness to place and others). What went before, and what follows is uncertain and unknowable. However, this temporality of human nature is one of the few things we can hold a level of certainty about; we were born, and we shall die (although we do not know when or how). Even those who choose to end their own lives have no guarantee what they will experience or whether they will survive. For each and every one of us our time on this earth is limited.

Existentialism places this temporality of 'being' at the heart of its thinking. In so doing, the short time in which we do exist takes on the utmost value. We must make choices about how we use that time and take responsibility for the decisions and consequences which flow from them, with the implications for ourselves, others, and the universe.

We may choose to drift through life in an unreflective manner, barely conscious of the passing of time and the value of each moment. However, we cannot delude ourselves that it is the 'nature' of existence that life just drifts by; instead we must accept that we have chosen to allow it to do so: it is our existential choice in choosing a life of drifting. Alternatively, we can choose to live in an existentially aware way, in which we continually question how we are experiencing and living our lives. We are conscious and reflective of how we approach and make the decisions we do, and so take full responsibility for our subsequent actions.

It is of course possible that drifting through life might constitute a reflected decision for a person. It may be perceived and experienced as meaningful by and to them, but then it probably would no longer be seen as 'drifting' but instead as a conscious decision not to engage with structured and determined living.

Humans seek to make their limited time meaningful. This meaning is not handed to us at birth as a universally agreed truth. Instead, each person is tasked with finding their own meaning. Some people may look to authorities or organised communities, sects, or religion for some structured meaning. However, from an existential viewpoint they are required to authentically engage with an inner discourse as to what extent the societal or organisational meaning on offer truly matches their own. They must consider whether their choices are ethical and meaningful to them. It becomes one of our key existential tasks to find our individual sense of meaning, in what is essentially a meaningless existence. Existentialism is concerned with finding self and meaning throughout life as we make choices based on our experiences, beliefs, and values.

In addition to the temporal reality of our existence and the need for it to be meaningful, existential thought requires us to both proactively and reflectively engage with the choices and decisions we make. We have freedom to make choices. This can be both a curse and a blessing. We cannot unthinkingly rely on laws, ethical rules, or traditions, but instead we must accept personal responsibility for our decisions, and the gains and the losses which flow from each of our choices. For most people these personal ethical choices will match the expectations of their cultural context. Existentialism does not give people the 'right to be selfish' and to do whatever they want; instead it gives great importance to the need to reflect and consider each choice and the consequences for self and others, as we are all beings-in-the-world-with-others.

Although there is a clear emphasis on personal responsibility and choice, there is an understanding that despite all being unique individuals, who experience and live our lives differently from anyone else, there are a number of things we share no matter how diverse our cultural, racial, or familial experiences may be. These are the things which make us human. Within the existential approach these shared 'existential givens' cannot be avoided but must be authentically acknowledged with the understanding that although we cannot prevent them existing, we retain choice over how we respond to them. These are universal givens which we all must live with.

I wish to briefly introduce some of these existential givens, as I shall return to them at points throughout this book. Holding all of these in mind in our encounters with ourselves and with others is an essential part of living fully and effectively.

## Existential givens

To be-in-the-world, humans, regardless of culture, race, gender, class, or beliefs must encounter some shared 'human givens'. Yalom (1980) defined four givens of the human condition: death, meaning, isolation, and freedom. I use slightly different words to present a broader understanding of the same ideas: death/time and temporality; meaning/uncertainty (with the human desire to try to make things certain and meaningful); isolation/relatedness (broadening it out to include both being-without and being-with); freedom/freedom and responsibility. I have added values and beliefs, and authenticity. It is worth looking at what existentialists understand by each of these givens, all of which are experienced emotionally, and make up our understanding of existential anxiety.

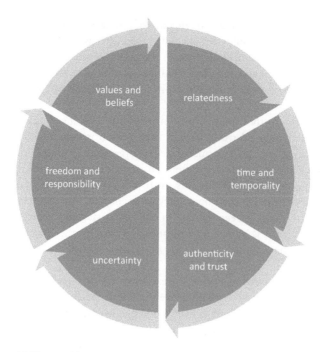

*Figure 3.1*  Existential Human Givens

## *Anxiety*

For existentialists 'anxiety' does not equate to 'worry'. Existential anxiety or angst is not 'the fretful state of mind that the English word anxiety usually refers to, but rather an apprehension of something beyond everyday concerns' (van Deurzen & Kenward 2005:6).

The awareness of the givens and the challenges they present can produce an anxiety that is all-pervading and never-ending. However, the very act of actively living means we will inevitably experience anxiety. Kierkegaard (1844:66) warns that, 'To venture causes anxiety, but not to venture is to lose one's self…And to venture in the highest is precisely to be conscious of one's self'. Kierkegaard described anxiety or angst as stemming from the 'dizziness of freedom' and the responsibility which accompanies it, writing that

> Anxiety can be compared with dizziness. He whose eye happens to look down into the abyss becomes dizzy. But what is the reason for this? It is just as much in his own eye as in the abyss, for suppose he had not looked down. Hence anxiety is the dizziness of freedom
>
> *(ibid: 61)*

We can choose to look, or not. He encourages us to embrace our anxiety because, 'Whoever has learned to be anxious in the right way has learned the ultimate' (ibid:155).

Kierkegaard saw the manner in which humans deal with anxiety as bound up with the problem of despair. As a Christian, he looked to God to help with the despair, believing that it could be overcome through the proper reaction to anxiety which is possible through 'resting transparently' in the power that established it. For many of us, who may be more aligned with Sartre's statement that God is dead, we cannot find escape from anxiety through the religious route.

If we cannot look to God, or a higher authority, we have to accept that we are the authors of our own lives and have agency. However, that agency does not come with a promise of certainty. For many of us, it is the uncertainty of life which leads to anxiety. We cannot control even our own lives; we cannot dictate where our lives start or where they will end.

Heidegger (1962) points to the ontological origin of existential anxiety as lying in our existence as Being-towards-the-end. The presence and inevitability of death is not seen as pathological, but a natural response to the nature of existence. He calls for us to live life with the resolute anticipation of death. In doing so we are living life authentically and facing our anxiety. This is a challenge which many seek to avoid. It is difficult for anyone to truly conceive of their own death and everything continuing without them. Tillich (1952:76) characterised existential anxiety as 'the state in which a being is aware of its possible nonbeing', listing three categories for the nonbeing and resulting anxiety: ontic (fate and death); moral (guilt and condemnation); spiritual (emptiness and meaninglessness). Tillich saw the last of these three types of existential anxiety, i.e. spiritual anxiety, as being predominant in modern times while he believed the others to have been predominant in earlier periods. Tillich differentiated between existential and neurotic anxiety with the latter serving as a distraction allowing us to avoid addressing angst. He argues that existential spiritual anxiety is part of the human condition and if resisted will be met with negative consequences, with the possibility to 'drive the person toward the creation of certitude in systems of meaning which are supported by tradition and authority' even though such 'undoubted certitude is not built on the rock of reality' (1952:20).

Modern writers see the presence of existential anxiety as a call to re-examine our lives and address its meaning and purpose (van Deurzen 1997; Spinelli 2007). Spinelli warns us that existential anxiety is not avoidable as it is present in 'all reflective experiences of relatedness' and that, 'the dilemma of existential anxiety is not so much that it is, but rather how each of us "lives with" it' (2007:27). When we embrace it, it still remains with us; if we reject it, then it causes more anxiety. Amit Ray (2015) wrote, 'If you want to conquer the anxiety of life, live in the moment, live in the breath'. Anxiety is always future-focused. Failure to understand and live with our anxiety means we focus on potential future failure or success, rather than on the truth of today. This fear can freeze us. We need to understand and heed the knowledge that 'our anxiety does not empty tomorrow of its sorrows, but only empties today of its strengths'. (Spurgeon 2015:207). We carry our anxiety with us throughout our existence, and in many ways, it serves as a 'call to arms' requiring us to find meaning and to live authentically.

## Authenticity

When looking at anxiety I hope I have already shown the very clear link with living authentically. Existentialists consider anxiety and authenticity important as they show basic truths about the human condition. Our everyday lives tend to be full of social convention and busy-ness (being-in-a-situation). These can be seen as ways of attempting to avoid taking responsibility for our own lives and forms of self-deception.

It is not only existentialists who are concerned with this; trying to live a life of truth is a universal concern. Shakespeare in *Hamlet* (Act 1, scene 3, 78–82) has Polonius give this last piece of advice to his son, Laertes, 'To thine own self be true, and it must follow, as the night the day, thou cans't not be false to any man'. Being authentic requires us to be genuine, original, not a fake (Concise Oxford English Dictionary, eleventh edition, 2008). It has roots in Greek philosophy;

'To thine own self be true' with the Oracle of Delphi calling for an individual to 'know thyself'. Existentialism would also require us not just to *know* ourselves but also to *be* ourselves.

The need to hold true to oneself and one's beliefs and values, despite external pressures, is central to existential thought. Its centrality of authenticity is evidenced in the works of existential thinkers and writers such as Kierkegaard, Heidegger, Nietzsche, and Sartre, amongst others. It belongs in all aspects of our engagement with self, others, the world, and beyond. It is more than a mere characteristic or property but is related to our very *being*. In turn, our *being* governs our doing. If we are attempting to work, or indeed live/be in an existential way, we must do this authentically. This is not easy. Most of us have at time felt the pressure to appear to be a certain kind of person, to adopt a particular role or mode of living, or to ignore our own moral and aesthetic objections, in order to feel that we belong and thus enjoy a more 'comfortable' existence. We can choose to note that we are doing this, and acknowledge that this is the case, or we may choose to ignore it, and live in what existentialists term 'bad faith'. Socrates pointed out 'the unexamined life is not worth living'; it wouldn't be possible to live an authentic examined life. We must authentically and openly examine how we are choosing to be.

Unfortunately, being oneself is far from easy. It may look much easier and attractive to not be oneself. Kierkegaard focused on a belief that authenticity is reliant on an individual finding authentic faith and becoming true to oneself. Although a Christian, he developed the idea that the media and Church-led Christianity present challenges for an individual trying to live authentically. He saw the media as supporting a society that does not form its own opinions but utilises the opinions constructed by the news. Today's social media has increased the belief that it is alright, or indeed necessary, to create a 'false self' for public consumption. For Kierkegaard, organised religion is a tradition that is passively accepted by individuals, without authentic thought. Kierkegaard's idea of authentic faith can be achieved by 'facing reality, making a choice and then passionately sticking with it'.

For Kierkegaard the most natural way of not being oneself is to live life only *aesthetically*. By this he meant a life devoted to the pursuit of pleasure and the avoidance of pain, choosing to follow one's desires and passions. He wrote, 'The aesthetic "conception of life's meaning and aim" is this: "that one must enjoy life"' (1992: 493). This seems a very dogmatic way of dividing what is authentic and what is inauthentic. I believe that a person who reflects on and then knowingly chooses the *aesthetic* life may well be making an authentic decision. However, to live a life which was only full of enjoyment and passion is likely to prove impossible as it would be hard to avoid all pain, and impossible to avoid death. Ignoring those truths is what would make it inauthentic. Kierkegaard also suggests that such a life would inevitably become boring. 'How terrible is tedium-how terribly tedious...all I see is emptiness, all I live on is emptiness, all I move in is emptiness' (1992:53). This leads him to suggest that such a life is inauthentic: 'everyone who lives aesthetically is in despair whether he knows it or not' (1992:502); '...it is always despair to have one's life centred in something whose nature it is to cease to be' (1992:531). Kierkegaard does not seem to consider that in accepting the inevitability of pain and death it could be an authentic decision to live life *aesthetically*. Kierkegaard valued authenticity highly and saw life's task as being to know and to be oneself, even when there was a price to pay. He considered not knowing who you or being who you are leads to the most common form of despair.

In order to achieve authenticity, a person must face reality and form their own opinions of existence. As an atheist, Nietzsche rejects the role of religion in finding authenticity, instead calling on us to find an understanding of truth without relying on virtues or conventional morality. The individual is required to stand alone and take responsibility for actively shaping his own beliefs. For Nietzsche, the authentic man transcends the limits of conventional morality in an attempt to reflectively decide for himself about good and evil. He rejects the idea of religious virtues due to the lack of questioning by the individual and warns us to avoid what he calls 'herding animal morality' by which he means going along with the majority in order to avoid isolation, but instead calls for us to be a free-thinker if we wish to find authenticity.

Though coming from different starting points, the commonality of Kierkegaard and Nietzsche's existential philosophies is the responsibilities they place on the individual to take an active part in the shaping of one's beliefs, and then to be willing to act on that belief.

Sartre was also concerned with the challenge of being authentic. Believing that a human being first comes into existence and then continually defines itself, he saw individuals as responsible not only for their identities, but for the way the world presents itself in their experiences. It follows that authenticity requires taking full responsibility for our life, choices, and actions. He saw the recognition of our freedom and choices as a 'vertiginous' experience, potentially so uncomfortable that it can feel unbearable, causing some people to choose to live inauthentically, or as Sartre would describe it, to live 'in bad faith': a form of self-deception, rather than engage with life. He recognised that people may choose to stay in situations where they feel they are not able to be or act authentically. This may be due to fear of the uncertainty of stepping out from the common view or accepted way of being and tackling a more authentic and possibly precarious existence. Most of us will have found ourselves at times in a situation where we choose inauthenticity, we may have stayed in a relationship because we feared being alone rather than because we felt an authentic love or commitment to the other person, or we may have remained in a job that didn't match or indeed challenge our values, leaving us feeling uncomfortable because we feared giving up the security or the material benefits the job brought us. These decisions are not in themselves bad, but to be authentic they must be recognised for what they are. Not to recognise this would mean living in 'bad faith'. Instead, Sartre calls for us to recognise the idea of being true to the inescapable tension at the core of the human spirit.

Authenticity, it is almost needless to say, consists in having a true and lucid consciousness of the situation, in assuming the responsibilities and risks it involves, in accepting it...sometimes in horror and hate' (Sartre 1948: 90). Sartre recognises that to live authentically may be uncomfortable but what about the alternative? To live in 'bad faith' (*mauvaise foi*) Sartre offers the story of the Parisian waiter, a skilful and supercilious character. This waiter is able to balance his tray 'putting it in a perpetually unstable, perpetually broken equilibrium which he perpetually re-establishes by a light movement of the arm and hand'. He moves beautifully but robotically. Sartre sees he is playing a game; he is playing at being a waiter in a café. He and we know what playing at a waiter requires. In G.K. Chesterton's tale 'Queer Feet', Father Brown moves between playing the part of a waiter and playing the part of a club member in a gentleman's club. We all have times when we choose to play a part. Sartre would consider that we are in bad faith when we *portray* ourselves through the prisms of our class, job, race, gender, culture, history, family, and early influences, be they conscious or unconscious. To turn it on its head, living in good faith requires us not to make excuses and to take responsibility for our thoughts and actions.

For Heidegger, authenticity equated to 'mine-ness' or 'being one's own' (*Eigentlichkeit*) which is the idea that we not only 'have' but 'are' possibility, that 'we can own ourselves, or seem to do so, or we can lose ourselves, or never own ourselves, all based on how we each individually define our own "who am I"' (Mandic in van Deurzen & Hanaway 2012). This belief calls us to challenge any illusion we hold that we are defined by circumstances, or external factors, and to take responsibility for what we choose to do and how far we choose to progress towards our potential. Heidegger did not see being authentic as requiring exceptional effort or disciple but requiring a shift in attention and engagement, a reclaiming of our self rather than just falling in with the norm. 'The challenge is to bring ourselves back from our lostness in the *they* to retrieve ourselves so that we can become our authentic selves' (Sherman 2009:4). Heidegger sees us having special moments of clarity or clear vision in which we are aware of our own ethical conscience. He calls listening to this ethical inner guide 'resoluteness', a state which allows us to be authentic. These moments do not produce permanent change as remaining authentic is not an easy task. We are always subject to the possibility of falling under the sway of 'the they' (*das Man*), an impersonal entity that takes away our freedom to think independently. To live authentically requires us to resist and outwit this influence. This is hard as *das Man* is so nebulous and not a separate entity. If we allow others/*das Man* to take responsibility for important decisions, it takes away our personal responsibility. As Arendt (1994) warns, this means that we slip into banality and so fail to think. We must find a way to tap into our voice of ethical conscience: the authentic self and wake up to our Being. This may result in setting us aside from everyone else. It may feel very lonely to be at peace with our own truth and to act accordingly.

Some more recent writers, such as Erich Fromm writing in the 1900s, do not call for the rejection of behaviour which is in accord with societal mores if it results from personal understanding and the approval of its drives and origins, rather than a desire to conform and be accepted. Fromm considers authenticity to be a positive outcome of informed motivation rather than a negative rejection of the expectations of others. He described Sartre's absolute freedom as the illusion of individuality, as opposed to the genuine individuality that results from authentic living. He warned us that not acting spontaneously or genuinely resulted in us creating a pseudo-self from which feeling of inferiority can grow. As a psychiatrist he warned others in his profession not just to accept someone as 'well adapted', as they may have needed to give up their 'self' in order to become the person they believed they were meant to be. He believed that on the other hand those considered to be 'neurotic' may be those who were not ready or willing to surrender completely to the battle for self.

As indicated, authenticity is a difficult state to achieve and maintain, due in part to social pressures to live inauthentically, and in part due to a person's own character. It has been described as a revelatory state, where one perceives oneself, other people, and sometimes even things, in a radically new way. It certainly requires self-knowledge, as authenticity is the reflection of one's inner values and beliefs, reflected in one's behaviour. It may be good or bad. Goffee & Jones (2005) describe authenticity as a quality rather than an individual or personality trait. If you are authentic in your actions, then others' perceptions and beliefs must develop about your authenticity and others must attribute it to you.

It is questionable as to whether there is such a thing as a fully authentic person. Both Erickson and Heidegger speak of the 'level' of authenticity in a person, as people are never entirely authentic or inauthentic, but rather seek to achieve a level of authenticity. We may strive to become authentic but may need the help of others in realising our potential. Authenticity has been criticised for what is seen as its potential to focus solely on one's own inner feelings and attitudes, so creating a self-centred preoccupation with oneself which can be anti-social and lacking compassion for others. Indeed, Lasch (1979) points out similarities between Narcissistic Personality Disorder and authenticity. According to Lasch, narcissism and authenticity are characterised by deficient empathic skills, self-indulgence, and self-absorbed behaviour. This does not fit with an existential understanding of authenticity which requires an authentic acceptance of relatedness and the necessity of others in our existential understanding of being-in-the-world-with-others. We are responsible for our decisions and actions, but to be authentic we must consider the implications of these actions not just for ourselves, but for others, and indeed for 'things', such as the environment.

## Freedom and responsibility

Our struggle with freedom is evidenced throughout history and literature. In the Book of Genesis in the Bible we find Adam and Eve faced with freedom and free will. God gives the couple dominion over all things in the Garden of Eden, other than the tree of knowledge from which they were commanded not to eat the fruit. They choose to disregard this command and suffer the consequences.

The notion of freedom has occupied philosophers for years. The concept of freedom is an important one because we must decide whether individuals are free and what implications that brings for the way we live our lives. Existential philosophers have been particularly drawn to these questions as the presence of freedom has such an impact on existential anxiety and the challenge to live authentically that it is interwoven within all the existential concerns.

Having freedom is not easy to manage and its existence frames the way we live our lives. Sartre (1948:34) sums up its challenge when he writes, 'Man is condemned to be free…because once thrown into the world, he is responsible for everything he does. It is up to you to give [life] a meaning'. He gives a compelling account of existentialist freedom in which he describes freedom as a 'doctrine of action' which pushes a person to find themselves again. Each time a decision is made, and an action taken we create a new set of givens and must deal with the positive and negative outcomes, the gains and losses which our decision will bring. In Sartre's words, the intention of existentialism is not to plunge humans into despair but to allow them to realise themselves as truly human, defined as such through our understanding and acceptance of our personal freedom. Sartre believes that all of us are always free to choose and therefore *must* choose and be responsible for our actions. He uses the example of being in a war to illustrate this. In times of war, it may seem that most of the conscripted soldiers have no freedom as they are forced to fight, but despite this, they do have choices. They could choose to run away, or commit suicide, or find reasons to disqualify themselves from service. The reason they end up fighting in the war is because they considered the consequences of their options and the implications of each potential choice before deciding that fighting is the best choice. It may be the best choice for one person because they see it as carrying the potential to defend their country, for them to be a hero, and live their beliefs and values, while for another it may be the best choice because they do not want to dishonour their family or their country, or face imprisonment or death if they choose not to fight. Although the choices may not be attractive, if they choose to fight it is because they have freely chosen to do so.

Although the belief that we are all free is paramount to existential understanding, there are times when we are not free. We are not free to decide if we will be born, nor can we choose the family or circumstances which we are born into. Existential thinking accepts that there are circumstances in which our freedom is limited. Heidegger termed this 'thrownness/ *Geworfenheit*', acknowledging that we are 'thrown into the world'. We may not have been in control of 'deciding' to exist, but for Heidegger, once in the world we are in complete control of our existence.

Sartre defines the same concept as 'in-itself', both a limitation and a condition of freedom. It is a limitation in that a large part of one's facticity consists of things one couldn't have chosen, but a condition of freedom in the sense that one's values most likely depend on it. However, even though one's facticity is 'set in stone' (as being past, for instance), it cannot determine you as a person: the value ascribed to one's facticity is still ascribed to it freely by that person. As an example, consider two men, one of whom has no memory of his past and the other who remembers everything. They both have committed crimes, but the first man remembers nothing about this, leads a rather normal life while the second man, feeling trapped by his own past, continues a life of crime, blaming his past choices and experiences for 'trapping' him in this life. There is nothing inevitable about his committing crimes, but he ascribes this meaning to his past. We have all experienced the sense of being 'trapped', but this is never totally or truly the case. We have the power and responsibility to take agency of what brought us to any given situation. We have possibilities and potentialities for freeing ourselves from our 'trap' or choosing not to and accepting our 'fate'. Unfortunately, the resulting freedom can sometimes seem as unattractive as the 'trappedness'.

Accepting things and choosing not to make a choice is impossible. Like it or not, we are responsible for making decisions. To not make a decision is to make a decision. If we have responsibility for ourselves and there is no definitive authority, then we embrace the twins of freedom and angst. Existentialists cannot look to God to make rules for them and so remove the possibility of choice. Without God or some form of grand plan we cannot pretend that our lives are subject to fate or are mapped out for us. There is nowhere to hide and nobody to hide behind; how our life turns out is purely our own doing and not due to external forces beyond our control. This leaves us to formulate for ourselves what is 'right' and what is 'wrong'. Each of us must decide for ourselves what our personal morality is and authentically abide by that in making our decisions, or knowingly choose to act against our own values.

Once we make a decision, we are not trapped by it. In existential freedom one may change one's values. We may deepen our knowledge about something or have an experience which challenges the continued validity of a belief or value. We are responsible for our own values, regardless of society's values or of those who surround us. The focus on freedom in existentialism is related to the limits of the responsibility one bears, as a result of one's freedom: the relationship between freedom and responsibility is one of interdependency. In making a decision, accepting responsibility and taking action we transcend ourselves and make a future-oriented commitment. It can feel very uncomfortable because freedom can create anxiety and anguish. Fromm argued that 'freedom from the traditional bonds of medieval society, though giving the individual a new feeling of independence, at the same time made him feel alone and isolated, filled him with doubt and anxiety, and drove him into new submission and into a compulsive and irrational activity' (Fromm 1995:89). This alienation from place and community, and the insecurities and fears entailed, helps to explain why people may choose to seek the security and rewards of authoritarian social orders such as fascism.

Frankl (1905–1997) offers us very powerful and concrete examples of our freedom. Frankl survived for several years in concentration camps, including Auschwitz, only to discover that his parents, brother, and wife were all murdered in the camps. He has written eloquently about the need we have to find meaning in life and execute our essential freedom even in seemingly the most hopeless of situations. He discovered that even when it seemed that the Nazis had taken everything from him, they could not take away who he was – the freedom of being. 'We who live in concentration camps, can remember the men who walked through the huts of others, giving away their last piece of bread. They may have been few in number, but they offer sufficient proof that everything can be taken away from a man but one thing: the last of human freedoms – to choose one's attitude in any given set of circumstances, to choose one's own way' (Frankl 1985:86)

We retain the ability to choose our attitude, even in the most difficult of situations. This is essentially what true freedom is. It is our decision how we react to trials that determines our happiness. People can take many things from us, but they can never control our thoughts, emotions, or behaviours. Individuals choose whether to use their freedom for good or bad: 'In concentration camps…we watched and witnessed some of our comrades behave like swine while others behaved like saints. Man has both potentialities within himself…After all, man is the being who has invented the gas chambers of Auschwitz; however, he is also that being who has entered those gas chambers upright, with the Lord's Prayer or the Shema Yisrael on his lips.' (Frankl 1985:212–213). Remembering that both potentialities are available to us – good or evil – is a sobering thought. Despite prisoners sharing the same appalling circumstances it is clear that the kind of person each prisoner became was the result of an inner decision and not purely the result of camp influences alone. Any person can under such circumstances decide who and how they will be – mentally and spiritually. If we take a fatalistic view and reject our freedom, choosing to believe that our circumstances define us, we are forever held captive to them. This view is one of 'bad faith' as we can *choose* to believe that we have the freedom to do just that – to *choose*. This is our true freedom. We must remember that we may be thrown into situations we did not choose but 'When we are no longer able to change a situation, we are challenged to change ourselves' (Frankl 1985:135).

Rollo May reminds us that freedom is also a requirement in challenging and changing the status quo. The ability to experience awe and wonder, to write poetry, to conceive and develop theories, and create works of art presupposes the freedom to reflect and create. May also saw freedom as the mother of all values, as values develop from being free; they are dependent on freedom. Freedom is more than a value itself: it underlies the very possibility of the formation of values. May sets it within the value of relatedness, as he sees freedom as always involving social responsibility, occurring within a context of perception limits as the self always exists in the world with others. The capacity to confront these limits is part of freedom.

Once we have taken onboard the enormity of our freedom, we cannot sit back but instead must engage in a daily self-creating aspect of freedom. Simone de Beauvoir (1908–1986) warned that it is all too easy to seize upon freedom as our birth right and forget that each of us must rediscover it for ourselves.

When working with others as a coach or supervisor it is worth remembering May's words. 'Freedom is the capacity to pause in the face of stimuli from many directions at once and, in this pause, to throw one's weight toward this response rather than that one. The person becomes able to say, "I can" or "I will"' (May 1999:54).

## *Meaning*

If we look to the root of the word 'meaning' we can see that it is understood as essentially subjective. 'Mean' is understood as the way in which someone or something is conveyed, interpreted, or represented. So, meaning is created by the personal significance which an individual chooses to give to something physical or abstract. In finding something meaningful, the individual assigns a value to it and it takes on a significance for that person.

As we have seen, existentialism is a philosophy that emphasises individual existence, freedom, and choice. This freedom extends to 'meaning', in that we are free to form our own sense of meaning and to bestow meaning to things. Meaning is not handed down to us; humans must define their own meaning in life, and try to make rational decisions despite existing in an irrational universe. Heidegger in *Being and Time* considered the search for meaning to be 'the fundamental question of philosophy' (1962: 27), and it could be argued that he made this his lifelong project.

When Heidegger speaks of 'meaning' he is not primarily concerned with linguistic meaning, i.e. the way meaning operates in language, and relates to reality, but instead is focused on ontological meaning; that is, the meaning connected to the meaning of existing things in the world. It is all about connotation, intension, and attributes: 'Meaning is the 'upon-which' of a projection in terms of which something becomes intelligible as something; it gets its structure from a fore-having, a fore-sight, and a fore-conception' (1962:151). Some scholars have complained that Heidegger is not clear on his understanding of meaning and perhaps that should be no surprise, for as Weixel-Dixon (2020:16) pointed out 'the meaning of meaning is particularly elusive'. It cannot really be otherwise when it is the task of the individual to formulate meaning. A thing becomes meaningful to the individual because they are in some way drawn to it, '*everything we encounter is meaningful to us to some degree*. Even a piece of trash I briefly spot out of the corner of my eye has meaning for me – otherwise I would not have noticed it' (Polt 1999:25).

Although we must individually bestow meaning on things, we also experience 'collective meaning' which is shared within social groups and thus provides us with a sense of belonging. We have seen this very clearly in recent times with Brexit. The shock for those who lived in a certain area, shared a collective set of meanings and values, and expected a specific outcome was palpable when the result was declared. Remainers were left asking, why did others not share their understanding and the meaning they gave to the referendum question? Brexiteers were left wondering why the Remainers understood the meaning of Brexit in a different way to them.

Humans are meaning-making creatures. We seek – indeed crave – meaning. Joining a group, particularly one with a 'doctrine' like a religious or political group, offers us ready-made meaning. We do not have to struggle to find it for ourselves and therefore such group meaning can be very attractive to some people. For others, to take on group meaning without analytic and critical reflection can feel inauthentic, and therefore considered to be bad faith. Even Kierkegaard with his Christian faith warned that the meaning had to make authentic sense at an individual level even when set within a set of religious beliefs.

> What matters is to find a purpose, to see what it really is that God wills that I shall do; the crucial thing is to find a truth which is truth for me, to find the idea for which I am willing to live and die...I certainly do not deny that I still accept an imperative of knowledge and that through it men may be influenced, but then it must come alive in me, and this is what I now recognise as the most important of all
>
> *(Kierkegaard et al. 1967:34).*

For Kierkegaard, meaning does not equal knowledge, although both are important. Meaning, for Kierkegaard, is a lived experience, a quest to find one's values, beliefs, and purpose in a meaningless world.

Nietzsche saw life as holding no higher purpose or meaning, unless you decide to make something meaningful. He urges us not to chase the answer of the meaning of life, but instead to live creatively and boldly, abandoning religious or societal meaning, instead accepting the human will to power. He believed that we find power through actively choosing, and through authentic powerful self-expression, philosophy, music, literature, and the arts. If these did not provide the necessary meaning, he looked to the creation of the *Übermensch* or 'Superman' who creates his own meaning of life by inventing it and taking full responsibility. For those failing to reach the heights of the *Übermensch* he advised loving one's life, no matter what it has in it, embracing failures as well as successes.

Sartre too saw the world as being meaningless. Humans exist first before they have meaning in life and so meaning is something to be achieved through our interaction with our surroundings and ourselves. This brings self-responsibility over who we are and what our lives mean. So, meaning is without representation or bearing in anything or anyone else. It is something truly unique to each person.

As mentioned in the previous section on freedom and responsibility, Frankl found himself in a situation, that of a prisoner in the concentration camps, where one might have expected it would be very hard to find meaning. However, from his experiences he developed 'logotherapy', a type of psychological analysis that focuses on a 'will to meaning' as opposed to a Nietzschean doctrine of 'will to power'. Frankl identified barriers such as hedonism, affluence, and materialism to humanity's quest for meaning in life. For Frankl, the main motivation for living lies in our will to find meaning in life, and he believed that meaning was always to be found under all circumstances, even the most miserable ones. He saw that meaning could be created through work or doing a deed, by experiencing something or encountering someone or by the attitude we take toward unavoidable suffering. Frankl (1997) writes that a lack of meaning creates the paramount existential stress – an existential sickness: 'As to the feeling of meaninglessness, per se, it is an existential despair and a spiritual distress rather than an emotional disease or a mental illness' (1997:141). He warns that we cannot look to religion as a panacea to the existential challenges that we face. 'Religion is not an insurance policy for a tranquil life, for maximum freedom from conflicts, or for any other hygienic goal' (1997:72). He proposes two stages of meaninglessness. The first stage is the existential vacuum, characterised by a subjective state of boredom, apathy, and emptiness, in which one may feel cynical, a lack of direction, and question the point of life. Frankl named the second stage 'existential neurosis' and says symptomatic manifestations such as alcoholism, depression, obsessionalism, delinquency, hyperinflation of sex, or dare-devilry for example, will rush in to fill the vacuum. He saw modern man's dilemma as not being told by instinct or tradition what one must do while at the same time not knowing what one wants to do. He suggested this leads to two common reactions: conformity (doing what others do) and submission to totalitarianism (doing what others wish).

More recently, Yalom, who drew on Frankl's thoughts, sees meaning-in-life as an important psychological construct; one that relates deeply to all of us, to the point of being a matter of life and death. 'The human being seems to require meaning. To live without meaning, goals, values, or ideals, seems to provoke considerable distress. In severe form it may lead to the decision to end one's life' (1980:422). He focuses on the paradox that as human we need to have meaning in life, yet we exist in a universe that has no inherent meaning. He separates out the two questions 'What is the meaning of life?' and 'What is the meaning of *my* life?' In answer to the personalised question he writes, 'One who possesses a sense of meaning, experiences life as having some purpose or function to be fulfilled, some overriding goal or goals to which to apply oneself" (1980:423). In contrast, he offers no answer regrading a universal meaning of life, as there is no existential meaning to be found, as for there to conceive of one would imply some design existing outside of the individual, and therefore in conflict with the existential concepts of freedom and responsibility. As we have no predestined fate, each of us must decide how to live as fully, happily, and meaningfully as possible. He suggests that 'perhaps we can forgo the question, why do we live? But it is not easy to postpone the question, how shall we live?' (1980:427). He suggests we can choose to address the question of *how* through 'Self-Actualisation', 'Altruism', 'Dedication to a Cause', or via 'The Hedonistic Solution' of simply living fully, retaining one's sense of astonishment at the miracle of life, and searching for pleasure in the deepest possible sense.

We have seen that we are 'condemned to freedom' (Sartre 1963:290). It is equally true to say, as Merleau-Ponty did, that 'Because we are in the world, we are 'condemned to meaning' (2002:xix).

## Relatedness

An important aspect of our existence is that we share the world with others. It could be said that the world and I are within one another. We cannot choose not to be related, even when we are not with others in an embodied way, they continue to be significant. Even when people die we remain in a relationship with them; we may be conscious that they would have enjoyed a specific event, like a Manchester United win in the case of my father. We miss them when they are absent from significant events such as the birth of grandchildren, etc. We may take comfort from happy memories or feel sadness when we create new memories without them. We may still wonder how they feel about successes and failures we have and may wish to share news or new discoveries, books, or films with them.

Cohn (1997:13) pointed out, 'Relatedness is a primary state of being – we cannot choose a world without other people'. Relatedness argues that everything that exists is always in an inseparable relation to everything else. What we think, feel, and do arises not only from the interaction between our experiences, values, and beliefs within ourselves, but also from the interaction between self and others, and between self and world.

The existence of others may be a source of both our joy, and of our despair. We rely on others to form our self-concept. Without others we would not know who we are, we would have nothing to read our otherness from. I know I am not a child, nor am I elderly, because I have access to both those groups and can see and feel that although I may value their company; I do not *belong* in either – although I once did, as a child, and most likely will become an elderly person in the future and therefore be considered to be part of that group. Apart from giving us some form of validation, or indeed threatening it, other people may help us achieve what we desire, or they can also act as obstacles to our desires and ambitions.

Existing with others is not always easy. Existential thought starts with the belief that although humans are essentially alone in the world, we long to be connected to others and to have some meaning in another person's life. Given that we need to also face our aloneness –being born alone and dying alone, this presents us with a challenge. We need others in order to experience ourselves through their gaze, and so understand our own structure of being. We rely on others to help formulate our sense of identity. Sartre argues that it is through the encounter with the objectifying gaze of another subject, that we gain awareness of ourselves. Sartre poses the question of whether we would feel shame if others did not exist to define what shameful behaviour is and observe us acting in a way which could be defined by them as shameful. Is something more shameful because it is observed? Other people see us and form a perception of who we are; we see others observing us and add the knowledge of their perception to our own self-image. Throughout life our concept of ourselves is challenged by others; people seem to experience us in ways we don't understand, or we feel that to succeed in a particular context we must change who we consider ourselves to be. As others hold so much power over our sense of self, Sartre, in his play *No Exit (Huis Clos)*, first performed in 1944, declared, 'Hell is other people'. Ultimately, we need to come to acknowledge that we cannot depend on others for our identity and validation, and with that realisation we must also acknowledge and understand that we are fundamentally alone. This revelation causes anxiety in the knowledge that our validation must come from within and not from others.

In addition to this validating role, we may choose to experience others as fundamentally helpful in our search for meaning and in establishing a positive self-concept, or equally we may experience them as potential impediments to our existential or even concrete projects. Buber, a philosopher whose ideas had a major impact upon existential phenomenology, suggests we only exist as a relationship to the other and we have a choice in how we view the relationship between self and other. I can choose to experience 'The Other' as a separate object who gazes at, judges, and places meaning upon me; the 'I' can approach 'The Other' as an interrelated co-subject carrying the potential for mutually revealing new meaningful possibilities (Buber 1970, 2002). The first approach is that of an 'I–It' attitude, grounded in an object-focused stance of separateness and control, whilst the latter is an 'I–Thou' attitude acknowledging the co-created engagement and potentialities between different people. Buber calls the 'I–It' mode 'experience' in which a person collects data, analyses it, classifies it, and theorises about it. The 'It' as an object of experience is viewed as a thing to be utilised, known or put to some purpose. In experience we separate ourselves out from the other, seeing the other/our object as a collection of qualities and quantities, in a particular point in time. There is a necessary distance between the 'experiencing I' and the 'experienced It': the one is subject, and the other object. In this mode of engaging with the world the 'experiencing I' is an objective observer rather than an active participant. Buber titles the alternative 'I–You' mode; 'encounter' in which we enter into a relationship with the object, participating in something with that object, and so transforming the 'I' and the 'You' encounter. The 'You' we encounter is encountered in its entirety, not just as a sum of its qualities as it was in the 'I–It' dynamic. The 'You' is not encountered as a point in space and time, but, instead, it is encountered as if it were the entire universe, or rather, that is as if the entire universe somehow existed through the 'You'. Buber believed that we can enter into encounters with inanimate objects, animals, and other humans.

Of course, we may experience some individuals as being more like us than others, focusing on any commonality rather than any difference. This failure to acknowledge difference, in all its richness is dangerous as it can lead us to work from unexplored assumptions about others. Sometimes groups of people are categorised together as Other – those who have a different gender, race, political view, or culture from our own. Within these groups will be individuals whose personal experiences are very different from others in the group.

Even when we are not directly in contact with others, the knowledge that they exist impacts on how we see and operate in the world. As Sartre wrote, 'to live in a world haunted by my fellowmen is not only to be able to encounter the Other at every turn of the road; it is also to find myself engaged in a world in which instrumental complexes can have a meaning which my free project has not first given to them' (1958:654). We are aware that people will bestow meaning on my presence or absence. If someone I love is away, I may worry whether they are alright, or whether they are missing me, I may face concerns about being without them not just in that moment, but in the long term. They take residence in my mind; I am certainly not without them.

## Time and temporality

We are only on this planet for a finite time, so our very existence means we must engage with issues of time and temporality. Husserl considered time to be a lived experience. He saw the past made present through our memories, and the future to be present through our hopes, aspirations and fears for what may happen. In this way past, present and future co-exist. Merleau-Ponty (2002/500) reflects this in his statement, that time 'has meaning for us because "we are it"'. We can designate something by this word because we are at the past, present and future'.

For this reason, existentialists give space to consider 'time' the individuals' experience of time, and the meaning each individual gives to it. During the Covid-19 pandemic which we are experiencing as I write, we may have had more space to consider time and how to fill it. We have all experienced individual time when an hour feels like a day, or perhaps like a second. At the moment, many of us may be confused about what day it is, or what month we are in. We may have experienced time as going very slowly from day to day, and at the same time feel the months of lockdown are flying by. We may be more conscious of our temporality and sense each minute of our confinement as a diminishing of our lifespan or welcome the escape from the 'norm' to enjoy a fuller sense of time. Our usual way of marking and experiencing time has become limited by the current circumstances. We do not experience time tick by tick, as though we were metronomes, but it is set in the context of our emotional experience of contextualised time. We do not all share the same experience of what a minute or hour feels like.

The increased popularity of mindfulness practice has called for people to be 'in the moment'. This is extremely hard to do. In a physical way we are in the moment, in that our breath takes place in certain moments which can be measured by the clock and the calendar. Yet as humans we are most likely, while standing in the present, to be thinking about the past and the future. As Merleau-Ponty put it, 'each moment of time calls all the others to witness' (2002:79). We are often caught up in the decisions we have already made and the possibilities which await us. The span takes us from birth to death. It is the sense of limited temporal time which is of interest to existentialists.

Indeed, Heidegger (1962) describes our existence as Being-towards-death. He argued that time is neither objective or subjective and as it is formed and based in individual human experience, time is always our *own* time. He referred to this as *Zeitlichkeit* or temporality, identifying time as a human activity rather than an entity, and speaking of the time in which we 'ek-sist' (ek-stasies) through standing outside of ourselves, and uses the term *augenblick*, literally the blink of an eye, to describe the moment we oversee past, present, and future.

Sartre is also concerned with the experiencing of time. He refers to the past as 'in-itself' and fixed and the present as 'for-itself' and free. 'In short, the For-itself is free, and its Freedom is to itself its own limit', while he refers to the future as 'the continual possibilization of the possibles' (Sartre 1943:129).

One of our major existential challenges is to embrace the reality that our time on earth is limited and we shall all die. This is not a negative statement but instead is a challenge to embrace our temporality and to fully live in each moment we have. Throughout life we suffer a lot of 'small deaths' or losses: the death of hope, future, confidence, the ending of a relationship, job, or course. Although all of these carry the possibility of a resurrection and rebirth, at some level they can put us in touch with our feelings about death and mortality.

For the existentialist it is vital to work to create a healthy balance between an awareness of death/loss and the propensity to become overwhelmed and terrified by it. No human being can constantly hold the awareness of death. As Becker (2011) points out, such awareness would be too overwhelming and potentially drive people to neurosis or psychosis. Yet, he warned that to live life oblivious to the reality of death is as destructive as to live in constant fear of it. How we manifest our fear of death will be different in each individual. Otto Rank (2003) believed that some people seek to be heroic so that the rules of death no longer apply to them. The fear of death can lead people to feel a strong need to leave something behind as a form of immortality. This may be something they invest in their children or they may find it through their work projects. Becker suggested that Freud's investment in the development of psychoanalysis was his way to overcome death by creating something which would live beyond his death, so that at least his memory would never die. Many of Freud's writing and his dreams seem to show quite a high level of death anxiety. It is hard for most of us to contemplate the world beyond us, with time continuing without our presence. In many cultures the ancestor only truly dies when people stop remembering them.

Yalom (1980) also considered our responses to the reality of the existence of death. He suggested that there are two ways of denying death; either by becoming a 'rescuer' or through being 'special'. We may seek to take on the role of rescuer by being like many immortal comic book heroes or the gods of mythology by attempting to save people from death or from life's challenges. If we spend our time saving others we do not have to think of our own inevitable demise. Death becomes something which happens to others. If instead we take on the role of being special then we can falsely believe that life's rules, including death, do not apply to us.

Another way people seek to deny the reality of death is by avoiding living, in a vain attempt to stay safe. They may avoid investing in relationships for fear of being hurt, rejected, or abandoned. They go through life terrified of living because of their deep terror of death. In his play, *No Exit*, Sartre explores the deadness of lives led in moral cowardice, and the implicit message is, ironically, life-affirming.

Tillich (1952) writes of the tremendous courage required to live life in the face of anxiety and death. In order to experience the true beauty of life he believes one has to become vulnerable to death and anxiety. We often hear those are terminally ill speak of the new intensity of their shortened existence with an increased awareness of the vibrancy of colour, smell, and texture, which accompanies their acceptance of their temporality. Acknowledging our vulnerable mortality can be experienced as not hopeless but life-giving and enhancing, helping us to find a certain grandeur in its temporality. Recognising and accepting the absurdity of our selves can lead us to free ourselves from habit and convention and see a freshness which can be experienced as liberating. This can restore the passion to life.

Although we are unlikely to be dealing with physical death in our coaching work we will be dealing with transition, the passing of time, deadlines, time management, ambitions and hopes, and other time-related issues. Coaching itself is time-limited, both in terms of each session and the length of the contract and will inevitably have to address beginnings and endings.

## *Uncertainty*

Most humans crave certainty as a seemingly safe framework within which to live their lives. Indeed, many people find uncertainty difficult to bear and to some degree frightening. For this reason, they seek to reduce their experience of uncertainty to the bare minimum. However, this is not true of everyone because in some circumstances, people may find uncertainty attractive, and choose to seek out uncertainty-inducing activities such as sport. Indeed, any form of creativity requires us to start with uncertainty. To paint I may, or may not, have an idea of what a final piece will look like, but I must always start with a blank canvas of uncertainty.

In objective, scientific terms, uncertainty is seen as simply being unclear about the truth or falsity of factual statements. In philosophical terms it goes deeper than this. There is little we can be certain about. We can be certain about the fact that we were born, although for some people they may not know where, when, or in what circumstances. We can also be certain that we shall die. However, even for those seeking to end their own life there is uncertainty in whether this will succeed, and how it may feel. However, one thing one can agree on with certainty is that 'uncertainty is a certainty of existence' (Spinelli 2007:24).

Existential uncertainty is not overly concerned with the type of objective uncertainty which interests the scientists; even for them there is uncertainty encountered during the process of identifying what may be deemed certain answers. Existential uncertainty is concerned with the uncertainty we encounter in the course of living our life. It is not taken up with facts, but with the uncertainty involved in considering what we do in light of the 'facts' we are given (in more existential terms, the 'limitations' or 'thrownness'). We are required to be reflective and consider what the facts mean to us, set within our value systems, and in present and future contexts. Our personal reflection on the facts allows us to make an authentic choice based on how they may affect us and others.

The lack of an innate and indisputable certainty can cause anxiety. This is often pathologised and we may seek to discover what is making us anxious and make a judgement as to whether the level of anxiety is 'normal'. Existential uncertainty is not attached to a specific event nor does it just happen *to* us, it *is* us. We are fundamentally uncertain in our very being. Indeed, it could be said that uncertainty is the nature of what it is to be human.

Our humanity requires us to accept that we cannot look to others to provide us with certainty. It is the responsibility of each of us to ask ourselves how we live with uncertainty, rather than deny its existence. Without certainty we have to find our own way of making life meaningful and living it authentically. We project ourselves towards future possibilities knowing that there is no certainty that particular future will exist for us, or how those possibilities might develop. The very act of acknowledging and moving towards a multitude of possibilities creates uncertainty which cannot be overcome through trying to gather information. We cannot avoid projecting ourselves into possibilities, as to do so would be the equivalent of defining ourselves as dead. Through our projections we say 'yes' to exploring some of our potentialities whilst rejecting countless others. We can never know what it would have been like if we had made different choices. The very nature of 'possibility' is that it is grounded in uncertainty. Since human existence is predicated on possibility, human existence is necessarily uncertain, and we have no choice but to engage with it if we are to move through life.

Our desire for some certainty means we will work hard to find it. We may choose to look to one person to provide it for us, which may explain why some people are content to take a very passive role in a relationship, even to the point where the certainty of continued abuse seems preferable to the uncertainty of moving into the unknown. Others may look for certainty in religion, cults, political groups, or other places which seem to have clear answers. They may appear to offer a pact between believing, joining, and the offer of a collective meaningful certainty, if one does not deviate from the beliefs, behaviours, and rituals of the group, and the acceptance of giving our individual power across to another person or deity. However, much as it may be desired by some, both religion and science fail to dispel uncertainty because human existence is fundamentally uncertain. Any form of existence that isn't uncertain wouldn't be human or authentic.

Accepting that we are without certainty may feel negative, but this is not the case. For us to live authentic, creative lives we require the presence of uncertainty. If everything was certain and we knew exactly what to expect our existence would be very boring. To go back to that blank canvas: if I knew exactly what it would look like when I finished painting on it, what would be the point in that activity? The artist would no longer exist but be replaced by a robot who could guarantee the outcome, with no emotional investment in the process. We undoubtedly need 'things' which can produce objects with a level of certainty, but they would be machines rather than humans. The very development of the object produced, stems from uncertainty, with an individual having an idea, which they believe has the potential to work, yet cannot be certain that it will.

To eliminate uncertainty would be to eliminate our humanity and our creativity. As this modern age pushes for more certainty, and it can seem weak to say, 'I don't know', we become less and less equipped to deal with uncertainty and be willing to take on the risks of being creative. This may lead to people feeling pressed into making more and more inauthentic statements.

## Values and beliefs

In our search for meaning, we need to develop a value-led framework from which to lead our lives. This may be self-created, 'inherited' from one's family or culture, or drawn from religious, organisational, or group rules and structures. Our values govern our behaviours and our ambitions. It is our values and beliefs which help create meaning and are also the touchstone for us in defining what is meaningful to us as individuals. 'The creation of values is intrinsic to the existence of our being' (Strasser & Strasser 1997:87); and it is 'inauthentic to believe that we are able to abstain from forming and holding judgments nor from making value judgements' (van Deurzen-Smith 1987:238).

Just as there is no ultimate and universal meaning to which we can cling, leaving us to find meaning for ourselves, we are also tasked with forming our own set of beliefs and values. As Nietzsche wrote, we are required to make re-evaluation of all values (2012:265–266). This view is shared with other existential writers. Heidegger opposed value ethics as he saw values as existential evaluations of specific conditions, not as essential givens (van Deurzen & Kenward 2005). De Beauvoir, and Sartre too, called on us to use our freedom to determine for ourselves how to evaluate our existence. De Beauvoir (1947) placed this in the context of ambiguity and describes how we reassess and change our values as we experience new things. For her, the experience of living in Nazi-occupied Paris brought about a 'conversion' through which she felt she could no longer afford the luxury of focusing on her own happiness and pleasure but needed to interact with her context, believing that when faced with 'evil' one must take a stand. De Beauvoir believed existentialism with its emphasis on freedom and truth held a call for reciprocity and responsibility which challenged the terrors of an authoritarian world. Sartre also emphasised our freedom to create and define our own values. Once established, then we must live by those values. To not do so would be to act inauthentically and in bad faith, pretending that something other than ourselves controls our behaviour. Given that we must be true to our values, it is important to note we are still required to continually check that these values still hold and remain meaningful for us. If this is no longer the case it then becomes inauthentic to persist with them and as Nietzsche warned us, we are required to create a new set of values and to live by those, for the period they remain valid. This is not to suggest that we constantly change values, many remain the same throughout our lives, but we must consider the truth of them in reference to time and context. If I value loyalty highly, what is my ethical position if faced with a boss who is behaving in a way which I consider damaging to myself and or others? Does loyalty require me to remain faithful to them, or does my value of truthfulness and a desire for integrity require me to call out such behaviour? It is not unusual for one of our values to be in a paradoxical relationship with another.

In evaluating, forming, and adopting our values we do not start with a blank sheet. From our birth we are surrounded by familial, societal, and cultural beliefs and values. Some people go through life without questioning these and unreflectively adopt them as a defence against uncertainty, and the lack of universal meaning. For those who choose to reflect on the majority values and beliefs which surround them and so find that they are not an authentic fit with their own thoughts, life can be challenging, so many people choose to silence their doubts. Being true to one's own authentic beliefs and values may set one aside from family, friends, and community. Their collective values provide them with a measure of inauthentic safety and certainty which will be extended to those around them if they embrace their values. They will not take kindly to having those values and beliefs questioned as this would require them to reflect on their truthfulness and relevance and so threaten that sense of communal security.

Existentialists do not celebrate that there is no universal set of values given by family, God, or others but on the contrary, may think it is distressing that God does not exist, 'because all possibility of finding values in a heaven of ideas disappears along with Him; there can no longer be an *a priori* Good, since there is no infinite and perfect consciousness to think it' (Sartre 1996:459). Life would be easier if we are given universal, indisputable values around which to frame our existence. However, to be authentic we have to accept this isn't the case but that we ourselves must take on the responsibility for forming and living by our values.

I have already mentioned the need to frequently check in with ourselves and re-evaluate our values. We may become very comfortable with our values and not wish to question them.

Over time we can find that certain actions or behaviours work for us and are consistent with our current value system. If we re-evaluate the value, there is a danger that we may also need to change our behaviour, which may result in feeling uncomfortably vulnerable, or even lost. Unfortunately, it is very easy to become stuck in the behaviours and the values which inform our actions, even when they are no longer working for us as they have just become habit. When this happens, these values and behaviours become what existential-phenomenological theory terms 'sedimented'. Just as the dregs of coffee which can become stuck in the bottom of a percolator, the dregs do not shift by simply shaking them, we need to put in some work to clear them away. It is possible to clear them away completely, but it is not easy. The same is true of values, beliefs, and behaviours.

These sedimented beliefs, rely on the belief in the primacy, or correctness, of one particular perspective over all others. However limited or irrational they may be, it will take a great deal to override their interpretative power. Spinelli (2005) sees sedimented beliefs as the foundational 'building blocks' of our constructed self. Even when we are aware of how restrictive they may be, we are reluctant to free ourselves of them, as in addition to providing a defence against uncertainty, they have also helped to define our self-construct. To look authentically and openly at how true our commitment to a certain belief or value remains challenges us to ask just who we are. If I have blithely been going through life with an unreflected self-concept, the realisation that I may have been doing so 'under false pretences' can cause a seismic shock to the system. If I am not who I took myself to be then I am required to reassess all my decisions and actions, including who I have chosen to align with, both personally and professionally.

If our beliefs and values are challenged, or we perceive that they are under threat in some way, we may become very emotional. Many people try to avoid emotional reactions so will choose to not acknowledge, or to hide their feelings, when they feel under attack. Others may give full rein to their emotions and show fear, anger, sorrow, or confusion. The attack may be external coming from other people, organisations, or societal codes. When the challenge comes from those who we previously thought shared our values, the emotional reaction is intense. The challenge may equally be internal, and experienced when we find ourselves in 'bad faith' behaving in ways which go against our beliefs. Our values and beliefs determine our actions and self-concept. In a quote, variously attributed to Mathatma Ghandi, Lao Tzu, Ralph Waldo Emerson, and even Margaret Thatcher, we are reminded that 'Your beliefs become your thoughts, Your thoughts become your words, Your words become your actions, Your actions become your habits, Your habits become your values, Your values become your destiny' (Vasudevan 2015:4).

All of these concerns need to be considered in relation to the fact that human life is full of emotions and paradoxes.

## Emotions

The word emotion is taken from the Latin 'movere' meaning to move out, remove, or agitate, and has been in use in English since the 1500s when it was adapted from the French *émouvoir* meaning 'to stir up' or 'excite'. This etymology indicates the dynamism of the word and its nature as an experience which has movement, is transitory, and not a static state of being-in-the-world. We may speak of an angry person, but in fact they are a person *in the state of* anger. Humans are capable of quickly moving through a whole range of emotions, or of becoming 'stuck' in one emotion.

In *The Gay Science*, Nietzsche reminds us that, 'thoughts are the shadows of our feelings – always darker, emptier and simpler' (1974:179). This interconnection of thought and feeling is one reason why existentialists are interested in and write so much about emotions. Although at times we may experience emotions as negative or as obstacles to action, we are never and can never be without emotions. All emotions are said to be 'intentional', that is they are 'about' or 'in relation' to '*something*'. For example, we are not just angry, we are angry *about* something (Husserl 2006). 'Emotions are linked to our encounters with the four existential dimensions and are a way of engaging with the world' (Solomon 1993:143). 'They express our reactions, concerns and values and so convey 'existential messages' (Hanaway 2020a:94).

All the existential givens evoke emotional responses. Emotions and what they indicate are important in any existential interaction. Our life from birth to death is full of emotional experiences. It is an important aspect of our humanity that we have an emotional reaction to people, events, things, places, and even to abstract concepts and ideas. How we express emotions, and the level at which we feel them, will differ between individuals and in different contexts, yet even the quietest and most introverted character has emotions. I regularly recall how the late Dr. Freddie Strasser, a much-missed mentor of mine, would speak of a client who presented with the issue that he could not feel anything; that he was without emotions. Something which his wife and others regularly commented on. When Freddie asked him, 'How does it make you feel to not experience emotions?' the response was 'I feel very sad and angry about it...I feel different from other people'. Freddie's question very simply and quickly unveiled the truth that even the person who believed he did not feel anything had an emotional reaction of sadness, isolation, and anger, to his perceived lack of emotions!

Many institutions and individuals have expressed the view that emotions are a nuisance which we would do well to get rid of. Early thinkers like Aristotle are often presented as seeing emotions as the negative aspects of our humanity, something animalistic which needs to be kept under control by logic and reason. Craven (1996: 303) suggests this is a simplistic reading, stating that Aristotle saw emotions not as 'blind forces, but intelligent and discriminating parts of the personality, closely related to beliefs of a certain sort, and therefore responsive to cognitive modification'. He saw them as valuable forms of intentional awareness; that is, an emotion is related to something. However, this still implies a hierarchy by which the logical, rational, and cognitive aspects can modify the emotions through discourse. The growth of interest in emotional intelligence is challenging the view, previously common in many organisations, that the workplace has no place for emotions, and in order to get the best from employees and keep productivity high emotions should be eliminated.

We do not have the choice of whether or not to eliminate emotions, as we cannot live in this world, conscious of all of the above, and not experience an emotional reaction. The relational aspect of our being is fraught with emotional anxiety, which in itself is a felt embodied emotion. We love people, we hate people, we are indifferent to people, and other people will have an emotional response to us. We have emotional reactions to things and to ideas. If this were not the case, we would not be human, life would be less interesting, and we would learn less about ourselves.

We are all emotional. Emotions are always present but there is often a desire to conceal them. Some people are more comfortable expressing emotion than others. Emotions play such a big role in our lives that there are more than 600 words in English, not the most emotional language, to describe them verbally, not to mention 43 facial muscles to express them physically. There are strong cultural and gender differences in the way the expression of emotion is encouraged or suppressed. One thing we can be sure of is that there will be an emotional response.

In existential and phenomenological thought emotions are seen as a gift to the person experiencing them and the person observing them. Our emotions usually express what really is important to us and are related to our values and self-esteem. For this reason, they provide a short cut to what is really important to a person and are often more eloquent than words.

Emotions not only reveal an individual's worldview, but also disclose the diversity of each individual. Existential and phenomenological thinkers write powerfully about the importance of emotions. In brief, they explain that in addition to being intentional, in that they are always about something, they reveal the 'world-view' of the person, i.e. what makes them tick, their beliefs, values, and assumptions regarding oneself, others, the world, and the cosmos. They are always present and are informative to self and others.

We have already considered the centrality of one emotion in the existential thinking, that of anxiety or angst. In 1844, Kierkegaard wrote about anxiety in *The Concept of Anxiety* (sometimes translated as 'The Concept of Dread'). In it, he recognised anxiety/angst as the emotion which dominates our existence, as we will almost certainly experience dread and despair if we live inauthentically.

Nietzsche (1882) not only acknowledged the inevitability of emotions but also welcomed and celebrated passion and all forms of emotion as evidence that a person was fulling living their life. For him, emotional experience was valuable and informative rather than pathological and should be cultivated rather than eliminated.

For Husserl emotions offer us insight into the worldview of another person. As stated earlier, they are intentional, in that they are about something; I am happy because…, I am angry about…, etc. They may be a response to an external event or can be internal, stemming from stimuli such as a memory or a belief. He sees 'the intentionality of emotions as connected to their cognitive content and thus sees the connection between emotions and evaluation, and emotions and reason'. (Arroyo 2009:11–22). We are not 'out of control' when we are emotional. To see the expression of emotion is to literally see the emotion itself (or at least part of it) and not merely an expression of the emotion.

Heidegger calls for us to live life resolutely and argues that emotions are not tied to an event but are one of the ontological givens through which we form our *Befindlichkeit*, or state of mind. They represent the way in which humans respond to finding themselves in a world to which they must become attuned. We become attuned through feeling, making meaning of, and then speaking of our world (disposition, understanding, and discourse). It is emotions which start this journey of attunement.

In 1939, Sartre produced his *Theory of The Emotions*, indicating the importance he gave to their consideration in his thinking. In it he calls for a rejection of a purely inward-looking attitude towards emotions, and instead sees the need to adopt an outward-looking attitude in which emotions are conceived within the context within which they arise, and so are meaningful and help us to form reality as we experience it and facilitate the navigation of difficult aspects of our reality. As Sartre puts it, an emotion is '…human reality itself, realizing itself in the form of "emotion"' (2004:12). Sartre praised psychoanalysis for recognising the significance of emotions, but he does not agree that they represent the unconscious unveiling of repressed desire. For Sartre, for emotions to have significance the individual needs to be aware of the emotion's finality. Emotions inform and guide us,

> We can now conceive what an emotion is. It is a transformation of the world. When the paths before us become too difficult, or when we cannot see our way, we can no longer put up with such an exacting and difficult world. All ways are barred and nevertheless we must act. So, then we try to change the world; that is, to live it as though the relations between things and their potentialities were not governed by deterministic processes but by magic.

*(2004:39–40)*

Merleau-Ponty is concerned with emotions in their embodied state, not merely as a hidden internal experience, 'I do not see anger or a threatening attitude as a psychic fact hidden behind the gesture, I read anger in it. The gesture does not make me think of anger, it is anger itself' (2002:214) and expands this by stating,

> I perceive the grief or anger of the other in his conduct, in the face or his hands, without recourse to any 'inner' experience of suffering or anger, and because grief and anger are variations of belonging to the world, undivided between the body and consciousness, and equally applicable to the other's conduct, visible in his phenomenal body, as in my own conduct as it is presented to me
>
> *(2002:415)*

Merleau-Ponty seems to reject the idea of a split between the 'inner' emotion and its 'outer' behavioural expression and considers emotions to be undivided between the body and consciousness, denying that emotion and expression are merely causally related.

More recent existential writers also stress the importance of emotion. May saw anxiety as fundamental to our existence. In 1950, in *The Meaning of Anxiety*, May considers the complexity of emotions; for example, he does not present anxiety as negative but calls for a distinction to be made between existential anxiety and neurotic anxiety. He sees neurotic anxiety as being a disproportionate response to a threat, or the result of an intra-psychic conflict, whereas he sees existential anxiety is a normal part of the human condition. It is not the existence of the anxiety which is the problem, but how we experience it and what we choose to do with it. This complexity can be seen in all emotions. The existential interest in emotions does not stop with anxiety, although it is anxiety which is often initially experienced and expressed and which needs to be deconstructed in order to be understood.

Tillich (1952) called for us not to fear or repress emotion, but to live courageously, acknowledging that courage flows from fear, making courage the affirmation of our being in the face of the ever-present threat of our non-being. In this way emotions do not merely spring from experiences, but also push us on through and into new experiences when we can find the courage to own them. They are the springboard for our living fully. They are about something and project us forward into something, if we find the courage not to be engulfed by them.

Van Deurzen shares this view of emotions as complex and multi-layered yet ultimately creative and activating. They are what it is to be human, and the tensions and paradoxes which accompany them create energy and push us forward to change. She warns us not to create a hierarchy of emotions or to consider some to be negative and unhealthy whilst elevating others as positive and healthy. Many Western cultures seem to value happiness above all else and may suggest that emotions such as sorrow or anger should be avoided. For van Deurzen the difference in emotions is not between positive and negative but between those emotions which 'move us away from our value and downwards towards loss and depression' (van Deurzen & Arnold-Baker 2005:113) and those which 'move us towards our value and upward towards anxiety' (ibid).

Suppressing an emotion to a place of non-recognition means we are not listening to ourselves because as we have noted, all emotions are intentional and tell us something about what is important to us. To deny our emotions means that we are not only living inauthentically with ourselves but also in relation to others. People who care about us will experience the embodied emotion even if it is not verbally expressed. We must compassionately hear out and sit with our emotions rather than immediately seek to silence them.

Strasser (2005) devoted a whole book *Emotions; Experiences in Existential Psychotherapy and Life*, to revealing 'the intimate relational nature of emotions' (2005:2), considering every emotion to be revelatory, 'a manifestation of an aspect of our worldview', (ibid:24) through which people can 're-discover and re-acquaint themselves with some aspects of their worldviews and with their ambivalence...' (ibid: 24). He stresses the essentially relational aspects of emotions, seeing them as a revelatory gift to those working with people.

human reality itself, realizing itself in the form of 'emotion" (12). Indeed, once we switch fran introspectionist to a phenomenological method of inquiry, the term "psychological state" seemto misconceive the subject matter because it understands emotions as things (or quasi-things) that literally populate the interiority of our minds. In contrast, Sartre refers to the emotions as

not in so far as they are pure facts'

When working with emotions, it is worth remembering that they are embodied, and we are given access to them through our observation and attunement to another's body language. We are capable of experiencing more than one emotion at a time; one emotion may be in the foreground and the other in the background, but like focusing a single lens reflex camera we can focus our attention on either emotion. These emotions can be paradoxical and sit in conflict with one another. I may feel hatred or anger for a person because of something they have done, at the same time as feeling love for who they are holistically or concern for the difficult position they were in which resulted in them taking action of which I disapprove. Just to make matters more complex we can experience emotions about emotions, often that emotion is guilt: I shouldn't feel angry with this person – they had no choice; I shouldn't feel frustrated with this person – they are doing the best they can; I know this person did not mean to hurt me – but they did. Being able to acknowledge and hold all of the above, in our encounters with ourselves, and with others, is an essential part of living fully and effectively.

Emotions are not simplistic but can be complex, contradictory, and paradoxical, and so cannot be experienced as fallible resources. 'They can be unstable, and misleading, through what Sartre called the magical transformations of the world, those voluntary ways in which we alter our consciousness of events and things to give us a more pleasing view of the world' (Hanaway 2020a:94). Sartre regards these 'transformations' as a form of 'escape-behaviour', ways of avoiding some crucial recognition about ourselves. To explain this Sartre offers an elegant and simple example in Aesop's fable about the fox and the grapes. Despite trying hard, the fox cannot reach the grapes. Rather than acknowledging its failure, the fox reframes its emotional experience, deciding that the grapes were sour anyway, and therefore not desirable. However, it is not the chemistry of the grapes that has changed. What has changed is the fox's attitude and its emotional investment in accessing their sweetness. The fox has come to look at the grapes as sour, in order to convince itself that it didn't want them anyway. So too, Sartre generalises, our emotions are strategies we may employ to avoid action and responsibility, and thus 'flee from freedom'.

An individual is made up of heart, soul, and body. All of these are brought together in out emotional relationship to self, others, and the world. Existentially it would be impossible to work a person without acknowledging their emotional being. Emotions provide us with an entry into the individual's rich worldview.

## *Paradox*

In addition to experiencing our world through emotions we have to contend with a world which is both complex and often paradoxical. An existential practitioner would see existence itself as paradoxical in that, if we are to live life fully, we must do so with the constant knowledge that life will end. 'To put meaning in one's life may end in madness, but life without meaning is the torture of restlessness and vague desire; it is a boat longing for the sea and yet afraid' (Masters 1915:64). Some writers will distinguish between what they consider to be a logical paradox and an existential paradox, but we do not need to take time here to look at the difference.

Life is full of contradictions and paradoxes of all kinds which must not be denied but welcomed as true tensions to be confronted and explored. Humans hold the capacity to live with, and in, a paradoxical existence, constructing meaning to create a unique, personal world, to which they bring both subjective and objective awareness. Nietzsche, Kierkegaard, May, and others believed 'the paradox of human existence should not be resolved because choosing to emphasise one pole to the exclusion of the other can result in behaviour that is either too expanded or too limited' (Krug & Schneider 2016:18). One of the tasks of a supervisor is to encourage supervisees to engage with such tensions, noting any focus on one pole or the other and so develop objective and subjective awareness and balanced behaviour. The ability to move between objective and subjective, between contradictions and paradoxes, may be unsettling but is also creative and brings energy to a person's way of being. Many of us get stuck in the uncomfortable feeling of confronting two or more opposed 'true' experiences. I may love my partner, but when they do something which severely displeases me, I may hate them; I may feel justified in that anger and at the same time feel guilty about feeling it. I must accept that I truly hold those paradoxes in the same moment.

We must learn to live fully in a world where we live to die; where we are significant and insignificant at the same time; where the present moment is eternal, yet fleeting. To be authentic we must accept that both poles are active and engage with both. We are tasked with finding meaning and living courageously in this paradoxical state and not being engulfed or frozen by it.

# 4

# PHENOMENOLOGICAL INVESTIGATION

When applying existential thought to practical ways of researching and working, the approach forms a natural fit with phenomenology. Phenomenology grew out of the carnage of World War One (1914–1918). Eagleton (1983:54) described the aftermath of the war as a time in which previous ideologies and cultural values were tested, leaving 'a myopic obsession with the categorising of facts; philosophy…torn between such a positivism on the one hand, and an indefensible subjectivism on the other; forms of relativism and irrationalism…rampant, and art reflected this bewildering loss of bearings'. This called for a new philosophical method which 'would lend absolute certainty to a disintegrating civilization' (Eagleton 1983:54). Into that gap stepped the German philosopher, Edmund Husserl (1859–1938), who despite the origins of phenomenology being traceable to Kant, Hegel, and Brentano, is regarded as 'the fountainhead of phenomenology in the twentieth century' (Vandenberg 1997:11). Although Husserl's transcendental approach is relatively well-known, it is worth noting that at least seven types of phenomenology have been identified. The *Encyclopedia of Phenomenology* (Kluwer Academic Publishers 1997) lists them as:

1. **Transcendental constitutive phenomenology** – how objects are constituted in transcendental consciousness by setting aside questions of any relation to the natural world.
2. **Naturalistic constitutive phenomenology** – how consciousness constitutes things in the world of nature, assuming with the natural attitude that consciousness is part of nature.
3. **Existential phenomenology** – concrete human existence, including our experience of free choice and/or action in concrete situations.
4. **Generative historicist phenomenology** – meaning, found in our experience, is generated in historical processes of collective experience over time.
5. **Genetic phenomenology** – the genesis of meanings of things within one's own stream of experience.
6. **Hermeneutical phenomenology phenomenology/post-phenomenology** –interpretive structures of experience.
7. **Realistic phenomenology** – the structure of consciousness and intentionality as occurring in a real world, largely external to consciousness.

Max van Manen (2014) offers us a contemporary view, with even more types and a list of the writers most associated with them. Based on van Manen, I have drawn up the following table to illustrate the historical developments.

Despite some differences, the core elements are consistent, so rather than analyse each one, I shall return to Husserl to continue my description of phenomenology.

Husserl challenged the belief that objects in the external world exist independently and that the information about objects is reliable, instead proposing that people can only be certain about how things appear in or present themselves to their consciousness. Other than that, there was no certainty, and the external world was reduced to the content of the individual's consciousness. This meant that realities should be treated as pure 'phenomena' and the providers of absolute data. Husserl himself named his method 'phenomenology' considering it to be the science of pure 'phenomena', with the aim being to return to the concrete. This has often been captured by the slogan 'Back to the things themselves!' (Eagleton 1983:56; Kruger 1988:28; Moustakas 1994:26).

*Table 4.1* Phenomenologies (Hanaway 2020a)

| **Beginnings** | | |
|---|---|---|
| | Transcendental | Husserl |
| | Personalistic & Value | Scheler |
| | Faith & Empathic | Stein |
| | Ontological | Heidegger |
| | Personal practice | Patočka |
| **Strands & traditions** | | |
| | Ethical | Levinas |
| | Existential | Sartre |
| | Gender | De Beauvoir |
| | Embodiment | Merleau-Ponty |
| | Hermeneutic | Gadamer |
| | Critical | Ricœur |
| | Literary | Blanchot |
| | Oneiric-Poetic | Bachelard |
| | Sociological | Schutz |
| | Political | Arendt |
| | Material | Henry |
| | Deconstruction | Derrida |
| **New thoughts & unthoughts** | | |
| | Technoscience/Post-phenomenology | Ihde |
| | Learning | Dreyfus |
| | Sense | Serres |
| | Ecological | Lingus |
| | Fragmentary | Nancy |
| | Religious | Chrétien |
| | Philological | Agamben |
| | Radical | Marion |
| | Techno-genetic | Stiegler |
| | Ecstatic-poetic | Gosetti-Ferencei |
| | Objectivity | Figal |
| | Evential | Romano |

One of his students, Martin Heidegger (1889–1976), developed hermeneutic phenomenology. Initially his thinking was in alignment with Husserl's, but he later challenged several key aspects of transcendental phenomenology giving more focus to phenomenological inquiry, with the need for interpretation before understanding, thus placing greater importance on the researcher/listener. Husserl was interested in the nature of knowledge (an epistemological focus), while Heidegger was interested in the nature of temporality and being (an ontological focus). This makes him more interested in the relationship between an individual and their 'lifeworld', believing that individuals' realities are invariably influenced by the world in which they live and that individuals already have an understanding of themselves within the world, even if they are not consciously aware of it. From this we get the concept of *Dasein* or 'Being there' with the idea of the dialogue between a person and their world, understanding that humans cannot experience a phenomenon without referring back to their individual background understandings. The *Dasein* concept therefore 'allows humans to wonder about their own existence and question the meaning of their Being-in-the-world' (McConnell-Henry et al. 2009:9). Essentially, Heidegger's hermeneutic phenomenology is focused on 'what it means to be' or 'Being-in-the-world' which is explored through seeking to understand those deeper layers of human experience obscured beneath surface awareness, and how the individual's lifeworld, or the world as they pre-reflectively experience it, influences their experience.

Both Heidegger and Husserl were concerned with exploring the 'lived-world' in terms of an 'average' existence in an ordinary world. Schutz (1899–1959) went further in suggesting that 'the human world comprises various provinces of meaning' (Vandenberg 1997:7). We can begin to see the coming together of key existential concerns and a phenomenological approach, with the ideas further explored and expanded on by the likes of Jean-Paul Sartre (1905–1980) and Maurice Merleau-Ponty (1908–1961) amongst others.

However, after flourishing in the first two decades following the Second World War, phenomenology did not immediately establish itself as a viable new approach to psychological research, as according to Giorgi (cited in Stones 1988:141), 'no phenomenological praxis or a systematic and sustained way of working, had been developed'. The approach was somewhat forgotten until the 1970s, which finally saw the development of the required praxis, providing a methodological realisation of the phenomenological philosophical attitude.

This emphasised the key task of phenomenological research as being to 'describe' the phenomena as accurately as possible, without looking to existing frameworks, but instead remaining true to the experience. Welman & Kruger (1999:189, quoted in Vallack 2021) described phenomenologists as being 'concerned with understanding social and psychological phenomena from the perspectives of people involved'. In other words, the primary interest was in the lived experience and the way 'ordinary' individuals attended to their 'ordinary' lives. This may seem very unscientific, and indeed Vandenberg in van Manen (1997:41) pointed out that the approach may come more easily to poets and artists than to scientists:

> [Phenomena] have something to say to us – this is common knowledge among poets and painters. Therefore, poets and painters are born phenomenologists. Or rather, we are all born phenomenologists; the poets and painters among us, however, understand very well their task of sharing, by means of word and image, their insights with others – an artfulness that is also laboriously practised by the professional phenomenologist.

The approach calls for those using a phenomenological approach to be open, and to avoid assumptions, even if these flow from well-established and accepted theories. This means that phenomenologists will try to avoid techniques or follow chronological steps. If they were to do so there would be a danger that there could be 'a great injustice to the integrity of the phenomenon' (Hycner 1999:143). However, this does not mean that there are no guidelines.

Although the individual's experience of the phenomenon is the starting point, phenomenologists, in contrast to positivists, believe that we 'cannot be detached from our own presuppositions and should not pretend otherwise' (Hammersley 2000). The key task of those using a phenomenological approach is to be aware of their assumptions and prejudices and seek to put them to one side in order to best focus on the phenomenon and so ensure that 'the phenomenon dictates the method (not vice-versa) including even the type of participants' (Hycner 1999:156). Husserl used the term 'bracketing' to describe this process of putting aside prior assumptions. It calls for deep and intensive listening and observation and dialogue directed to a deeper understanding of the person's unique experience, feelings, beliefs, and convictions. Wherever possible people are invited to describe their lived experience in a straightforward and simple way, allowing the listener to bracket their own assumptions and gain entry to the worldview of the other person.'Husserl called the freedom from suppositions the *epoche*, a Greek word meaning to stay away from or abstain' (Moustakas 1994:85) which allows for a true, open, and respectful 'inter view' or interchange between people.

There is no prescriptive framework for phenomenological research or for a phenomenological interchange. Indeed, most phenomenologists would avoid the concept of data analysis, believing that 'analysis' can have dangerous connotations for phenomenology as the 'term [analysis] usually means a 'breaking into parts' and therefore often means a loss of the whole phenomenon' (Hycner 1999:161). However, Hycner did identify what he saw as identifiable elements or phases including:

Bracketing and phenomenological reduction
Delineating units of meaning
Clustering of units of meaning to form themes
Summarising each interview, validating it and where necessary modifying it
Extracting general and unique themes and making a composite summary

Although these are usually referred to in the context of research, they are also to some extent valid when taking a phenomenological approach to coaching and supervision and so worth a brief overview here.

## Bracketing and phenomenological reduction

I have already introduced the requirement to bracket one's assumptions (including previous understandings based on scientific theories, knowledge, or explanation; truth or falsity of claims made by participants; and personal views and experiences) in order to be truly present to another person and their unique experience. Husserl also speaks of the process of 'phenomenological reduction'. The word 'reduction' is perhaps an unfortunate one. When used philosophically it has nothing to do with the reductionist natural science methodology and does not imply diminishing something, but instead returns to the Latin root and meaning – to restore or return something to a more primordial mode. Husserl is speaking of the use of *epoche* or bracketing to affect a specific shift in attitude in the perception of external and internal objects to reveal not only the phenomenal nature of objects, but also transcendental subjectivity and intersubjectivity. This means that we are asked to take no position with respect to the ultimate (existential) reality but simply to witness what is presented and describe it as such. One could say that in this way the facts are 'reduced' to the way they stand out as presences. In recognising this, the phenomenologist must also recognise their own embeddedness in intersubjectivity. Husserl claimed that when one examines the phenomenal ground of what it means to be an 'I', one discovers that it is impossible to have a sense of 'I-ness' without an accompanying sense and expectation of 'you-ness' or 'other' and that at the core of the sense of 'I', there is the experience of a plurality of 'you's' which Husserl termed 'co-subjectivity' (*Mitsubjectivität*). I recognise my commonality with others and also my difference. Gurwitsch (1966:443) described this as the way by which 'the psychologist, in analysing his own conscious life, becomes aware of its relationship to, and connectedness with the conscious life of other persons…in his very experience of himself as a human being are implied references to other human beings, to an open horizon of humanity…and co-subjectivity (*Mitsubjectivität*). Experience of oneself proves to be inseparable from that of others'. In this we can see the phenomenology of empathy (Husserl 1982; Scheler 1970; Stein 2008; Zahavi 2010).

## Delineating units of meaning

In this stage the listener/researcher tries to understand the meaning behind the statements that the speaker/interviewee makes. To a large extent this starts with an individual judgement call regarding which theme in the material offered should be deconstructed first. As Hycner (1999:150–151) states '…in this step…the phenomenological researcher (is) engaged in something which cannot be precisely delineated, for here he is involved in that ineffable thing known as creative insight'. All themes are equally important and when choosing which to follow the listener need to make a very honest assessment of their own meaning-making, their presuppositions and prejudices, in order for these to be effectively bracketed. Perception is the primary source for gathering such data, and perceptions emerge from looking at things through many 'angles', which Husserl terms 'horizons'. Through horizonalisation an initial meaning is identified but from there the horizon continues to extend and open up new perspectives. Horizons are unlimited.

## Clustering of units of meaning to form themes

In research, units of identified meaning are identified, and the researcher tries to elicit the essence of meaning of such units within the holistic context. Colaizzi (1978) refers to this as the researcher's 'artistic' judgement. Often there is overlap in the clusters, which can be expected, considering the nature of human phenomena. By interrogating the meaning of the various clusters, central themes are determined. All themes are equally valued and by following one and deconstructing it the likelihood is that it will take you to the same key as would be found by choosing to follow any of the other themes which are identified.

Unlike many research methods, there is no computer software package which can be turned to when working phenomenologically because 'it is not an algorithmic process' (Kelle 1995:3).

## Summarise each interview, validate, and modify

Having grouped the material from the interviews into meaning clusters the phenomenological researcher would then seek to summarise them within the overall holistic context. The aim is to reconstruct the inner world of experience of the subject, indicating the individual's own way of experiencing the elements of the existential dimensions including spatiality, temporality, materiality, and spirituality, which Hycner (1999:153–154) reminds us 'must be understood in relation to others and to the total inner "world"'. The researcher would then check the validity of their findings with the interviewee and make any modifications which may be necessary.

## General and unique themes for all the interviews and composite summary

Finally, the researcher must identify themes common to all interviews and also the significant differences. Where there are such differences, care must be taken not to cluster common themes. Unique and minority differences provide an important counterpoint in the research.

By this point Sadala & Adorno (2001:289) suggest the process 'transforms participants' everyday expressions into expressions appropriate to the scientific discourse supporting the research'. However, it is important to remember that 'good research is not generated by rigorous data alone...[but] "going beyond" the data to develop ideas' (Coffey & Atkinson 1996:139). We should also take heed that as Husserl asserted, 'Ultimately, all genuine and, in particular, all scientific knowledge, rests on inner evidence' (1970:61) and therefore for Husserl subjective and objective knowledge are intimately intertwined. For us to understand the reality of a phenomenon it is also necessary for us to understand the phenomenon as it is lived by a person.

When working phenomenologically within the coaching context we are remaining true to a process of phenomenological investigation through which we seek to understand and describe the essence of a phenomenon by exploring it from the perspective of the client; that is, the person who has experienced it. We are seeking to understand, as far as possible, the meaning of any described experience, in terms of *what* was experienced but also *how* it was experienced. However, it is worth remembering as Douglas Adams pointed out, 'Human beings, who are almost unique in having the ability to learn from the experience of others, are also remarkable for their apparent disinclination to do so' (1990:120). So, coaches are not taking on an easy task when choosing to use an existential phenomenological approach. The coaching approach does not call for the discipline of a phenomenological research but will be aware of the same elements and use the same philosophies.

# 5

# THE EXISTENTIALLY INFORMED COACHING APPROACH

## What do we mean by existential coaching?

In a previous book, *The Handbook of Existential Coaching Practice* (Hanaway 2020a), I have given an explanation of what we mean by existential coaching. One requirement of an existential phenomenological approach is to bracket assumptions. In that spirit, I am bracketing the assumption that those of you choosing to read this book are doing so because you already understand the existential coaching approach and just wish to see how it can be used in supervision. So, in order not to work from that assumption, I have decided to firstly introduce the existential coaching approach to those of you who may not already be well acquainted with it.

Existential thought is centred on the human lived experience and so concentrates on our experience of 'being' in the world on a temporal journey. It is concerned with how we experience our lives, and how we approach and make decisions, taking full responsibility for the implications of each decision. In common with other coaching approaches, it aims to facilitate the development of an increased understanding and new perspective on the way we live, to increase the client's awareness of themselves, the world in which they exist, and the future that they want, whilst also considering some new questions about life.

Existential coaching is not solution-driven and instead expresses caution in providing solutions. It suggests answers will be more profound and more beneficial to the client when the coach stays still and pays attention to what is in front of them rather than working to 'fix it'. If the client finds their own answers, they are likely to be more meaningful, and the client will have more commitment to any plan of action they may formulate.

Although having its roots in philosophy, existential coaching, and providing room for philosophical debate and contemplation, the approach is ultimately one with 'an entirely pragmatic objective: to help people to live their lives with greater deliberation, liberty, understanding and passion' (van Deurzen & Hanaway 2012:xvi). Although we are each a unique individual, and as such will experience our lives differently, there are a number of givens which we all share, and which an existential approach suggests we cannot avoid. Our experience of being born alone and ultimately dying alone whilst seeking to create a meaningful journey between those two points can result in anxiety. Although drawing on philosophy, the approach provides a very practical framework for an approach to coaching. A client may seek companionship in their journey of meaning-making, and benefit from a coaching relationship which facilitates the exploration of our being, and the dilemmas and challenges that will inevitably be encountered as we forge our unique path.

The existential approach can be used in all areas of coaching including life, business, executive, and leadership coaching. It can be the main focus of the work, or elements and themes can be used within a more integrative coaching model. I have already covered the key focus areas for existentialists in Chapter Three. Existential coaching uses the same philosophical framework and focus, drawing on the work of Heidegger, Sartre, Kierkegaard, and others to underpin its coaching approach. It also draws on more recent philosophical practices including philosophical consultancy (Achenbach 1984, 2002; Hoogendijk 1991) and existential analysis (Längle 2011, 2014; Batthyany & Russo-Netzer 2016).

There is very little writing specifically on existential coaching until the early 2000s when some existential thinkers turned their attention to the use of what may be termed 'applied' existential thought in areas such as coaching, consultancy, leadership development, and conflict resolution (Berg 2006; van Deurzen & Hanaway 2012; Echeveria 2013; Hanaway & Reed 2014; Längle & Bürgi 2014; Hanaway 2018; Johner et al. 2018; Jacob 2019; Hanaway 2020a, b).

The approach works with all the same issues as other coaching approaches, but an existential coach may focus particularly on existential issues such as anxiety, authenticity, freedom, responsibility, purpose, meaning, paradox, and dilemma, all set within the framework of 'being', which is relational and emotional. People may present for coaching with a number of concrete and practical dilemmas, but these may have roots in more existential concerns. This is something many other coaching approaches may choose not to focus on, fearing that it may divert the work away from any concrete problem the client is facing.

## *The role of phenomenology in existential coaching*

In addition to the existential concerns, existential coaching employs a phenomenological method of enquiry stemming from the philosophical traditions of Edmund Husserl, Martin Heidegger, Maurice Merleau-Ponty, Jean-Paul Sartre, et al. In Chapter Four, I have outlined how phenomenology provides a framework for a practical tool for exploration. However, let us briefly look here at what phenomenology brings to enrich the coaching experience.

Phenomenology is concerned with the study of structures of experience, or consciousness. In more recent developments of the philosophy of mind, the term 'phenomenology' is often restricted to the characterisation and experience of sensory qualities. In literal terms, phenomenology is the study of 'phenomena', the way things appear in our experience, with the meanings which we individually attach to them in response to our own thoughts, perceptions, and experiences. Experience is not just about sensation but is a much richer field, calling for us to address the meaning things have in our experience; notably, the significance of objects, events, tools, time, the self, and others, as these things arise and are experienced in our day-to-day 'lived-world'. Therefore, phenomenology is about conscious lived experience. At the heart of existential coaching lie the questions of how we give meaning to our experiences, how we invest in the challenge of finding meaning going forward, and how we are in touch with, and are willing to authentically explore our experiences. All of these aspects of the way in which we live an embodied, temporal existence are of relevance to existential coaching.

Phenomenology provides a coach with a way of studying the structure of various types of experience ranging from perception, thought, memory, imagination, emotion, desire, language, bodily awareness, embodied action, and social activity. Such experience involves the directedness of experience toward things in the world, the property of consciousness, that is a consciousness of or about something. Husserl called this 'intentionality'. Our experience is directed toward, represents, or 'intends' things only through particular concepts, thoughts, ideas, images, etc. These make up the meaning or content of a given experience and are distinct from the things they present. They are revelatory with regard to how we live in the world as an embodied being, set within a time, social, and cultural context, and expressed through our actions and our verbal and bodily language. Given its revelatory potential, phenomenological investigation is an important gift to the coach, as it can help in identifying what is important to the client. All of our struggles are interconnected with recurring existential themes within our understanding of our worldview and can be accessed through the phenomenological approach. Although the word may be hard to say, and many people may stumble over it, the practice is simple and based on common sense, drawing on the innate interest we have in our fellow human beings.

Van Deurzen and Hanaway (2012:8), in relation to existential coaching, describe the objective of phenomenology as being

> to gather information and understanding carefully. This is always done from multiple perspectives: we do this by going round the houses and investigating different aspects and different interpretations of reality until a true picture emerges. Phenomenology is the science of the way in which things appear to us. It proceeds by systematically describing a phenomenon from different angles until we can intuitively grasp its essence in quite a new way.

This emphasises the patience which the approach requires and how challenging that can be for coaches or clients looking for quick or sure solutions. The power remains with the client, with the coach acting as the guide who has access to certain maps but cannot guarantee that the routes shown are still open or are suitable for the individual client. The terrain may prove exciting to some, and terrifying to others.

Spinelli, another existential writer, psychotherapist, and coach also draws on the phenomenological existential approach in his coaching work. On his website (www.plexworld .com) he describes the approach as being 'practically focused and highly accessible…developed from a set of interconnected principles designed to assist clients to more effectively respond to the dilemmas of living and act in greater harmony with their chosen goals and aspirations'. He sees its core function as being to 'address those areas of conflict and tension that restrict our potential for personal achievement and diminish our ability to engage in fulfilling relationships with others'. Again, there is no promise of a speedy solution.

For many coaches the phenomenological method presents a number of challenges. Not only does it actively avoid coming up with any quick solution, or presenting linear or chronological pathways for the client, but it also necessitates the coach to 'bracket' their assumptions. It calls on the coach to be aware, and sensitive to their own prejudices and expectations. This may result in the coach feeling naked and vulnerable, as these assumptions may include beliefs we have accepted or developed in relation to set theories, and system-led training. The existential coach cannot so easily draw on generic techniques and exercises, instead placing more emphasis on the lived relational experience.

For this reason, some existential coaches are reluctant to use many standard exercises, tools, or psychometric tests. They may feel that they detract from the uniqueness of the individual and can lead to labelling and the forming of assumptions. However, there are some tools which are aimed at exploring some existential ideas around meaning which may start a deeper and more individual dialogue with the client and I shall expand on these in future chapters. An existential coach may not wish to use the tests in their entirety as systematic 'tests', but they may be useful in enabling coaches to formulate and clarify questions or explorations they may wish to discuss with their client.

The coach is called upon to be authentic and open in their working relationship with the client, focused on the client's way of being-in-the-world and studying the 'phenomena' of the moment. Existential coaches do not take the position of expert. They cannot be too quick to jump to the conclusion that they are understanding their client or the dilemmas they bring. The coach will seek to explore and clarify before tentatively offering their understanding, in a way which invites the client to question and further clarify that understanding, rather than place the client in a position where they may feel the need to too quickly agree that the coach has indeed understood the complexity of their unique lived experience. This means that the existential coach is less reliant than some other coaches on diagnostic or test-driven reductive explanations. Instead, they must commit to explore the client's perception, thought, imagination, emotion, bodily awareness, embodied action, linguistic, and social activity in relation to any presented dilemma. In doing so, they will attempt to identify and bracket any of their own assumptions, including any solution to the client's dilemma which may seem all too obvious to the coach. If such a solution was that obvious, there will be a reason why the client has not thought of it themselves. Facilitating the client's exploration of the reasons why that solution was not identified, will require the coach to openly and uncritically enter the client's worldview and seek to gain understanding of the underlying blockages and resistance. To explore the client's emotional response and reasoning, the coach will take a patient approach, combining active listening with tentative feedback and summarising, encouraging the client to challenge both the coach, and themselves in their exploration of ways forward, looking at the potential pathways in relation to how meaningful they may be, how well they may fit with the client's authentic self and with their values and beliefs.

## The role of the existential concerns in existential coaching

As we are beginning to see from the above, the phenomenological approach begins to unveil issues which relate to the existential givens. For any individual client, different givens will be more important at a particular time. In the same way, different existential coaches may place greater emphasis on one of the givens.

In identifying four key ideas which lie at the heart of existential coaching, Spinelli starts by placing his emphasis on the need to focus on meaning. Without knowing what was meaningful to the client the coach may embark on many unhelpful journeys, based primarily on what would be meaningful to the coach. Spinelli suggests that to find out what is meaningful for the client, rather than for the coach, requires a joint exploration of the client's worldview, including their values and beliefs, needs, wants, hopes, and aspirations.

He engages with the paradox that we may experience contradictions in all these areas noting that, 'our worldview contains competing and contradictory attitudes and stances that provoke conflict between our wider life-oriented needs and goals and our work-focused objectives, responsibilities and development plans' (www.plexworld.com). To try to ignore these contradictions is inauthentic and disrespectful to the complexity of the uniqueness of the client. It is a requirement when working existentially to acknowledge and explore the contradictions, paradoxes, ambiguities, or ambivalences which the client may present. This facilitates the client to become more aware of their uniqueness, whilst recognising thrownness, and the commonality of the existential givens. In this way they are more connected to their own underlying worldview and better able to identify and to challenge their own contradictions, seeing and acknowledging these internal conflicts as the start of creative progress. Throughout the coaching process the client's sense of where meaning lies may shift and change and so the coach needs to continually reassess what is meaningful and explore the obstacles which the client is encountering in finding meaning in their current situation.

So, for Spinelli, perhaps the most vital ingredient of existential coaching is the provision of a safe, mental space for a client to find their own meaning. It is not the role of the coach to suggest, or supply that meaning for the client. This would be impossible as they do not have full access to the internal or external space of the client's world. Even when there may be similarities in the coach and client's worldviews, how those views have been formed will differ and will be experienced differently within the social, emotional, environmental, and spiritual elements of the individual's world. When a coach perceives a similarity with the client this calls for the coach to be even more vigilant in bracketing their assumptions. If we consider someone to be 'like us' then we may not give the same energy or attention to deconstructing our understanding and exploring the differences between the worldview of the client and our own. A coach cannot understand the client's world better than the client, and so will not seek to impose change; such pressure can cause the client to retreat from their own self exploration, as Spinelli points out, 'Existential Coaching recognises that the less we feel required (whether by others or ourselves) to alter something in our lives, the more willing and able we become to consider the possibilities and worth of change – and then act accordingly' (ibid).

Jacob (2019) shares Spinelli's view of the importance for existential coaching in creating a place for the client to explore the meaning, paradoxes, and opportunities within their worldview. Jacob also emphasises the need to acknowledge and work with existential anxiety and the need for authenticity, writing, 'Existential coaching is a place to think, ponder, reflect and explore the human condition in the context of a specific goal. It helps clients to identify areas of self-deception (blind spots), to create more opportunity and choice, and to live a more authentic and full life in spite of (and indeed because of) inevitable existential anxiety (angst) that accompanies living in this world with other people' (Jacob 2019:17).

Having focused on meaning, Spinelli turned his attention to the inevitable contradictions and conflicts which will present during an exploration of meaning, and he names dealing with conflict as another of his four areas of focus. It is inevitable that in any dilemma we are faced with a conflict between the myriad potentialities involved in each of the different ways of moving forward which may be identified. With every pathway we choose, we are abandoning others. With every gain there is a loss. However, conflict presents us with an opportunity for creativity and development (Hanaway 2020b). If we do not engage with it, we miss a chance to progress, and instead choose to opt for the status quo.

Expressed conflict helps us to see what is really meaningful and important to an individual. Usually, conflict occurs when our self-concept or values are perceived to be under attack. We value both of these and will fight to defend them. The conflict may take the form of an internal struggle, or it may bring us in direct connection with the existential concern of relatedness, and the ways in which we are in agreement or disagreement with others. One of the challenges of relatedness is that we can choose to see another person as an obstacle to our project, or alternatively as a facilitator towards our goal.

The existential coach will not ignore any conflicts, but instead will see them as ways of uncovering the important issues and clarifying the client's stance towards those concerns. This willingness to go beyond the more positive coaching models, and engage in depth with tensions, paradoxes, and possibly with despair, not colluding with a way of thinking which is linear and causal, is expressed by Spinelli when he wrote, 'unlike many other coaching programmes that only focus upon broadly positive, self-actualising qualities and possibilities for each client,

Existential Coaching's approach also recognises and gives equal emphasis to the divided stances, aims and aspirations that may well exist as competing values and beliefs held by each client' (ibid).

If the coach fails to address the issues and sources of dividedness and conflict, this may render any coaching intervention simplistic, and meaningless to the client, and result in the client feeling not listened to, misunderstood, or that one aspect of their thinking is being considered unacceptable or unhelpful, and so is being rejected or ignored. If this happens then the coaching is doomed to failure, or possibly can only offer a brief and inadequate resolution. Rather than resulting in just an unsuccessful coaching session, the experience may be damaging for the client, and provoke greater levels of uncertainty, potentially leading to an increased sense of hopelessness or unacceptability.

Relatedness in the coaching process is certainly not all about conflict. We are not able to exist without others, we desire for our life and being to have meaning for others, although we realise that we cannot solely depend on them for our validation and must learn to live with the knowledge that we are fundamentally alone (Yalom 1980). Despite the need to acknowledge this aloneness, Weixel-Dixon (2016:20) suggests that 'it is **not** possible to be totally isolated, nor is it possible to be **fused** with another person; we stand always in relatedness, in some form'. This is something which Bugental refers to, using the dimensions of 'a-part-of' and 'apart-from' (1992:239). At all times we are never, and can never, be truly detached nor totally connected.

The existence of other people helps define who we are and who we are not. They can give us a measure as to how alike or different we feel ourselves to be from others. I recognise my gender or race only because I encounter those who differ in that way from me. If such differences did not exist, I would not be able to identify myself as female or white, as there would be nothing to set myself alongside for consideration. To identify oneself or others by these crude labels is of course dangerous, as words such as 'female' or 'white' do not tell us anything about how individuals experience being labelled in this way, whether by themselves or by others. For one person being 'female' may carry a great deal of meaning. It may be a positive experience they can relate to. For another, it may be a word, or an assumed generic experience, coupled with a set of expectations which they do not relate to. For some a label may be empowering, for others restricting. Whether we like it or not, people will try to label others, they will seek both commonality and difference. As an existential coach I must work not to do so, but to attempt to listen to discover how the client experiences their own being.

The immediate relationship in play in any coaching relationship is that between coach and client. As well as two roles, those of coach and client being involved, it is a relationship of two people. I have already mentioned the need for the existential coach to take care in respecting difference and not jump to any assumption that they are like the client in any way. Any similarities and differences must come from exploration during the coaching, rather than preconceived ideas. An existential coach must cultivate a sensitive awareness of, and to individual and cultural diversity, and welcome the richness this brings to the coaching experience. Quite often the material the client brings will include issues relating to others, who the coach can only experience through the lens of the client and therefore as projections.

Time and temporality can also be an important reference within existential coaching. How the client is experiencing, and consciously noting time gives insight into their worldview and their own phenomenological positioning. Indeed, our worldview is not static but continues to develop and refine as a result of our experiences, reflections, and interactions with others. The client's internal sense of time passing and the goals they may have achieved, or failed to have achieved, may form a theme within the coaching content. Externally defined time is often an issue with clients starting with their experience of time in and between sessions. Do those times feel right, too long, or too short? Externally measured time is a common concern in presenting issues. A client may feel pressured by imposed deadlines or may feel that time lies heavily, or moves too quickly; they may measure time by personal or organisational milestones determined by what they have achieved. The client may also have expectations of where they should be in life by a certain age, be concerned about the aging process, or wish to proactively prepare for change, be that promotion or retirement. The existential coach will work with these elements of transience and change, just as any other coach would, but they would set them within the context and acceptance of the temporality of life.

For some people time can feel like a source of certainty. Time will move forward; it will not stop. However much the experience of time may hint at certainty, we have no certainty in how it will be experienced. As befits an approach centred on uncertainty, existential coaching does not offer time-based solutions. Some coaching approaches offer a fairly speedy search for a solution to the client's presenting problem – their 'external reality – the outer game' (Bluckert 2006:48). It can be tempting for a coach to try to come up with such suggestions for solutions, feeling that to do so demonstrates their skills and validates their title of coach and the payment they receive. This can lead to the coach to too quickly form the belief that they have fully understood the complexities of the client's issues. Existential coaching seeks to illuminate and deconstruct these complexities rather than seek quick answers and so is willing to actively engaged with the lack of certainty. The client's level of comfort with uncertainty may indicate how they interact with the world and their level of need for structure and a belief in a universal truth. Existentialists will not find an authentic place for certainty but urge us to accept the uncertainty of our existence and look to find meaning within the limitations of our existence.

The existential approach will require the client to accept their freedom and responsibility. This means acknowledging the decisions they have made so far and exploring the implications for themselves and others of any decisions they make and act on as a result of the coaching. If the client chooses to stay in a difficult situation the coach will ensure that they acknowledge that this is a choice. Even refusing to consider change or take any action, is a choice. There is no 'easy get-out clause' for the client in existential coaching.

The depth to which existential issues will be explicitly explored with an individual client is dependent on the nature and length of the coaching contract, the level of trust between coach and client, the relevance of existential themes to the focus of the coaching work, and the client's willingness to enter into discussion of these areas. There will always be existential issues present but the coach does not need to label them as such and will be sensitive to the needs and requests of the client.

Some of the above may seem somewhat ungrounded when considered against some of the more common presenting coaching issues. The table below indicates the concreteness of the approach grounded in everyday experience and dilemmas. One can see that many of the issues are attached to one or more given.

Existential coaches will use the emotions which are presented, or notably absent, as pathways to a deeper understanding of the importance of the issues the client brings. They will not aim for a cool professionalism with the coach as holder of knowledge, but instead will consider themselves to be a fellow being facilitating the client's journey or project. If a client expresses an emotion this will not be closed down or seen as a distraction but will be explored so that coach and client can use the intentionality of the emotion to clarify what is important for the client in the coaching project. The coach will encourage the client to be open to their vulnerability and to any 'negative' or 'difficult' emotions they may be experiencing not only within the presenting issue, but also within the coaching session. Emotions are important tools in an existential approach. An existential coach needs to develop a trusting working alliance with their

Table 5.1 Examples of the Relationship between Common Issues in Coaching and the Existential Givens

| Common Presenting Dilemma | Existential Given |
|---|---|
| Feeling paralysed in professional or personal life | Anxiety |
| Being afraid of making a decision and acting on it | |
| Being paralysed by the knowledge of the temporality of existence | |
| Fearful of change | |
| Feeling isolated as the values and ethos of a group/ family/organisation differ from one's own | Authenticity |
| Feeling the need to play a part to gain respect or validation, or as an attempt to be accepted | |
| Being afraid to express one's view | |
| Feeling stuck | Freedom and Responsibility |
| Issue with authority rather than recognising one's own power | |
| Reluctance to delegate | |
| Reluctance to accept responsibility for actions | |
| Feeling there is no reason to continue with life/ job/project | Meaning |
| Feeling that one's meaning is not aligned with those around you | |
| A feeling of isolation and loneliness | Relatedness |
| Issues with others, e.g. family, colleagues, etc. | |
| Sense of time passing one by | Time and Temporality |
| Judging one's achievements by age or chronological expectations | |
| Issues around change, e.g. professional restructures, aging, different phases of life, change in relationships with others, e.g. aging parents, independent children, redundancy, retirement, promotion | |
| Desire to control self, others, and environment | Uncertainty |
| Plans and structures – desire for or rejection of certainty | |
| Disagreements with others including differences between organisational and personal values | Values and Beliefs |

client, within which the client feels secure about expressing all their emotions in relation to the focus of the coaching. This can be hard to establish when the coaching has not been directly commissioned by the client but by the client's employer. They may feel reluctant to talk about any negativity towards their employing organisation or individuals within the hierarchy or anger about their treatment or frustration with organisational structures and demands. The coach must make it safe to explore such fears.

## *The Existential Dimensions*

In addition to considering the client's presenting issues, and the content of the coaching sessions, in relation to the 'givens', an existential coach may also explore the ways in which things are being experienced within what are termed the 'existential dimensions' to which I have made reference in earlier chapters. Although existentialism does not divide people into types, it will explore the way in which an individual is 'in the world' at a particular stage, and consider how this can be placed on a 'map of human existence', which itself can be divided into the four dimensions; social, physical, psychological, and spiritual (Binswanger 1963; Yalom 1980; van Deurzen 1988).

An existential coach will see the dimensions as places to find meaning. In some areas meaning may be easily identified, whereas others may be more problematic. The dimensions consist of the *Umwelt*, which is concerned with the physical world, and promotes questions on how we relate to our environment, nature, physical body, the physicality of others, and the world of sensations; the *Mitwelt* which is concerned with social interactions, how we relate and communicate to others, our sense of belonging or of isolation, and how we interact with society as a whole; the *Eigenwelt* or psychological dimension, which is concerned with thoughts, memories, self-identity, similarities, and differences from others, and the *Überwelt* or spiritual dimension which is focused on beliefs, intuition, values, meaning, and purpose.

A coach may use these dimensions as a map to uncover a more holistic picture of the client's being-in-the-world, and the values and beliefs underpinning their behaviours. It may be apparent that the client more richly inhabits one dimension, or totally ignores another. It may be fruitful for the coach to note and reflect with the client which dimensions are given more priority, and whether the client is happy with this. If the informed client is content with only inhabiting some of their dimensions, it is not the role of the coach to try to change this but merely to identify it and explore with the client what might be the implications, thus providing the client with a platform to understand and consider past and future action.

An existential coaching supervisor will use the above understanding of existential coaching as a framework for their supervisory role. I shall explore how this would work in a practical way in the following chapters and through the use of some case examples.

# PART THREE

# 6

# BRINGING AN EXISTENTIAL APPROACH TO SUPERVISING COACHES

Supervision provides the opportunity for the supervisee to look afresh at their client's narrative, their own assumptions and biases about that client, and the quality of their relationship with the client and their coaching practice. It allows a safe place for the coach to explore any doubts or concerns that affect their ability to fully engage with the client. Existential coaching supervision is not a distinctly different discipline to other models of coaching supervision. It covers the same grounds and holds the same responsibility which one would expect in any supervisory relationship. It does, however, place its emphasis on the existential elements within the work which the supervisee presents, and so is usually more focused on the more 'philosophical' considerations than most models, but this is not at the exclusion of the concrete and practical dilemmas the coach and client are working with. This more philosophical approach suggests a dialogic approach to supervision (two people attending, listening, and exploring), as distinguished from monologue (where one person speaks and the other listens) and duologue (two people speaking to each other but only superficially listening). The listening will be to both the noema (directional, concerned with the content and the 'facts') and the noesis (concerned with the individual's experience of the content – their cognitive and affective meaning-making). In any dialogue

> there will always be the "top line" through which we deliver a primarily factual narrative
> of events which happened, and a deeper "bass note" consisting of the emotions that
> were generated. Just as in different styles of music, for some people their bass note is
> more prominent or "noisy", whereas for others it will be their top note which is more
> easily heard. To fully appreciate the "music" in what people say we must hear both top
> and bottom notes; facts and emotions.
>
> *(Hanaway 2020a:95)*

Existential psychotherapy already has a well-established model of supervision which existential coaching draws on (van Deurzen & Young 2009; Krug & Schneider 2016). It is a requirement for those in existential psychotherapy training, and for established practitioners to receive supervision. This means the models are built on the expectation that practitioners will be engaged in, or will have completed, many years of training in the approach, something which is not always true of coaches. This lineage with its emphasis on the philosophical, means that existential coaching supervision needs to be in tune with the values, theories, and practice of existential thought.

Because of its philosophical framework, existential supervision has been described as 'a joint philosophical enterprise' (van Deurzen & Young 2009:1) which calls for the supervisor and supervisee to engage in a unique and embodied way. Moja-Strasser (in van Deurzen & Young 2009:32) emphasises the role of embodiment when speaking of herself as a supervisor stating, 'I do not remain in my head, rather I respond from my whole being – thoughts, emotions, sensations and so on'. As Merleau-Ponty (2002) and Sartre (1996) constantly remind us, we are always present in an embodied form and meet others in their embodied state, therefore we have to acknowledge that a meeting of 'bodies' is part of both the coaching and supervisory experience. This, of course, links us to the existential given of relatedness, we are relating as supervisor and supervisee, as two unique individuals who are not just embodied brains, but are embodied complex organisms, with emotions, sensations, assumptions, and experiences. The importance of relatedness and the centrality of what it is to be human is at the centre of the existential approach to supervision. Madison (2008:1) writes, 'As an existential supervisor, I try to create an environment that sustains the "humanity" and mutuality of the supervisory relationship, combining respectful collegial rapport with moments of profound experiential depth'. Madison calls for existential supervisors to not only be alert to inherent power dynamics but to take a humble approach: 'the humility of un-knowing' calling for it not to be sacrificed 'in order to claim authority based solely upon years of experience or psychological "evidence"' (ibid). Such an unknowing stance can enable existential supervisors 'to exhibit a general willingness to question much of what passes unquestioned in contemporary therapeutic practice' (ibid).

Both supervisor and supervisee will bring all of these aspects into supervision. I have written earlier about the need to be aware of any assumptions, and as Yalom (1980:25) suggests 'so far as possible one must "bracket" (or set aside) one's own world perspective and enter the experiential world of the other'. In the supervisory relationship this is a layered requirement, with the need for the supervisor to be aware of, and bracket their own assumptions about theories and processes, about their relationship with the supervisee, and the material the supervisee brings. The supervisee needs to consider their own assumptions about expectations, for supervision, of the supervisor, and assumptions about the client and their narrative. If both parties can succeed in doing this it presents the opportunity for the supervision to be a simple and 'pure' experience which is neither 'esoteric or highbrow' (Krug & Schneider 2016), allowing supervisors to 'engage in this way of being with their clients and supervisees – it simply means being present, accepting, empathic, and attuned to the meanings clients and supervisees have made about themselves and their experiences' (ibid).

If we remove any assumptions or expectations of superiority in experience or knowledge, we are better able to meet and treat the supervisee as an individual and fellow traveller on the uncertain existential journey, instead of a role or classification. This calls on the supervisor to draw on all aspects of self in a real and authentic way. As Krug & Schneider (2016;19) point out, 'presence and curiosity cannot be cultivated when abstract models of human behavior or clinical diagnoses are projected onto clients or supervisees'. Supervisors must concern themselves with 'being with' and 'being for' supervisee's rather than 'treating', 'doing to', 'teaching', or 'instructing'. Madison (2008) links this approach to the concept of 'evocative' supervision. 'Evocative' supervision connotes an experiential-existential stance that prioritises implicit experiencing and by its nature is not quantifiable. Anything I say is not 'it' but only an attempt to point towards 'it' (ibid). Madison is drawing on the phenomenological research of van Manen (2002), a Canadian psychologist, who described his research as 'evocative', seemingly from the term *evocare*, which is concerned with the act of bringing to mind and creatively imagining through word or image. This moves existential supervision away from the 'clinical' and requires the supervisor to attend to 'the bodily flow of experiencing as it arises in shared understandings that are never solidified by explanation' (Madison ibid).

This idea of a meeting on many different levels, which informs the existential supervision experience may involve more discussion and disclosure than some other supervision models as it considers the two participants, supervisor and supervisee, to be engaged in a joint exploration of the client's material, rather than the relationship being one of master and apprentice. The supervisor is a fellow explorer, not an expert, but will openly, yet tentatively, offer ideas, questions, and sometimes suggestions to the supervisee for them to consider from their own experience and knowledge of their client. The process is a creative and non-didactic one in which the supervisor is willing to acknowledge their own state of 'unknowing', and to bracket any assumptions about there being a 'right' way to work with the client, other than openly, respectfully, and ethically. Moja-Strasser also stresses that in addition to unknowing, the supervision involves 'a process of unlearning, letting go of previously held assumptions…' noting that 'if you are capable of letting go to this extent you can find "the secret of the art of helping others"' (Moja-Strasser in van Deurzen & Young 2009:32).

An existential supervisor is less likely to offer suggestions for the use of techniques or tests but will seek to jointly explore the client's material in relation to their being-in-the-world, and may use the existential dimensions, and existential givens to illustrate or note aspects of the client's being which may have relevance to their presenting or unfolding issues, and to explore these through a form of phenomenological investigation based on Socratic and hermeneutic questioning. As Krug & Scheider (2016:8) remind us, the 'phenomenological method challenges the assumption that humans can be adequately understood in terms of some theory, whether it is a mechanical, biological, or psychological one'.

This dialogical approach with its philosophical basis means that clients and supervisees are considered to 'need experiences not explanations' (Reichmann quoted in Ehrenwald 1992:392). This is a challenge for supervisor and supervisee alike, as it requires an approach which does not fit neatly into any standardised model and is willing to operate in an uncertain space. Many supervisees desire clear instructions from their supervisor, hoping for a 'if you do this, this will happen' in response to the dilemmas they bring to supervision. This does not fit well with the existential approach, with existential thinkers such as Yalom (2003:34) believing that standardisation can make the work 'less real and less effective'. The reasoning behind this is partly because of the existential view of the uniqueness of each individual and of each relationship which are individually interpreted and constructed. What may be a standard approach or exercise which works for one person, in one situation, may be completely meaningless for another individual who finds themselves in the same situation. This may be because the two people draw on varied personal experiences, hold differing beliefs and values, leading to an individualised and unique experience of being, and a different meaning being attached to it. With these differences, for the person to react authentically, the resulting thought process and actions are likely to be very different. The supervisor, and indeed the supervisee, cannot know what is 'best' for the client. The supervisor can only experience the client through the supervisee's lived encounter with their client, which is itself filtered through their assumptions, training, modality, and their personal and professional experiences, and of course through the client's understanding, and their willingness to be open and authentic with the coach/supervisee.

The existential supervisory experience will encompass the emotional responses the supervisee has towards their clients and will explore the emotions the client is expressing, or maybe only hinting at during the coaching. It will not look to keep things neat, linear, or chronological, and will be willing to take the 'scenic route', allowing space and time to explore any irregularities of response, any paradoxes, contradictions, and dilemmas, highlighting both possibilities and limitations. In working in a non-linear way, the supervisee is encouraged to look at the client's dilemma from numerous angles and to keep returning to a point deconstructing it further and experimenting with different views in order to; as van Deurzen & Young (2009:3) noted, to 'over-see' their own work. Of course, during this journey the supervisee and supervisor must not lose sight of the client's reality and their presenting issues. With trust in the supervisor, the supervisee can then openly explore any blind spots they may have in their work with this client, returning to this often to verify and clarify the main objective of the exploration.

Supervision is a creative and innovative encounter between two (or more) individuals in which the participants are 'more artists than technicians (in that) they bring to bear a wide variety of sensitivities and skills so that their clients can release their latent potentials for fuller living' (Bugental 1992:264). They draw on their experience and creativity to give the supervisee a richer palate from which to explore the world of the client. It pulls from the internal worlds of the supervisor and supervisee, based on existential philosophical ideas, rather than theory.

Without an easy recourse to generic well-worn, tried and tested techniques and exercises the existential process is more challenging for the supervisor and supervisee. Bugental (1992:264) recognises this complexity, describing the need for the supervisor to be a 'virtuoso' weaving together science, philosophy, and art in a multifaceted approach, whilst van Deurzen & Young (2009:6) describe the role as that of a 'philosophical guide' providing a clear and safe place to re-think and re-experience what has happened in the coaching sessions.

## Orbit of existential supervision

From the above, we can see that existential supervision is not primarily concerned with finding a linear route to the solution to any problem, be that the client's, or the supervisee's. Instead, it will draw on the existential givens and dimensions to more fully explore the issues and implications in the client's dilemma, and in the possible solutions. In doing this, existential supervision will seek to cover a wide orbit, starting with, and regularly returning to the client's presenting issue, but also engaging with the supervisee's values and assumptions, the level with which the supervisee and their client are comfortable with uncertainty, the meaning the client and supervisee are attaching to the client's narratives, and the individual elements of that narrative, and the level of authenticity evidenced in the client and their dilemma. The supervisor will seek to model good practice through the quality of the supervisory relationship, aiming to hold a high degree of presence and authenticity. Krug & Schneider (2016:5) pointed out that, 'presence, congruence, and empathy are ways of being; they cannot be taught, but they can be modeled and valued'. Given that this is the case, Krug and Schneider see a place for 'the supervisor to bring in examples from their own practice thus treating the supervisee as a fellow traveller and cultivate a collegial, non-hierarchical atmosphere' (2016:60).

As with all supervision models, the existential supervisor will facilitate the supervisee's clarification of any ethical or professional problems. Given that existential philosophy places emphasis on the development of an individual code of ethics and requires the individual to carefully consider their moral stance and actions, I have devoted the following chapter (Chapter Six) to a more in-depth consideration of the place of ethics in existential coaching supervision.

In my chapter on existential supervision for Bachkirova and Clutterbuck's new edition of *Coaching & Mentoring Supervision* (due for publication early 2021, OUP), I devised a diagram to show the orbital fields of existential supervision. I have amended this slightly for this book. It can serve as a reminder of what supervisee and supervisor may need to cover during supervision.

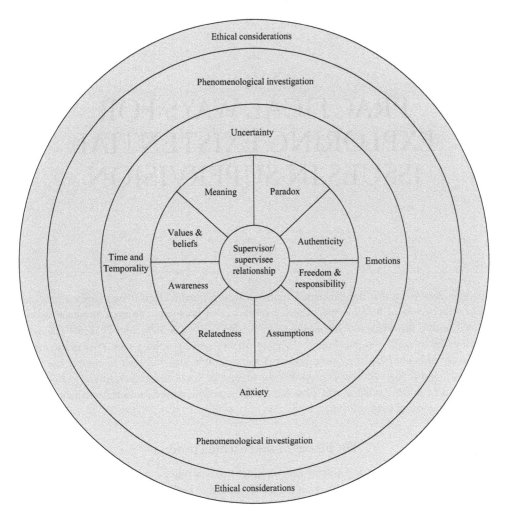

*Figure 6.1* The Orbits of Existential Supervision

Having given an overview of what an existential supervisor may draw on in developing their practice, I wish to move on to offer some practical ways in which existential matters may be explored in a supervision session. This moves it from the philosophical and theoretical into practice. I intend to show that these existential concerns, which some people may see as rather esoteric, are a very practical tool for the coach and supervisor.

# 7

# PRACTICAL WAYS FOR EXPLORING EXISTENTIAL ISSUES IN SUPERVISION

We have discovered that the existential approach to supervision offers 'fewer explanations and more experiences of being – specifically experiences of how one cultivates presence within oneself, within the other, and within the relational field' (Krug & Schneider 2016: 59–60), with much of the learning coming through dialogue. An existential coaching supervisor is also aware that every individual has their own preferred learning style and will seek to respect this. This means that existential supervisors may offer the supervisee visual frameworks, literary references, or embodied practice, such as role play, within the supervision session. In this chapter I give a brief description of some of these.

## The phases of the coaching process

The supervisor will want to consider the whole of the supervisee's coaching relationship with their client. They will draw attention to existential aspects in each phase of the coaching process, from first meeting and contracting through to ending.

### *First meeting*

A client may come to work with a coach through a direct personal contact. The coach may have been recommended to them or the client may have read about them on their website or through their blogs or articles. The client will already have some 'information' from which to start building a picture and forming assumptions about what the coach may be like, both professionally and personally. The supervisee will be encouraged to explore any preconceptions the client has formed about them in order to creative an authentic working alliance with themselves and the client.

Not all clients choose their coaches. Some have the potential coach chosen for them by the organisation which pays for the work. The client may be offered the opportunity to choose a coach from a number who they can meet for a 'chemistry session', after which they can choose the coach who they feel most comfortable to work with. The supervisor will seek to ensure that the supervisee is sensitive to any perceived lack of freedom the client may feel in relation to the coaching contract. The supervisee may also need to explore their emotional reaction to being chosen over other coaches.

Even at this stage the process is encountering existential issues. The issue of freedom is already in play, with both coach and client having the ability to say 'yes' or 'no' to working together. Such a decision is unlikely to be without consequences which should be explored as part of the coaching process. Any assumptions which the coach forms about their potential client would also need to be acknowledged and bracketed. Once the client and coach have decided to work together then it is usual for a contract to be agreed.

The first meeting is likely to be emotional for both sides as it is a meeting of two flesh and blood beings who will be uncertain what to expect and be caring of their self-concepts. The supervisor will encourage the supervisee not to ignore their emotional reaction to the client, even if it is only to bracket it, and to note any expressed or indirect emotional responses from the client.

## Contracting

The supervisor may guide the supervisee through the contracting process which will clarify and challenge assumptions. The supervisor may also wish to have a contract with the supervisee, which may be verbal or written. Contracts usually cover what the focus of the work will be (if indeed there is a focus); the boundaries; the timings; the fees, etc. An existential practitioner may also wish to include something on the approach and ethical stance. The contract is the start of the coaching journey and immediately brings both parties (or in some cases a third party: the commissioning agent) in touch with the existential issues of relatedness, freedom, and accountability, with the acknowledgment that they are individuals in relationship to one another, with complimentary or contradictory needs and wants.

Often the contract is in existence before the supervisee starts working with their supervisor, and the supervisor will not have had a role in drawing it up. However, the contract can be revisited throughout the coaching process to check on its continued relevance and this would form part of supervisory discussions. The supervisee and supervisor may also choose to review their own contract on a regular basis.

A more detailed exploration of the existential elements in a contract can be found in Hanaway (2020a:53–54).

## Coaching sessions

The main tools used in the existential supervisory discussions of coaching sessions are phenomenological investigation and open dialogue. During these discussions the supervisor bears in mind the existential givens and dimensions. Through exploring these, a more holistic picture of the client's being-in-the-world and the values and beliefs underpinning their behaviours can be formed. This means that any decisions the client makes can be done so with full knowledge of their relevance to the client's values and needs and to their authenticity, making it more likely that they will be genuinely committed to meaningful action.

## Existential dimensions

Through exploring the different ways a person operates in the social, psychological, physical, and spiritual areas of their lives one can form a deeper understanding of a client's way of relating to self and others and where they place their priorities. Even when remaining authentic, we all know that we do not always feel the same, or act the same in all contexts, or with all people. We choose to share different aspects of ourselves, needing to feel more secure before sharing some things. We may be confident about singing and dancing at a party, yet not choose to do so in the workplace. We choose to share our most intimate thoughts and desires with chosen individuals, whilst with others we are content to just skim the surface.

Existential writers (Binswanger 1963; van Deurzen-Smith 1987) have used the concept of a map of existence, comprising of four dimensions, to help us to holistically explore a person's worldview. Binswanger (quoted in May 1994:288) gave the reason for this:

> It is a question of attempting to understand and to explain the human being in the totality of his/her existence. But that is possible only from the perspective of our total existence: in other words, only when we reflect on and articulate our total existence, the "essence" and "form" of being human.

He suggested three modes of existence: the *Umwelt* (the 'around world'); the *Mitwelt* (the 'with world'); and the *Eigenwelt* (the 'own world').

The *Umwelt* is concerned with the physical aspects of our existence, how we relate to our environment, and the givens of the natural world around us. Included in this is our attitude to, and relationship with the body we have, the concrete surroundings we are in, the climate, objects, and material possessions, others' bodies, our bodily needs, health, illness, and mortality.

The *Mitwelt* is focused on social presence and our relationships, with our attitudes and reactions to our social context, and how we relate to each other in the public world. It also includes responses to the culture we live in, and the class, race, and gender we are identified as belonging to, and by default those we are not considered to belong to. Our authenticity can be tested in this dimension with the willingness we wish to accept or reject this communal labelling, and to what extent we can tolerate others, or being alone.

The *Eigenwelt* is about our personal and psychological aspects, how we understand and relate to ourselves, and create our own meaningful personal world. How we may identify ourselves may be in conflict with how other see us.

Van Deurzen (1987) added a fourth dimension, the *Überwelt*, which focuses on our spiritual realms. This covers how we make meaning, relate to the unknown, and so create our values and personal ethical code. It brings us in touch with the tension between purpose and absurdity, hope and despair, and is the dimension in which we face the void and the possibility of nothingness.

When working with a client the nature of the contract may be that we are focused on one dimension. However, if we ignore the other dimensions, we will not access a full picture of the client's worldview, and so may miss important aspects of their 'being-in-the-world', an absence which will impact on the coaching work. A client may also identify one or more of the dimensions which are undeveloped and as a result may wish to give them some attention. It may become evident that the client gives more attention to one or more of the dimensions or may fail to consider one at all. An existential supervisor may invite the coach to note this, and to consider exploring with the client why this is, and whether they are happy with it. The purpose is not to encourage the client to change this but for the client to be authentically aware that they are choosing to prioritise one or more areas and take responsibility for those choices. The supervisor may also identify areas which the supervisee may be missing in their exploration of the client's worldview and check the supervisee is not caught up in assumptions or are rushing to solutions rather than actively listening to the client's concerns and ideas.

It is sometimes useful for the supervisee to make a note of the client's way of inhabiting their dimensions. Some supervisees have liked to do this using a triangular diagram. The dimension which is most evident would be shown at the base of the pyramid, with the one least consciously inhabited at the top. The distance between lines varies for each client and may change over the different sessions. Some supervisees return to their original diagram at the end of each session to note the changes. Below is an example which a supervisee brought to supervision following their first session with Julian.

After six sessions Julian's priorities shifted, and the changes were marked on the original diagram (see figure 7.2). The most important dimension had shifted from the *Eigenwelt* at the beginning of the coaching work, to the *Überwelt* by the end of the work. There is no hierarchy attached to what is important and it is not the task of the coach to make the client change their priorities but to ensure they are aware of their choices and take responsibility for them.

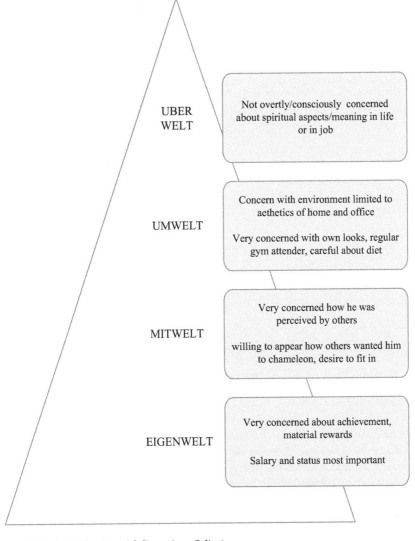

UBER
WELT

Not overtly/consciously concerned about spiritual aspects/meaning in life or in job

UMWELT

Concern with environment limited to aethetics of home and office

Very concerned with own looks, regular gym attender, careful about diet

MITWELT

Very concerned how he was perceived by others

willing to appear how others wanted him to chameleon, desire to fit in

EIGENWELT

Very concerned about achievement, material rewards

Salary and status most important

*Figure 7.1*  Client's initial existential dimensions (Julian)

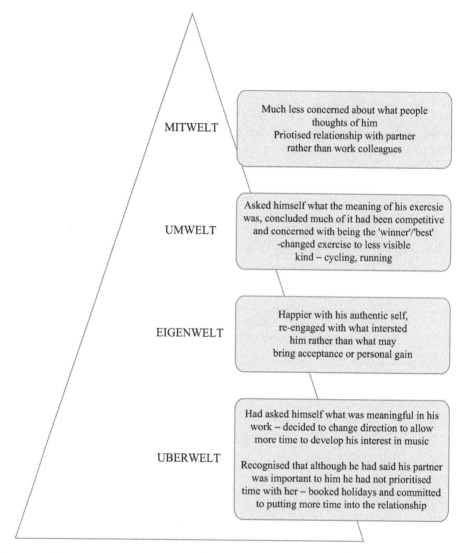

MITWELT — Much less concerned about what people thoughts of him
Priotised relationship with partner rather than work colleagues

UMWELT — Asked himself what the meaning of his exercsie was, concluded much of it had been competitive and concerned with being the 'winner'/'best' -changed exercise to less visible kind – cycling, running

EIGENWELT — Happier with his authentic self, re-engaged with what intersted him rather than what may bring acceptance or personal gain

UBERWELT — Had asked himself what was meaningful in his work – decided to change direction to allow more time to develop his interest in music

Recognised that although he had said his partner was important to him he had not prioritised time with her – booked holidays and committed to putting more time into the relationship

*Figure 7.2*   Client's initial existential dimensions after six sessions (Julian)

## Existential givens

An existential supervisor may also use the existential givens as a framework for the supervisee to check the thoroughness of their understanding of those aspects of the worldview which the client allows them access to, whilst remaining aware of those which the client does not choose to share. The client may be consciously choosing not to bring those aspects into the coaching, or they may be unaware of them themselves. The coach does not dig for aspects which are consciously held back but may feel it is relevant for the client to note their absence in their narrative.

## *Anxiety*

Our awareness of life's uncertainties and the challenges of living life fully and authentically can bring existential anxiety. It will undoubtedly be present in coaching. If it is not readily evident this may indicate that the client is not very reflective or willing to truly acknowledge life's challenges. Despite this, it is not the role of the coach to push a client to examine or expose those anxieties. The supervisor's role is to ensure that the supervisee is not evading any anxiety which is present in the client or indeed in themselves. The supervisor would also help the supervisee consider whether the level of any anxiety is appropriate to work with in coaching or whether the client needs additional help or support.

## *Authenticity*

As we have noted, one cause of anxiety is the challenge to live authentically. Unfortunately, this is not easy to do. Many people can feel uncomfortably conscious that in parts of their life they are merely 'going through the motions', rather than being authentically connected to their thoughts and actions. Kierkegaard suggested that not being oneself leads to the most common form of despair, and not living authentically is in Sartre's terms to be living in 'bad faith'. I can certainly relate to those feelings of despair which I have felt when I have been in a group in which someone speaks 'for all of us', thus making an assumption that I am in agreement with their remarks. I am left with a choice: to speak out, and in so doing to risk isolating myself from the others or be governed by my need to defend against loneliness, resulting in me remaining silent, and so, being in bad faith.

Experiencing some level of bad faith can cause a person to feel wretched, and they may turn to coaching to explore their difficulties and the options open to them. Some people may only become aware of inauthenticity through reflection during the coaching. This may result in a stark realisation that others in their professional or personal groups have different values to them or attach different meanings to things and situations. We may become aware that we have taken on a work role because we originally shared the values and meaning of the organisation, only to find that these values change. Without reflection, we may continue to live as though the work is still meaningful and in line with our values, when this has ceased to be the case. If this happens, we are likely to feel a level of discomfort attached to inauthentic living.

The supervisor may draw the supervisee's attention to a number of areas concerned with authenticity which they could explore with their client, e.g.:

- To what extent is the client remaining true to their values, beliefs, and sets of meaning?
- What factors are obstacles to their authenticity?
- What are their plans to overcome these obstacles?
- Are they happy with the balance and appropriateness of what they disclose of themselves to others?
- Is their current level of authenticity causing anxiety?
- Are there any identifiable paradoxes which make authenticity difficult?

## *Freedom and responsibility*

We often complain that we have too little freedom, but when we do recognise it, it may feel overwhelming and we may wish to deny it because with freedom comes responsibility. Freedom also requires us to act; in fact Sartre (2007) referred to existential freedom as a 'doctrine of action'. It is not unusual for clients to present as though they have no agency, for if they are without agency they cannot be expected to act and in not acting they falsely believe they are not responsible; however, as expressed earlier, to do nothing is to *choose* to do nothing and it is because we have freedom that we have that choice. The supervisor will look to the coach to challenge any such delusion. It may be that the client does not wish to use their freedom and accept their responsibility, and the supervisor would encourage the supervisee to challenge this stance. It may equally be an issue that the client does recognise their own freedom but seeks to deny or limit the freedom of others. The supervisor may enable the supervisee to address the following points with their client:

- To what extent does the client recognise and acknowledge their freedom and agency?
- Do they take on too much responsibility?
- Do they take responsibility away from others?
- Do they find it difficult to share or delegate responsibility?
- Are you, as coach taking too much responsibility and not encouraging the client's creativity and agency?

## Relatedness

It is impossible for any coaching process to not include issues concerning a number of relationships. Amongst these will be: how the client and coach relate; the people involved in the dilemma the client brings to coaching; significant others in the client's life; and how any decisions may affect them. Even presenting issues which initially appear detached from involvement with another will involve other people and their worldviews. A client may complain that they cannot remain in their post because they disagree with the strategies which are being put in place. This, of course, has the client and their wants, needs, values, and meaning at the centre but also involves, even if indirectly, the person who devised the strategy and to whom it may be very meaningful, and whose self-concept will be tied to it. It also involves colleagues who may have a response to the client leaving, and those others who may be affected by their decision positively or negatively, e.g. their family for whom there may be financial and/or emotional repercussions, and who no doubt will have an emotional response, e.g. fear for the future; grateful that the client is removed from the stress; relief that they have made a decision.

In supervision, another relationship is brought into play, that between the supervisor and the supervisee. The supervisor will bear this in mind and consider how the context of the supervision may affect this. If the supervisee is a trainee, they may have had little choice of their supervisor and may feel the need to please and not challenge them, particularly if a report from the supervisor plays a part in them successfully completing their training. The same is true when the supervisor is appointed by an organisation to offer supervision for a number of their employees.

The supervisor will facilitate the supervisee's awareness of the issue of relatedness in their encounter both with the supervisor in supervision, and with their encounter with the client in each coaching session. They may use a number of invitational queries to facilitate reflection and challenge, such as:

- How do you see your relationship with the client?
- In what way has that relationship changed over the time you have been working together?
- What relationships have you identified that hold significance in the client's presenting dilemma?
- What meaning is attached to these relationships?
- Does the client value relationships?
- Does the client like solitude?
- Are there problematic relationships with specific people?

- What lies at the heart of the difficulty, e.g. different values and meaning, competition, etc.
- Is the client aware of other relationships which will be affected by any decision they make?
- Which relationships are most meaningful to the client?
- Does the client's way of relating align with their values?
- Do you recognise anything in our relationship in supervision which mirrors the relationship you have with your client?

## Time and temporality

We are all conscious of time, whether it is external time, as measured by the clock or the calendar, or internal time, how time feels, e.g. it is 'flying by', 'dragging', 'stuck', etc. For many clients it is their relationship to external time which brings them to coaching. They may feel under pressure due to deadlines, that they have not achieved personal milestones, or are struggling with the aging process with changes in their body and their physical strength, and the prospect of retirement and death.

An existential supervisor encourages the supervisee to consider the client's internal experience of time. If we consciously accept that our time is limited and will inevitably end in death, each day can take on added significance and we may choose to consider how much time we are prepared to give to non-meaningful actions, conflicts, and worries. This turns time from a potentially negative enemy to a marker of creative space with an invitation to live life fully in every moment.

The supervisor may use a number of invitational queries about time and temporality to encourage the supervisee to facilitate reflection and challenge. For some of us time passes by without any real acknowledgment from us that it does so. A supervisor may enquire how their supervisee is encouraging the client to authentically engage with temporality. A powerful and very challenging way of doing this can be by inviting the client to identify what age they think they may die and asking them to consider where they currently see themselves to be on the journey between birth and death. If an individual identifies 70 as their final age, and they are now 40, reflecting on this puts them in touch with the 30 years they consider are left to them and so encourages them to reflect on what is important to do with that time. Even more challenging would be to ask the client to write what they would like said about them in their obituary, and then ask them to write an obituary as if they had died yesterday. This followed by asking them to write their ideal obituary, set sometime in their future. By identifying how they would like to be remembered, what they would have liked to achieved, and then comparing it with the obituary detailing how their life has been so far, a coach can help a person see what steps they need to take to make life as meaningful as possible.

On a practical level, time will be present as an issue in the coaching contract. The supervisor may ask the supervisee to reflect on time-related aspects of the coaching relationship:

- Do coach and client respect any time boundaries agreed in the initial contract?
- If not, why not?
- Do sessions feel as though they go quickly, or do they drag?
- Does it feel as though the time is used creatively?
- How easy is it for the client to live in the moment?
- Can they use mindfulness and mediation?
- Is the temporal nature of the coaching relationship acknowledged and the ending discussed?
- What does the supervisee feel and think about the ending?
- To what extent does the client recognise their freedom in relation to use of time?

- To what deadlines is the client working?
  - Are these externally imposed?
  - Are they self-imposed?

## *Values and beliefs*

We inherit values and beliefs from our families and our culture. Over time we will reassess these and form variations on these beliefs or create new ones. Our beliefs provide a structure for our meaning-making and a baseline from which to consider our actions. The supervisor will expect the supervisee to gain understanding of the main values and beliefs held by the client. Failure to do so would mean the supervisee may waste a lot of time working in a way which will prove meaningless to the client and so considering actions which the client cannot agree to authentically. The client may verbalise agreement to the coach to either please, or appease, but without a congruence between the proposed actions and their beliefs it is unlikely that the client will fully commit to action.

As has been noted, values and beliefs can become 'stuck' or sedimented and the client may find it hard to let go of them. Our beliefs have helped to form our self-construct and so create a perception of stability and security, guarding against uncertainty and doubt. So, it is not surprising that any challenge to these values is highly likely to be met with fear and strong resistance. Should our values be attacked in some way, we are likely to have an emotional reaction. A coach exploring sedimentations may be perceived as attacking unless they show great sensitivity. A supervisor would work with a supervisee to identify ways of sensitively challenging, using holistic awareness of the client's worldview and ways of communicating, 'hot buttons' and sensitivities, so that the client sees the coach's action as enabling and creative rather than destructive. The supervisor will also work with the supervisee to enable the client to identify internal threats which may occur when the client finds themselves thinking or acting in conflict with their own values. By facilitating the client's early identification of this, the supervisee can enable the client to address these threats to their authenticity.

Sedimented values can hinder the momentum of the coaching and so need to be sensitively explored and never ignored. If a client unquestioningly places loyalty high on their list of values, they may feel the need to remain loyal to an institution or individual no matter what, and to follow their rules or behaviours, even when those actions are destructive, and have veered away from the client's other values. The supervisor will look to the supervisee to identify any such confusion around paradoxical values and behaviours, and to explore with the client what is most powerful and meaningful in the current situation and to find the courage to challenge their own sedimentations.

It is a common paradox, often encountered in coaching, that we want to change yet we also wish to remain the same; we may seek excitement but also crave safety. However, 'one cannot change "bits" of the sedimented self-construct without its effects being felt by the whole, as it alters the entire structure' (Hanaway 2018:86). A small earthquake may not result in evident visible damage but under the surface the tectonic plates will have shifted and those who felt the quake may not look different but will surely feel different.

The supervisor may offer a number of queries to enable the supervisee to consider their work on values and beliefs:

- How does the client define their values?
- Are there any of the client's beliefs and values which are inconsistent with your own?

- If so, how will you work with this?
- How comfortable is the client in communicating their values to others involved in their dilemma?
- To what extent does the client feel their values are at odds with those of significant others, including relevant organisations?
- Can you identify values and beliefs which have become sedimented and no longer serve the client's goals?
- Can you identify paradoxical values in the client's material?
- Can you provide a safe space to explore sedimented values, which may allow the client to reframe or let go of them?

## *Uncertainty*

Auguste de Villiers de L'Isle-Adam (2000:62) described uncertainty as 'a quality to be cherished, therefore – if not for it, who would dare to undertake anything?' The fear of uncertainty is a common reason for inaction and clients may look to their coach to provide certainty. Indeed, a supervisee may also look to the supervisor to offer a degree of certainty in how they should practise. Of course, this is something neither the coach nor the supervisor can authentically do. Indeed, perhaps one of the biggest mistakes a coach or supervisor can make is in thinking that there can be an antidote to uncertainty (Levitathan 2011). New coaches particularly can suffer from the desire to prove themselves and their professional worth by offering suggestions which imply certain outcomes. They may believe that to do so conveys professional knowledge and confidence. However, this is the opposite of the truth. Professionally confident and competent existential coaches will not offer certainty, as this would be to act in bad faith, can be dangerous, and goes against existential thought. The willingness and ability to fully engage as a human being, in a state of unknowing and to openly explore the client's dilemma as a co-traveller, rather than to pretend to be an expert, with all the answers to hand, is the real mark of the confident, authentic coach.

A supervisor will work with a supervisee to embrace uncertainty as a creativity playing field for their interactions with the client, and in so doing not to be afraid to own their own state of uncertainty and unknowing, as appropriate. As von Clausewitz (quoted in Williams et al. 1993:150) points out it, 'although our intellect always longs for clarity and certainty, our nature often finds uncertainty fascinating' and 'understanding how to act under conditions of incomplete information is the highest and most urgent human pursuit'. Enabling the supervisee to courageously enter into the realm of uncertainty and engage with the client in the pursuit not of certainty, but of the creative opportunities it allows us to consider, is an important element in supervision.

The supervisor may support the client in finding questions for their own and their client's self-reflection, e.g.:

- How good am I in handling uncertainty in my day-to-day existence?
- How do I respond when someone challenges my ideas and plans?
- How important is it to me that my clients experience me as knowledgeable?
- How do I react if I do not know something?
- How do I react when I make a mistake, or I am misunderstood?

Having considered these in relation to themselves, they can then look at them in relation to the client and consider how they can increase the client's tolerance of uncertainty and eventually welcome it and the creative possibilities it brings.

# *Meaning*

It is not unusual for clients to present for coaching because they are searching for meaning in their professional and/or personal life. Others may never have found a meaning to lose! Yet others may have only just posed themselves the question of what is meaningful for them. Vos (2018:67) suggests a number of different categories in which we look for meaning:

- Materialistic-hedonistic concerned with:
    - Basic survival needs; housing, finance, etc.
    - Professional, educational, and social success
    - Aesthetics and enjoyment, peak experiences, and pain avoidance
    - Health
- Self-orientated:
    - Resilience
    - Self-efficacy
    - Self-acceptance
    - Autonomy
    - Creativity
    - Self-care
    - Authenticity
- Social:
    - Feeling socially connected
    - Belonging to a community
    - Following social expectations
    - Altruism
    - Giving birth and taking care of children
- Larger:
    - Goals, purpose, aims
    - Personal growth
    - Temporality
    - Ethics
    - Spirituality
- Existential-philosophical:
    - Being alive until death
    - Uniqueness
    - Connectedness with others and the world
    - Individual freedom
    - Gratitude for the gift of life
    - Responsibility

An existential supervisor may use questions, like those below, to start a discussion on the supervisee's work with meaning:

- What elements does the client need for something to be meaningful?
- What elements of their current situation are meaningful for them?
- Does the client feel that the same meaning is attached by others to the current situation?

- What would need to change for the client's current position to become more meaningful for them?
- To what extent does their current dilemma and the possible outcomes fit with their overall understanding of meaning in their whole life?

The supervisor my also offer queries which can be used directly with the client, focused on what the client's life goal, life quest, destiny, and calling is perceived to be.

No doubt my own ambivalence towards formal questionnaires and exercises is apparent in my writing; however, there are questionnaires available which also aim to explore a client's meaning-making, which can be used directly with the client.

One such is Steger's Meaning in Life Questionnaire (MLQ) which seeks to measure two dimensions of meaning in life: Presence of Meaning (how much respondents feel their lives have meaning), and Search for Meaning (how much respondents strive to find meaning and understanding in their lives). A client may be asked to rank statements such as those below, on a scale ranging from absolutely true to absolutely untrue:

- I understand my life's meaning
- I am looking for something that makes my life feel meaningful
- I am always looking to find my life's purpose
- My life has a clear sense of purpose
- I have a good sense of what makes my life meaningful
- I have discovered a satisfying life purpose
- I am always searching for something that makes my life feel significant
- I am seeking a purpose or mission for my life
- My life has no clear purpose
- I am searching for meaning in my life

Weems (2004) also devised a questionnaire to explore Tillich's theory of Existential Anxiety through the use of twenty-one questions to which the client would answer 'yes' or 'no'. These include a number which are specifically aimed and uncovering the client's relationship to meaning, including:

- I never think about emptiness
- I often think that the things that were once important in life are empty
- I often think about fate and it causes me to feel anxious
- I know that life has meaning

Whether a supervisee chooses to use a questionnaire or is alert to the need to explore the client's meaning through less formal approaches, an existential supervisor would look to see that this was an important component in their work. If a supervisee does use questionnaires, they need to be sure they are not asking the client to give them information which the client has already given them either overtly or in some more subtle way. If this did happen the client would not feel heard and would lose trust in the supervisee/coach.

If a supervisee wishes to work on a deep level with the client's meaning, then the supervisor would need to check with the supervisee whether it was appropriate to do so with that particular client, their presenting dilemma, the length of contract, and the context of the work.

## *Emotions*

We have seen that emotions are important tools for a coach. As a painter, I think of every emotion as a colour which I can add to my palate, giving me more potential for sensitive creativity. The same is true for the coach; emotions add richness to the material the coach has to work with. As we have noted, emotions are intentional and never in isolation, and so they tell us about the *something* which generated them, or they are attached to. In learning this, we will discover more about the client's worldview through exploring the meaning of their emotions. 'In emotion…We can rediscover the whole of human reality, for emotion is the human reality assuming itself and emotionally – directing itself towards the world' (Sartre 1963:25). Emotions can be complex. The supervisor will encourage the supervisee not to grasp at the first emotional expression communicated by the client, as more than one emotion can be experienced. Sometimes these emotions may be in opposition to one another, e.g. a client may hold strong feelings of anger and rejection at losing their job and yet also recognise feelings of relief. Exploring these two conflicting reactions can enable the client to make a better-informed decision about their next action. There can be dissonance between what the client is saying and their emotional body language; a person may smile when they are feeling sad. Clients may hold more than one emotion about something – they may be angry, and at the same time disappointed and sad. They can hold emotions about emotions, e.g. feeling guilty because they feel angry. The supervisor would look to ensure that the supervisee was aware of multiple and sometimes conflicting emotions.

In supervision the supervisor will look to the supervisee to note both the client's factual and emotional narratives. In doing so, the supervisor looks to see if the supervisee is aware of their own emotional response to the client, and the meaning attached to that response, the role emotion is playing in the coaching sessions, and in the client's way of being-in-the-world-with-others. A supervisee too will have emotional reactions to their client and supervisor, which may form part of the material for supervision. The supervisor will encourage the supervisee to be alert for any sedimented emotions and to explore with the client why they have become stuck.

A supervisor may facilitate the supervisee's thoughts on the role of emotions in their client's situation, through querying the following:

- Are you, as coach, equally engaged with the client's emotional narrative (noetic) as you are with the factual narrative (noema)?
- What was the first emotion you were aware of in the client?
- What was your emotional response to the client?
- Is there a prominent emotion demonstrated in most sessions?
- Did you note any paradoxical emotional responses?
- Did you experience any dissonance between what was said by the client and the level and type of emotion they exhibited?
- What emotions does the client evoke in you and how did these show during the work?
- How are you as coach working with your own emotions?
- Was there a significant lack of emotion displayed by the client?

This exploration can develop an understanding of a client's 'being'; how they are in the world, and how they relate to it in all its complexity. This can be fed back to the client to provide a platform for them to understand and consider past and future action. Ignoring emotions means the coach is only hearing part of the client's narrative and so cannot fully address it in a meaningful way.

## *Paradox*

Existential thinkers are concerned with our quest to find meaning in an uncertain and temporal existence, full of contradictions, ambiguities, equivocations, inconsistencies, and unstated assumptions. Working with paradox is therefore an important aspect of an existential coaching approach and will be explored in supervision.

R. D Laing, in his book *Knots*, summed up the paradoxical nature of everyday existence, and the internal games we play in order to address the paradoxical. He wrote, 'I never got what I wanted, I always got what I did not want. What I want I shall not get. *Therefore*, to get it I must not want it *since* I get only what I don't want…I can't get it *because* I want it, I get it *because* I don't want it. I want what I can't get *because* what I can't get *is* what I want' (1970:30–32). At the time of his death in 2008, Dr Freddie Strasser and I were engaged on writing a book on paradox. Freddie saw paradox everywhere and considered any useful work with a client required an exploration of the paradoxes of the client's situation and their desires. Despite the age difference between us, Freddie's energy level and capacity for engaging with complex thinking late into the night far outlived my own by several hours. Freddie was interested in paradox in the psychotherapeutic context whilst I was keen to look at the ways in which this thinking could be applied in the time limited world of coaching.

In my conversations with Freddie, we found many different definitions of 'paradox', most of which focused on its nature as absurd or contradictory. The experience of paradox and particularly paradoxical desires can feel very lonely, but to ignore our contradictions is inauthentic. We may feel a sense of disintegration as we struggle to make sense of any conflicting 'wants' we may hold. Indeed, Laing (1970:42) claimed, such a confusing state leads to a state of ontological insecurity and anxiety, in which the individual loses, or never possesses, 'the sense of personal consistency or cohesiveness. He may feel more insubstantial than substantial and unable to assume that the stuff he is made of is genuine, good, valuable'. These feelings may cause a person to seek therapy or coaching without any conscious awareness that their discomfort flows from paradoxical goals.

May (1967) shared this interest in exploring the paradoxes and conflicts in our modern society. He considered the twentieth century as a time when psychological dilemmas were to the fore, with loss of identity, increased uncertainty and anxiety. May identified the key challenge as the need to engage with the ultimate paradox between freedom and responsibility. For May, it is in the engagement with the paradoxes involved in the dialectical process between these two poles that development occurs, and we see a deepening of human consciousness. He rejects the assumption, expressed by Skinner (1953), Rogers (1951), and others, that one can avoid the dilemma by taking one of its poles. This would be considered inauthentic; instead he believed that we must not simply learn to live with the paradox but are required to act on the awareness of this and use it creatively. 'The courageous living within this dilemma, I believe, is the source of human creativity' (May 1967:20). May believed in the unique human ability to comprehend paradox and to wrestle with dilemma. The supervisor would be looking to further develop the supervisee's ability to work with this with their client.

To identify and work with one's paradoxes may not be the most intuitive thing for many of us, as it may carry a great deal of discomfort. Sartre's concept of bad faith is intimately related to paradox. Bad faith with self-deception and inauthenticity inevitably involves an undeniable paradox – how it is possible to deceive oneself. We cannot truly deceive ourselves that we do not know something which we do. It is tempting to pretend that is the case when we do not like what we know and the implications which may follow on from that knowledge. At heart we know we are only choosing to pretend, no matter how hard we may try to convince ourselves otherwise. Sartre calls for us to stop lying to ourselves, seeing such an action as an act not just of bad faith, but of self-distraction, drawing our attention from the truth by seeking out evidence suggesting that the opposite is true. It is possible that self-deception may be used as a coping mechanism, but one without long-term benefit, but with long-term implications. A supervisor would encourage a supervisee to engage with any sense they may have that a client is involved in acts of self-deception and to explore what lies at the base of this action. The aim is not to criticise the activity but to explore all potential ways of addressing the dilemma without resorting to inauthenticity.

Kierkegaard saw all human experience as underpinned by paradox. He saw this tension as making life richer. In *Fear and Trembling* Kierkegaard drew on the Old Testament story of Abraham to explore how an individual is faced with the paradoxical. Abraham is given a paradoxical challenge by God. He is called upon to sacrifice his son at God's command. He must choose to be loyal to God or to his son. He has to decide between honouring life or destroying it. Thankfully most of us are not faced with such overwhelming challenges but paradoxes are inevitable and part and parcel of the complexity and challenge of existence.

Paradoxical dilemmas are often at the heart of the work of an existentially informed coach who will work to enable the client to recognise specific tensions that are at work in the client's life. This will include identifying any paradoxical tensions which are evident in the client's narrative of their understanding of choice and responsibility, and 'thrownness' Heidegger (1927). Thrownness has to be acknowledged, but never used as an excuse.

Human beings are often paradoxical. We can love and hate someone at the same time. We can want to move forward yet value the security of the status quo. Through enabling the client to see the paradoxes inherent in their dilemma, the coach can facilitate the client's exploration of their own values, identify their priorities, recognise the losses and gains in any decision, and to take responsibility for ensuing action and its consequences. In doing so they may need to recognise that it may be impossible for them to achieve everything they want to as some of their desires may be in opposition to others. This is often the cause of a client's feelings of 'stuckness'. Accepting that every gain brings with it a loss, and that by taking one route we are turning our back on another, at least for the short term is the first step to finding the courage to make decisions and accepting the responsibility for the outcome.

The supervisor will encourage the supervisee to identify any ambiguities, ambivalences, and paradoxes in the client's material. In understanding that they cannot have everything, the client can then make use of their freedom of choice and take responsibility, knowing that most gains carry a loss. It is important that the supervisee does not choose one part of the client's narrative and focus on it, ignoring other parts which may appear to be contradictory. All contradictory parts of the client's narratives must be fed back to them, e.g.

> you say you are determined to get your job back and can't wait to be back at your desk, yet at the same time you have told me you feel sick at the thought of going back through the office door, and never want to re-experience the stress you felt when you were there. There seems to be a challenge here – if you are reinstated, apart from feeling vindicated, you recognise that you may put yourself under stress, even make yourself ill again. How can this circle be squared? What is most important to you, feeling healthy and not stressed, or feeling you have proved your point about the unfairness of your treatment? It may be very difficult to have both these needs met.

If only part of what the client tells the coach is reflected back, then the client cannot make a meaningful decision. An existential supervisor would expect the supervisee to explore potential and existing paradoxes in their client's situation. This requires noting, rather than ignoring any paradoxical statements or goals, fully exploring them instead. It may be that a supervisee fears that to point out such difficulties distracts from the linear path to a potential solution thus complicating or prolonging the coaching and frustrating the client. However, to ignore contradictions makes it highly likely that any plan will become derailed further down the track and the client will be left disillusioned by the coaching process. This disillusionment may happen after the coaching has finished, and so the coach may be shielded from the client's feelings.

An existential supervisor will encourage the supervisee to gently challenge the client when they identify paradoxical desires, e.g.:

- I noticed that you said that you want X. How is this possible as you have also stated you want Y?
- If you get X what will you gain and what will you lose?
- What would it feel like if you got everything you want? Would there be any potential challenges?

## Frameworks for existential coaching: MOVER and CREATE

Following requests from supervisees and students, Hanaway & Reed (2014) drew together many of the existential coaching concerns and placed them within two frameworks for existential coaching practice, to be used in the way the commonly used GROW coaching model is used.

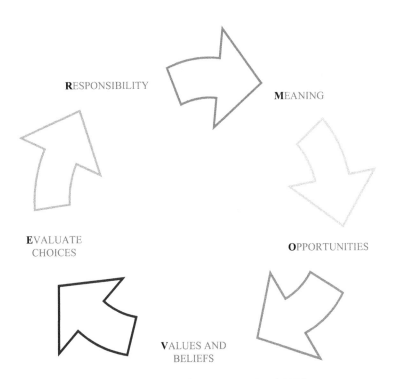

**R**ESPONSIBILITY

**M**EANING

**E**VALUATE CHOICES

**O**PPORTUNITIES

**V**ALUES AND BELIEFS

*Figure 7.3*   MOVER – existential coaching model (Hanaway & Reed 2014)

These models were originally created to act as an aide-mémoire for coaches' self-reflection, but they work equally well in providing a structure for supervisors and supervisees to jointly explore the supervisee's work with their client. They are not linear or chronological and so are represented by circular arrows. If any phase is incomplete or not fully understood the coach may have to return their focus to another phase.

**MOVER** focuses on the existential elements of the coaching session. As the name suggests, it reflects the dynamic nature of the coaching relationship with its commitment to change and movement. Even if this results in an informed decision not to move or change anything, it is done after reflection and with a considered acceptance of the implications of that decision for the client and others. This leaves no room for the client to deny their agency, freedom in making the decision, and the responsibility for the outcome. The framework starts with 'M' for 'meaning', as often people come to coaching because something, once meaningful, has lost its meaning.

---

**M    Meaning**

The meaning the client gives to their experiences is identified. This includes the meaning the client is giving to the coaching relationship. Attention is given to exploring where meaning sits within the presenting issue. It is also useful to engage the client in considering what it would mean to achieve their objective, or indeed to fail to achieve it.

**O    Opportunities and Obstacles**

The coach facilitates an exploration of obstacles in the client's dilemma. Understanding and acknowledging the temporality of the dilemma and the perceived obstacles is important to the process. Through reflective exploration the client can identify opportunities for new and creative action, and identify strategies for negotiating a way around obstacles, if indeed they are still perceived as obstacles.

**V    Values and Beliefs**

The coach needs to identify the client's values and beliefs. How the client defines what an obstacle is and what an opportunity is will be influenced by their values. To offer strategies which go against the client's values, means the client is less likely to follow through on the agreed actions. If they do so against their own values, they may experience a deep sense of inauthenticity. To operate ethically within the existential approach it is necessary for the coach to check whether 'the proposed action works with or against the client's value system and to ensure that the client has sufficient space to consider the 'fit' of the action with their core beliefs and values and the implications of that action on not just the practical but also the psychological and emotional dimensions' (Hanaway 2020a:51).

**E    Evaluation**

Once clients have explored the above, and potential ways forward are identified, they need to be **evaluated** in relation to the existential dimensions and givens and the potential implications.

**R    Responsibility**

At this stage, the client takes responsibility for the consequences for themselves and others, which flow from their decisions.

---

The process is completed through summarising the journey, including any paradox, ambiguity, or ambivalence which has been identified, so that actions can be taken in full knowledge and with full existential responsibility.

The second model **CREATE** is named to reflect the existential belief that life is a creative process within the parameters of the givens of existence. A process in which coach and client take responsibility for co-creating and defining their joint understanding of the coaching process

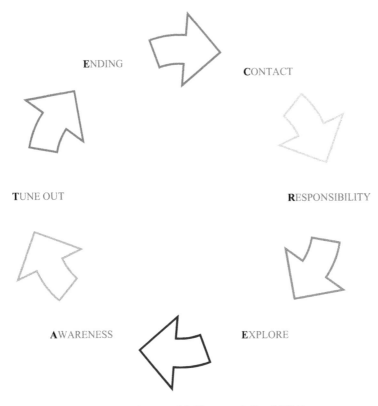

*Figure 7.4* CREATE – existential coaching model (Hanaway & Reed 2014)

through the awareness of the client's values and beliefs, allowing for dynamic and authentic choice.

Whilst the MOVER model is concerned with the existential content of the coaching work, the CREATE model focuses on the how; that is, on the process of facilitating the coaching session.

---

**C    Contact** (psychological and physical)
The 'relatedness' of the process starts before the client and coach even meet with their pre-assumptions about each other and the coaching process, with the uncertainty this will hold for both. In the physical meeting the coach will aim to create a 'clean' psychological and moral state, bracketing any judgement or assumptions.

**R    Responsibility**
The shared responsibility for the session, and the individual responsibilities held by coach and client or by supervisor and supervisee. The authentic accepting of responsibility for outcomes.

**E    Explore**
To explore what is meaningful for the client and the implications of actions for their authenticity, performance, and achievement. The focus of the exploration gradually shifts away from exploring and defining the coaching boundaries and goals, to focusing on the choices and possibilities available to the client and considering these in relation to the client's worldview.

(*Continued*)

*(Continued)*

**A  Awareness**

This is an important goal within the coaching process. Given its temporal nature, coaching provides the opportunity to encourage awareness and a willingness to engage with the existential anxiety attached to our temporal state. The supervisor will encourage the supervisee to be aware of their own perceptions and assumptions and to develop a deep awareness of those of the client through an exploration of the existential worlds.

**T  Tuning and Tuning Out**

Initially the coaching relationship requires the parties to build a trusting working alliance through developing an understanding of values. This can be termed the **'tuning in'** phase with the coach focused on understanding the client's worldview. The coaching relationship should reach a point where there exists sufficient trust for the coach to bring in elements of their own perspective, knowledge, and experience. The coach will not hide behind more generic techniques and exercises but will own what they choose to share, as their own, not as universal truths. This is termed **'tuning out'**.

**E  Explore and End**

This is concerned with what is meaningful for the client and the implications of actions for the authenticity, performance, and achievement of the client. The focus of the exploration gradually shifts away from exploring and defining the coaching boundaries and goals to focusing on the choices and possibilities available to the client and considering these in relation to the client's worldview and presenting dilemma.

The ending provides an opportunity to review the process and address anything which may have been overlooked.

## Reflective journals, case notes, recordings, etc.

If is not common practice for existential coaching supervisors to ask for case notes or recordings from sessions, but all supervisors are different and have different levels of comfort with uncertainty and taking a non-structured approach in a supervision session. This means different individuals may favour quite different ways of working, all flowing from the core existential concerns.

Some supervisors may choose to use checklists in supervision or may offer them to supervisees as a prompt or tool, particularly if they are new to the existential approach. Examples of what might be on such are checklist are:

- **Attending to process** (providing a safe and respectful space; working in the linguistic space and style of the client, etc.)
- **Presence** (being aware of one's assumptions; bracketing assumptions; being open and authentic; maintaining genuine active listening and interest)
- **Working in the here and now** (not being drawn into inappropriate therapy mode by over emphasis of the past)
- **The historical and immediate context** (the extent of its relevance)
- **Client's use of language** (factual or metaphorical; story-telling; lists; personal or professional)
- **Anxiety** (level of its presence in coach and client; its intentionality)
- **Authenticity** (self as Coach)
- **Authenticity** (of client in presentation; in their dilemma; in their action)
- **Emotions** (identifying what emotions are present and their intentionality; identifying what emotions may be expected but appear to be absent; noting one's own emotions in the session and their meaning)

- **Freedom and Responsibility** (to what extent the client is willing to explore and acknowledge these and explore them in relation to proposed action or non-action)
- **Paradox** (what paradoxes and contradictions are present in the client's presentation and narrative; whether these are being acknowledged by the client, and used creatively within the coaching process)
- **Meaning and meaning-making process** (what meaning is given by the client to their narrative and the elements within it?; where do they find meaning in life?; is this meaning compatible with their current context and ambitions?)
- **Choice** (what choices are the client aware of?; what choices are they choosing to ignore and why?; how do they experience choice? – anxiety-creativity)
- **Relatedness** (relational style; quality, consistency, challenges)
- **Self and world constructs (**in what way does the client experience self and others?; self-esteem; isolation; belonging; acceptance; abandonment; positioning other as opponent or facilitator)

The above can also act as a guide to the focus for any reflective journal or similar reflective approach the supervisee may wish to use.

### Ending

Given the importance in existential circles of acknowledging the temporality of life and taking note of time, an existential coach will carry an awareness of these elements as they work. The ending of each session and the ending of the coaching relationship are examples of an encounter with temporality. As such they will be acknowledged, and if necessary, worked with. The supervisor will also work with the coach to draw attention to the endings which the client may acknowledge or endeavour to ignore. These may include aging; personal or professional change which marks the ending of a phase of life and one way of being; redundancy; retirement; health issues, etc.

## Conclusion

Before moving on, it is worth noting that some existential practitioners have questioned whether there can ever be such a thing as existential supervision. Much of their disquiet is focused on how supervision is defined. Milton (van Deurzen & Young 2009:149–160) notes, 'the term "supervision" is problematic as it explicitly refers to a process whereby the supervisor "oversees and directs the performance of, the one who manages, controls, is in charge of, or is responsible for" the practice of another' (Mitchell 2002: 92). This definition implies that the relationship will be based on an authoritarian stance and that this is both possible and desirable (Strasser 1999). Milton goes on to say that in addition to problems with the definition 'the language used to discuss "supervision" is problematic as it contributes to a lack of critical thinking which has meant that the supervision literature has, at times, conflated what theory and policy say supervision *should* be with what those involved need or want it to be. Or maybe that it *can* be' (Milton in van Deurzen & Young 2009:150).

Many existential supervisors will shy away from defining what they do as a 'model' of supervision. Pett (1995) drew attention to the need to use a supervisory 'framework' rather than a formal model as a better way of providing an experience flexible enough to utilise existential insights. While Wright (1996) argues that the non-doctrinaire nature of existential-phenomenological supervision is both its greatest strengthen and its greatest weakness, and that while he may in some ways envy those models which appear to offer steady certainty, to remain authentic requires the trust in the continual uncertainty that goes with existentialism.

As you may have noticed, I too have tried to avoid the word 'model', feeling happier to speak of an 'approach', as this implies, for me at least, that what is offered in existential supervision is not something universal or concrete, carrying an implication that if the model is followed correctly certain results will ensue, but is indeed more of a pathway, or approach along which the supervisor and the supervisees travel together and openly explore the unknown, holding no preconceptions as to what they may discover. It is the centrality of the co-created relationship built on the openness and trust between supervisor and supervisee, which is the focus of existential writers such as Du Plock (2007) when they consider the nature of existential supervision.

I hope that this chapter has acknowledged these tensions, whilst suggesting that it is possible to create authentic existential supervisory practice, which holds true to existential aims, and at the same time accepts responsibility for working cooperatively and ethically with another, without creating a hierarchical relationship.

# 8

# ETHICAL CONSIDERATIONS IN EXISTENTIAL COACHING SUPERVISION

## What do we mean by ethics?

An important aspect of the supervisor's role is to enable the supervisee to work ethically. This is required of all coaches regardless of their theoretical approach. As coaches we are allowed into aspects of our clients' lives and trusted with their concerns and dilemmas and so we take on an ethical responsibility to our clients, any commissioning agency, and to ourselves.

Despite our shared humanity, we may have very different values and beliefs from which we devise our collective or individual code of ethics. Schwetzer (in Somerville 2006:124) drew our attention to the view that, 'ethics, too, are nothing but reverence for life. This is what gives me the fundamental principle of morality, namely, that good consists in maintaining, promoting, and enhancing life, and that destroying, injuring, and limiting life are evil'. To work respectfully with our clients, we must address ethical considerations. Somerville (2006:2) suggests that to discover a person's ethical stance we must give importance to 'stories, myths, poetry, imagination, "examined emotions", intuition –especially moral intuition – and the human spirit'. She suggests that although common sense, facts, and reason are not unimportant to ethics, the fact they are often assumed to be the **only** things which are important disregards the richness of the human spirit. I would suggest that this leads to many codes of ethics being mainly prescriptive, transactional, and concerned with avoiding the risks of litigation. They are not intended to speak to the spirit and yet it is our values and beliefs which should underpin our ethics and are essentially determined by our *Überwelt*; our spiritual world, through which we find meaning in some things and not in others.

There is nothing new in the requirement for those working directly with other people and holding special obligations to the public to need to adhere to a code of ethics. We only have to look to the origin of the term 'profession' which comes from the Medieval Latin *profession*, relating to the professing or taking of vows upon entering a religious order. This shows the spiritual origin and aim of committing to a particular way of being.

One of the earliest written ethical codes, carved into a massive stone pillar, dates back to as 1754b.c. The Babylonian Code of Hammurabi provides a code of laws, a collection of 282 rules and established ethical standards for commercial interactions and set fines and punishments. It recognised priests, physicians, servants, and tavern keepers as those holding jobs which carried a duty towards others. The code went so far as requiring physicians to set fees according to the social status of patients. In addition to professional issues, it addresses issues of household and family relationships, inheritance, divorce, paternity, and reproductive behaviour. However, embodied within the code is a structure of inequality, with punishments for someone assaulting someone from the lower class being far lighter than if the victim held a higher status. Women were also discriminated against, receiving punishment for behaviours for which men were not punished. Men were allowed to have affairs with servants whereas married women would receive severe punishment for adultery. The code contains some of the earliest references to the doctrine *lex talionis* sometimes better known as 'an eye for an eye' with a belief that the punishment should relate in some way to the nature of the crime. For example, the penalty for a doctor who killed a rich patient was to have his hands cut off, the very hands which had undertaken the medicinal work and accepted the payment for it.

The introduction of the Hippocratic oath in 400 B.C. is perhaps the first example of a code generated by a specific profession and covers such ethical issues as competence, sexual involvement with patients, confidentiality, and keeping patients and others from harm. It requires a reverence towards teachers and supervisors, requiring that they are treated as equal to parents with a duty of care flowing both ways. It also places a duty on followers to teach the secrets of medicine to the next generation. It was thought to be part of a rite of induction into a specific Greek medical guild-like community. The guidelines are still widely used and quoted by physicians today.

Other early codes include one created by Moses ben Maimon (1135–1204), Spanish-born Jewish physician and philosopher (often referred to in Western literature as Maimonides). Again, he focused on physicians, creating a prayer that emphasises their special ethical obligations, including not to thirst for profit or fame, and that one should gladly help all people, whether rich or poor, good or bad, enemies or friends. This brought in a holistic perspective with its emphasis on the need to see the human being, not just the illness.

Of course, we need more than ethical codes to prevent unethical behaviour. We see many examples of professional ethical codes being in existence but not adhered to or interpreted very differently than intended. An obvious example would be the Nazi doctors who performed horrific medical experiments on prisoners in Auschwitz during WWII. Indeed, they used 'ethical and scientific' excuses for their behaviour claiming that what they did was in the name of science, the search for truth, and in the quest to solve future medical issues. Despite their 'justifications' at the most basic they disregarded the ethical maxim, *primum non nocere* ('above all do no harm'). We did learn from this and as a consequence new codes of ethics were adopted in the late 1940s. Amongst these were The Nuremberg Code of Ethics on Medical Research (1946), Declaration of Geneva (1948), and the ethical code amendments by the American Medical Association (1948).

The study of ethics and the formulation of ethical codes comes from philosophical explorations of what it is to be ethical. In responding to an ethical dilemma in coaching it is useful to have some basic understanding of ethics and to understand the significance of the philosophy behind it. Any study of ethics will show that what is understood by and accepted as ethical behaviour is culturally, societally, and historically led, and so is constantly subject to interpretation.

Although any interpretation of ethics is set within its context, I am using the Remley & Herlihy (2000:174) description of ethics as '...a discipline within philosophy which focuses on human conduct and moral decisions within the context of particular relationships'. When writing of meta-ethics, I am using the term as it originated from the Greek *meta*, meaning after, between, and among and described in the Collins English Dictionary, (2003) as 'The philosophical study of questions about the nature of ethical judgment as distinct from questions of normative ethics, for example, whether ethical judgments state facts or express attitudes, whether there are objective standards of morality, and how moral judgments can be justified'.

## A professional code of ethics for coaching

It is not a simple task to become an ethical coach. Handelsman et al. (2005:59) drew our attention to the fact that, 'Becoming an ethical professional is more complex than simply following a set of rules or doing what one sees one's mentors do…(It) involves more than teaching certain professional rules to morally upright people who will easily understand and implement them'.

Coaching is a rapidly growing profession and as such continues to understand more each day about the ethical dilemmas its practice must address. Although Williams & Anderson (2006) consider Socrates to be the earliest recorded model of life and business coaching through his process of inquiry, the profession has grown from the development of individuals (mainly from two professional strands: psychology and business), to seeking ways to integrate knowledge and experience and broadening their area of impact with these early coaches mainly drew on the ethical codes of their previous careers to form a framework for their coaching practice.

### *Historical development*

Professional codes of ethics still mainly emanate from the individual profession's recognition that its members have a special obligation to the public. Coaching focuses on working directly with people, often at times when they may be particularly vulnerable. Coaches work from a philosophy of belief in the capacity for change and personal growth and see their role as being to facilitate such growth and to support individuals in their development. Whilst the work is based on the requirement for individuals to take responsibility for their choices and for coach and client to behave responsibly this cannot take place without the coach remaining aware of the responsibility the coaching relationship; not to bear this in mind is in itself unethical.

Not all professions have fully recognised their responsibility to their clients and are only forced to address it when change occurs, and ethical issues are recognised or reviewed. An example of this is the development of psychology, which was mainly an academic interest until WWII when psychology began to be applied not just theoretically but practically in clinical practice, and the need for a code of ethics was recognised.

By the 1990s and early 2000s the coaching phenomenon intensified with the creation of coach training schools and two major professional associations. With this came increasing awareness of a need for an ethical framework specific to the needs of the coaching profession. To become a recognised profession, coaching needed professional standards, definitions, ethical guidelines, ongoing research, and methods of accrediting. This resulted in the two key coaching organisations, the Professional Coaches and Mentors Association (PCMA) merging with the International Coaching Federation (ICF) in 1966 and developing a coaching code of practice. By 2004 the ICF had developed a set of core competencies, a code of ethics, a system of professional oversight, professional coaching credentialing, professional coach training accreditation, and on-going self-regulatory oversight.

The process of agreeing the first UK Statement of Shared Professional Values (Association for Coaching) began in 2008. The coaching bodies involved were the International Coach Federation (ICF), the Association for Coaching (AC), Association for Professional Executive Coaching and Supervision (APECS), and the European Mentoring and Coaching Council (EMCC). They agreed a statement of shared professional values which included the recommendation that every coach should:

- Be a member of a professional body suiting their needs
- Abide by a code of governing ethics and apply acknowledged standards to the performance of their coaching work
- Need to invest in ongoing continuing professional development to ensure the quality of their service and their level of skill is enhanced
- Abide by a duty of care to ensure the good reputation of the coaching profession

These points were backed up by seven guiding principles:

1. **Reputation**. Every coach will act in a positive manner that increases the public's understanding and acceptance of coaching
2. **Continuous competence enhancement**. Every coach accepts the need to enhance their experience, knowledge, capability, and competence on a continuous basis through continual personal development
3. **Client-centred.** Every client is creative, resourceful, and whole and the coach's role is to keep the development of that client central to their work, providing services which are appropriate to their needs
4. **Confidentiality and standards**. Every coach has a professional responsibility to apply high standards in their service provision and behaviour, to be open about methods and techniques used, maintain only appropriate records, and respect the confidentiality
5. **Law and diversity**. Every coach will act within the laws of the jurisdictions within which they practise and acknowledge and promote diversity at all times
6. **Boundary management.** Every coach will recognise their own limitations of competence and exercise boundary management

Most of the codes of ethics which coaches and supervisors are currently working to will contain these issues.

## *Ethics in individual and business or organisational coaching*

The above may cover most of the ethical dilemmas a coach may encounter in working with an individual client in a private setting. However, many coaches are commissioned through an organisation or company and so must also take note of organisational ethics. It was not until the 1990s that Solomon (1993), identified that excellence, even in business, begins with ethics. Much has been written on the topic of business ethics (Trevino & Nelson 1999; Ferrell & Fraedrich 2018; Fisher & Lovell 2009; De George 2006; Ciulla et al. 2007; Crane & Matten 2004). Within the work two broad themes can be identified. The first focuses on case studies and scenarios containing ethical issues. The second considers ethical models and ethical decision-making processes. The case studies reflect the business school approach to learning by observing and reflecting on real life cases. This contrasts with the psychological model of learning and research which is focused on research studies using empirical methods.

For business the main ethical dilemma is often seen as balancing competing interests: essentially a trade-off between interests of profit and consumer and stakeholders (Ferrell & Fraedrich 2018). The culture of the organisation sets its own ethical framework regarding the treatment of stakeholders. Coaches working within the business context have to work with any tensions between the commissioning organisation's ethical interests, the ethical interests of their client, and their own values and beliefs. Supervisors will encourage supervisees to address any differences and tensions which are present across the differing needs, views, and values, and determine how these will be tackled.

Values do not differ just between organisations and individuals. Kohlberg (1969) suggests that individuals have different levels of moral development; the lowest being punishment and obedience, the highest being universal ethical principles which include inalienable rights which apply to all. These elements influence the intended behaviour and actions of the organisation.

Jones (1998) drawing from earlier work by Rest (1986) identified four stages of a process for ethical decision-making:

- Recognise the moral issue
- Make a moral judgement about that issue
- Establish an intention to act upon that judgement
- Act according to intention

In coaching outside the business context, it is clear that the person being coached is the centre of ethical concerns and responsibilities; this is not always the case for business, leadership, or executive coaching. In these contexts, we have to consider who the client is – is it the individual in the room who the coach is working with, or the organisation who has commissioned the coach? The coach has to consider who, in the event of a conflict, should be put first. Passmore & Mortimer (2011) also identify another difference, that of collaboration. They suggest that while this features in nursing and business ethical codes, it is missing in coaching. I am not totally convinced that this is the case, as to make a significant difference leadership coaches have to collaborate with the organisation, taking note of elements such as organisational change plans and management training.

Whatever context the coach is working in they carry ethical responsibilities not just towards the professional status of coaching, to the commissioning organisation, and the client, but also to

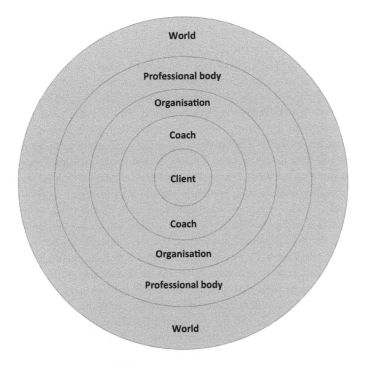

*Figure 8.1*  Circles of ethical responsibility

themselves. Indeed, existentially it may also be claimed that coaches carry responsibility beyond that; to the world in which we live, taking into account diversity and equality, environmental, time, and other broader issues. Within their commitment to self and to professional respectability they need to maintain and enhance their experience, knowledge, capability, and competence on a continuous basis through continual personal development and involvement in shaping policy.

It is worth returning briefly to the seven guiding principles of Shared Professional Standards (2008) considered earlier, and to look at them in a practical way, noting any ethical tensions which may be identified.

## *Reputation*

There are many different approaches and styles of coaching and coaching training programmes. They may differ somewhat in aims, and also to some extent on where they stand on the more complex ethical issues. Even between coaches themselves there may be a difference in the status awarded to some coaches and some coaching contexts, and to the professionalism of different coaching training organisations.

These differences may be confusing to clients, as the behaviour of some coaches may be experienced as unexpected and inappropriate, and therefore damaging to the professional status of coaching, e.g. some coaches may use embodied coaching approaches and so touch clients or manoeuvre their physical positions; others may be very vocal and loud and encourage, challenge, and be directive, whilst others may not. The coach needs to be clear about the style, boundaries, methods, and techniques they may use so that the client is always in a position to give informed consent at the time of contracting. It may be harder for a client whose coaching has been commissioned by their employer, and who is not personally paying for the sessions, to challenge or even not agree to proceed with a particular coaching style. Whether a coach proceeds when they know the organisation is happy with their approach, but the individual client isn't, can introduce an ethical tension into the work.

In today's society where social media has a high presence coaches may need to consider to what extent they publicise their personal values and beliefs. If the coach is working one-to-one with fee-paying clients it may benefit the clients to know more about the coach's views, but where the coach is paid by a coaching company, or by the employers of the client, then there may be objections to this. Coaching organisations may also feel that some public statements by coaches, particularly in the political arena, may risk bringing the profession into disrepute. Equally, some coaches may feel it is unethical to remain quiet about things they believe are important. They may look to their governing body to make public statements either supporting or condemning some political policies or actions. This can result in ethical tensions between client, coach, commissioning agent, governing body, and the public.

The individual coach's reputation will primarily be built on the relationships they develop with their clients and on the coaching work they deliver. Some coaches are very effective at marketing themselves through blogs, websites, podcasts, etc. but rarely actually work with clients. Other coaches will rely almost exclusively on word of mouth recommendations. Such coaches will build their reputation on their actions, they will 'walk the walk'. If they are working with a client to help them with their time management, they will not only offer them techniques which may help with this but will make sure that their own time management is excellent during the coaching relationship. If they are working with a client on enabling them to be more assertive, they will ensure that they allow the client space and opportunity to develop these skills, taking care not to rescue them or jump too quickly whilst at the same time modelling their own assertiveness skills.

I have written earlier about the need to make sure that the client knows what to expect. It is important to the reputation of a coach that they are known for delivering on their promises. Of course, there are always occasions where a coach may promise something in good faith and then find themselves unable to deliver. A coach with integrity will immediately inform the coach of possible problems and if something goes wrong to work to resolve the issues as quickly as possible or refund the client.

## *Continuous competence enhancement*

CCE, more often referred to as CPD (continuing professional development), can present a number of ethical issues. Some professionals will sign up for lots of conferences and workshops to gain the necessary CPD hours, whilst not engaging with the conference subjects and perhaps leaving as soon as they have their certificate of attendance. Individual coaches should value their own development and openly pursue opportunities which will encourage increased awareness and enhance their practice.

## *Client-centred*

Coaching starts with belief in the resourcefulness of the client. At times, the coach might feel they want to rescue the client or make it easier for them, but the coach is not required, nor has the right, to do the work for the client. This approach would be unethical and disempower the client. Ultimately it is up to clients to create and take responsibility for the life they want. The coach's responsibility rests with introducing them to the tools which will equip them with the ability to develop create results for themselves.

## *Confidentiality and standards*

### Confidentiality

When thinking about ethics the first thing most coaching students will think about is confidentiality. Having a keen sense of ethical awareness around confidentiality builds confidence and trust between coach and client. However, there are virtually no sectors in which total confidentiality can be offered. If there is a threat from the client towards self or others, if the client shares information regarding illegal activity or serious crime, the coach has a duty of care which may override confidentiality. The client needs to be aware of the extent and limitations of confidentiality when the contract between coach and client is agreed and where it is deemed necessary to breach confidentiality this should be discussed with the client. With GDPR and the Data Protection Act 2018 the coach also needs to have the explicit consent of the client to the making and keeping of records that contain personally sensitive information and to know who will make, keep, and have access to notes and records, how they will be kept, for how long, and for what purposes they may be retained/destroyed/disclosed.

### Standards

I have touched on the issue of maintaining high coaching standards under the previous heading of reputation. With regard to confidentiality the coach needs also to consider how and where to safely maintain appropriate records.

## *Law and diversity*

### Law

For those wanting to look in detail about law and ethics in coaching I would recommend Williams & Anderson (2006). Coaches have to work within many sets of laws or rules; those of the country in which they practise, those of their governing body, and those of any organisation they may work for. Sometimes, although fortunately infrequently, these can contradict each other, and the coach must form an ethical opinion for themselves.

### Diversity

Considerable thought has been given to how coaches work with diversity and respond to issues of gender, generational, cultural, national, and racial difference when working with clients (Passmore et al. 2013; Harris 2019). La'Wana Harris (2019) faces coaches with the challenging truth that people often worry that they must give up their power for others to have a chance and she points out that sharing power is not the same as losing it. At the time of writing, I can see this misunderstanding all too clearly in relation to the Black Life Matters movement and protests of 2020 following the death of George Floyd. For some white people they could not get beyond the mistaken idea that for black lives to matter it somehow indicated that white lives didn't! Harris introduced what she termed 'Inclusion Coaching' with a six stage COMMIT model in which commitment was made to:

- Courageous action
- Opening eyes and ears
- Moving beyond lip service
- Making room for controversy and conflict
- Inviting new perspectives
- Telling the truth even when it hurts

Although there is quite a bit of literature aimed at helping coaches identify their own prejudices and to be skilled in working with diversity, I could find little looking at the gender and race makeup of the coaching community itself. This was brought home very strongly to me when a coaching supervisee who was involved in setting up a new coaching course spoke to me about his difficulty in recruiting female or BME coaches with a known reputation to come and work on the course as trainers. I was a little surprised at his perception of there being a lack of female candidates, although I may suggest that they are less likely to self-publicise but sadly I was not as surprised by his failure to identify well-known coaches of black and minority ethnic background. Clearly this is an ethical issue which the whole coaching community needs to take note of and commit to change. I could not find any reliable breakdown of the ethnicity of coaches working in the UK. A code which requires coaches to 'practise and acknowledge and promote diversity at all times' must first look to its own professional make-up.

## *Boundary Management*

Ideally, at the start of the engagement, the coaching contract establishes the ground rules, the roles and responsibilities of the coach–client partnership. Setting boundaries stems from knowing who you are as a coach and what your understanding is of the coaching partnership is, what is acceptable or unacceptable for the client, you and any commissioning agency. These may be fairly easy to lay out at the contracting stage. However, Passmore & Mortimer (2011) estimate that less than half of coaches regularly set out the ethical or complaint guidelines to clients. This raises concern regarding possible negligence and may leave the client confused as to how to recognise whether they may have been treated ethically.

As the coaching relationship develops these issues may become more problematical. The coach has ethical and professional decisions to make about how much support or challenge to bring to the client. These can be a danger to withhold necessary support, particularly if the client is experienced a demanding or difficult. Equally, there is a danger of 'caring too much' and losing the role of coach to become a caretaker or rescuer. Both are disempowering to the client and can constitute unethical professional behaviour.

It is also possible to become too drawn into the client's story and lose objectivity, feeling you see yourself or someone you care about in the client. This may cause the coaching to lose focus and the work become side-tracked into discussions of subjects interesting to coach and client but straying from the focus of the coaching contract. Equally, a too close connection with the client can make it harder not to take their side on contentious issues, thus losing the neutrality of the coaching role. As I shall explain later, an existential approach would see everything within the coaching dialogue as relevant but would require the coach to be self-aware to relational dynamics and any possibility of collusion.

Most coaches are keen for their clients to like them and may find it hard to challenge clients when they breach boundaries by being late for sessions, not attending at all, expecting the session time to overrun if they wish it too, or taking calls throughout the session. Exploring these behaviours, rather than ignoring them, is part of the coach's responsibility to the client.

Coaches must also hold the boundaries of their professional role, not straying into those of counsellor, friend, mentor, or adviser. This leads to an ethical requirement for the coach to know when they are at the edge of their capability and knowledge and having systems in place to refer the client on if necessary.

It is also useful for the coach to have thought about, and conveyed to the client what, if any, relationship is appropriate outside of the coaching session, either during the length of the work together or after it has been concluded. The client's right to terminate the coaching process must be respected at all times. The coach also has a duty to terminate the contract if they believe they cannot offer the client their full attention because either the coach or the client has personal, behavioural, or emotional problems which mean they are not able to fully commit to the coaching work.

The supervisor must hold to ethical good practice with regard to all the issues discussed above. However, their ethical responsibility may extend beyond the life of their supervisee. Within the therapeutic professions the supervisor also has a responsibility to the supervisee's legacy and will hold contact details of supervisee's clients. They will agree with the coach what message should be given in the event of death or incapacity, and whether they will offer coaching to the clients, signpost them elsewhere, or make referrals.

I have already noted that codes of ethics change with time and context. This reflects the fact that as individuals and communities we change and may hold differing and changing ethical views and beliefs fitting with our experience, contexts, and increased knowledge. Even if we all prescribe to one code of professional ethics our interpretation of this code, even if the code remains the same, may change and differ from person to person. It is important to remember this when working with clients, taking care not to assume that our clients' values are written in stone like the Code of Hammurabi.

It is only with an understanding and commitment to ethical philosophical investigation, and in the context of this book, existential philosophy as a means of understanding behaviour, thought, and the nature of the universe, that coaches can identify their own existential value systems.

From there they can develop as coaches and become skilled in identifying and understanding the values of their clients. So, how might an existential perspective on ethics differ to what we have already noted?

## Existential perspective on ethics

We have already noted the existential requirement for individuals to take responsibility for their choices and for supervisor, coach, and client to behave responsibly. If a coach or supervisor fails to hold this in mind they are behaving unethically.

Kierkegaard (1985156) reminded us that there are always different pathways offered to us to choose between: 'I see it all perfectly: there are two possible situations – one can either do this, or that. My advice is this: do it or do not do it – you will regret both'. By this he was reminding us that with every path we choose not to take there is a loss of the potentiality that path carried. An important role in coaching and supervision is to openly recognise and explore all pathways that are open, together with their possible implications, gains and losses for the individual and for others. A coach or supervisor can be faced with an ethical dilemma when they (wrongly, or even rightly) believe that one path is preferable to another.

Although most people would agree with the need for ethical behaviour, for existentialists this is not enough. They would look to us to explore the question of why we should be ethical.

## *Why be ethical?*

Existential thought places a high value on authenticity and the desire to avoid operating in 'bad faith'. Bad faith (*mauvaise foi*) is a philosophical concept utilised by the French existentialist philosophers Simone de Beauvoir in *The Ethics of Ambiguity* (1947) and Jean-Paul Sartre in *Being and Nothingness* (1958:86–119) to describe the phenomenon in which human beings, under pressure from social forces, adopt false values and disown their innate freedom, thereby acting inauthentically. By acting in this way, sticking to safe default choices, and refusing to recognise other potential ways of being, a person is choosing to place themselves at the mercy of circumstances, thus functioning more as an object than as a conscious human being; in Sartrean terms, they are being more akin to 'being-in-itself' than 'being-for-itself'. Sartre sees bad faith as evidence of a deep confusion about one's own basic projects, attitudes, desires, and actions: in essence an act of self-deception. By acting in bad faith people are attempting to deny their freedom to make choices, instead adopting social roles and value systems which do not fit with being conscious human beings. However, even in doing this they are making a choice and thereby perhaps unconsciously acknowledging their freedom as conscious human beings. As Sartre saw it, we are condemned to our freedom. Whilst he would see freedom as the chief value of existentialism, he would consider bad faith or the failure to recognise and acknowledge one's freedom as the chief existential vice. De Beauvoir describes her belief in the contingency of existence in that there is no necessity that we exist and thus there is no predetermined human essence or standard of value. For her, human freedom requires the freedom of others for it to be actualised. It would be bad faith not to recognise this.

This leaves open the possibility that an individual's innate 'authentic' response may be to act in a way which society and others might perceive as unethical. This adds an additional challenge when we consider what it means to be ethical from an existential perspective. We are led by our values to demonstrate preferences and choices from an array of possible actions and attitudes. Freedom goes hand in hand with the requirement and responsibility to make choices. The concept of 'choice' is important in existential ethics and requires us to understand 'the inner demand for justification as a self-imposed necessary relation between actions and judgements by and within the same individual' (Barnes 1971:83). Just as we are not handed an answer to what constitutes the meaning of existence but have to discover this for ourselves, in relation to our own unique experience of existing, neither are we offered an answer to what is truly ethical. Instead, we need to establish our own ethical framework to overlay those of the organisation or individual we may be working for and the codes of ethics of a professional organisation to which we may belong. In choosing an individual code of ethics the individual still holds a responsibility for their choice and identify the reasons for their choice. Such reasons

might be one grounded in the denial of being responsible, or the 'source' of this decision: this would therefore be an article of 'bad faith' in the Sartrean tradition.

If a coach argued that freedom to choose is an existential value (as demonstrated in opting not to be bound by any ethical considerations) and declares this to a client or commissioning organisation it might be concluded that the person is acting authentically. If the client knowingly chooses to work with such a coach, the client is taking responsibility for their choice. However, if the coach operated without ethical boundaries and did not declare this as their way of working, they would be operating dishonestly and inauthentically and would be responsible for the outcomes.

To claim as a general principle that it is fine to be 'unethical' and to deny any evaluation, self-imposed or otherwise, is a contradiction: it is still a choice to value one thing over another. It could be argued that there is some semblance of a value system operating in this instance, but if the individual refuses to acknowledge their choices as attempts to serve their chosen value, they fall into self-deception, and the ground of authenticity is again lost. There is no escape from the freedom to choose.

It would seem that it may be possible to be authentic, while not ethical: by refusing any attempt to justify one's choices or actions. Barnes's claims that, 'critics are right who have pointed out that authenticity of and by itself does not necessarily result in what may properly be called the ethical life' (ibid). The ethical stance remains an authentic stance, even if only an ideal to be strived for and never finally attained. It takes into account the demands and obligations of being-in-the-world with others, of being accountable and responsible far beyond any anticipated effects (Barnes 1971; Becker 2011).

Being responsible for our ethical choices is a necessity in the quest to be authentic. Sartre (1963) questioned whether there was any need to be ethical at all claiming that 'There is indeed no reason why a man should do this (be ethical), and he gets nothing by it except the authentic knowledge that he exists…' He sees ethical choices as a response to meaninglessness and authenticity, as in freely choosing to assign meaning, and value, a purpose to existing is created. 'You are free, therefore choose…No rule of general morality can show you what you ought to do: no signs are vouchsafed in this world. The Catholics will reply, "Oh, but they are!" Very well; but is it still myself, in every case, who has to interpret the signs' (ibid). Whether God exists or not we are each responsible for how we interpret and live by the values we recognise, even when these stem from organised religion or society.

At one point Sartre expressed a desire to develop a systematic survey of existential ethics, but this never happened. He came to the conclusion that it was probably impossible and irrelevant, as ontology could not formulate ethical norms. Despite this, ontological theory does carry moral implications, as we are always faced with making a choice whilst holding individual value and beliefs to which the choice may or may not conform. These choices have implications for self and others. We can only look to ourselves to authentically create values, beliefs, and ethical choices by which we judge ourselves. Knowing this creates anxiety. Codes are theoretical: life is very practical and concrete, and it is down to each one of us to live our temporal lives authentically, taking ownership of all we do in the time we have.

Once we have formulated our ethical code, things don't get easier. A complication of an ethical dilemma lies in the fact that one or another value is destined to be compromised in a particular situation. It is often unclear whether any particular ethical choice is good or evil as either may has negative implications for somebody. To behave ethically we must consider our motives and all the possible implications for all those who may also be affected; indeed Heidegger (1962) reminds us that we exist within a with-world so it is unavoidable that we are responsible for all our actions and their effect on others.

We can see the tension of the need to rely on ourselves for an internal moral code played out in Kierkegaard's book *Fear and Trembling*, where he explores the ethical dilemma within the biblical story of Abraham, which I referred to earlier. Abraham is not, and can never be, entirely confident that God has chosen to communicate with him with the aim of instructing him to kill his son and so act in direct opposition to that all that has been deemed righteous. Abraham must rely on himself to make an ethical judgement. There are no external guidelines he can look to for help in this situation. He can only draw on his own limited understanding and his own personal experience of his relationship to God. Whatever he chooses to do, he will suffer the consequences of his action. It is with 'fear and trembling' that he approaches this decision, without a generalised code of morals to support him. In Abraham's case, his choice was vindicated by an archangel sent from God. Most of us will not receive such reassurance. Instead, the outcome of our deliberations and actions is often accompanied by feelings of both guilt and justification. We are solely accountable for our choices: we may adopt, freely, a codified system of ethics, but the choice to abide by such a code is strictly our own. This understanding and acceptance of 'ownership' of one's decisions is fundamental to the existential perspective.

Our temporal nature brings another ethical challenge. Any choice we make can only be made once, at a particular time, and in a unique situation. 'We cannot decide a priori what it is that should be done...choice always remains choice in the situation...' Sartre (in Kaufmann 1956:306). This is important to hold in mind throughout the coaching process, a process which should be an ethical, authentic, innovative, and creative enterprise.

Given that we now have professional codes of ethics for coaches, what other specific challenges need to be borne in mind when bringing an existential approach to coaching? We cannot just look to the professional codes, nor can we look to religion for our ethical stance; as Sartre pointed out, 'God is dead. Let us not understand by this that he does not exist or even that he no longer exists. He is dead. He spoke to us and is silent. We no longer have anything but his cadaver. Perhaps he slipped out of the world, somewhere else like the soul of a dead man. Perhaps he was only a dream...God is dead.' (Jean-Paul Sartre, *Situations*, 1948:280). Indeed, for many people the first thing which springs to mind in relation to Sartre is this concept that God does not exist. This has led people to assume that therefore everything is permitted and that existential approaches are not high on ethical boundaries and may even consider ethical codes to be inauthentic. The inauthentic rejoinder, in Sartre's view would be, 'If God did not exist it would be necessary to invent Him' (ibid). God's absence does not exclude ethics, rather it provides the necessary condition under which a genuine ethics becomes possible. If God exists then everything would be predetermined, and if this were the case then we could not consider ourselves to be free. To accept absence of God we are forced to take responsibility for our actions, and this requires an ethical code, be it overt, external, and collective, or internal, subjective, and individual. Any denial of this is bad faith.

One cannot be truly authentic without considering the context of one's decisions and the possible implications on others. These represent ethical approaches of psychological coherence and integrity which are likely to be present in the coaching relationship. To live a full authentic life in which one is true to oneself rather than merely being alive can be a real challenge to many coaches living in the real world of conflicting desires and demands. For the coach, helping the client to acknowledge their choices and responsibilities is in itself an ethical exercise.

Williams & Anderson (2006:285) wrote that a person entering the coaching profession 'might assume that being effective and making ethical choices means obtaining some training and learning about the ethical code of conduct for coaches. However, ethical behavior involves a more comprehensive journey'. For a person wishing to coach from an existential perspective that journey is a philosophical one and will throw up many dilemmas along the path. Krug & Schneider (2016:109) sum up the ethical aim of existential supervision as being to help to sensitise the supervisee 'to the many social, cultural, and political contexts that may bear on his or her work with clients. This means helping... develop a multilevel awareness of what traditionally are called *transference* and *countertransference* issues but in existential terms are issues of *encounter*' May (1969). Krug & Schneider (ibid) identify a number of ethical breaches which a supervisor may have to attend to, including 'presumptions about client's attitudes or dispositions that do not dovetail with the phenomenology of their presentations...(witting or unwitting) imposition of values on client; ...imposition of...own personal needs or conflicts on clients; ...lack of atonement to client's fears or aspirations that short-change clients' capacities to explore...'

## Ethical issues within each of the main existential concerns

Having looked in an earlier chapter about the main existential concerns, it may be useful here to explore what ethical issue may be contained in each of these.

Beauchamp & Childress (1994), in considering what makes a good coach, named integrity, compassion, discernment, and trustworthiness as qualities they would expect to find. Meara et al. (1996) echoed this, listing respectfulness, integrity, prudence, and benevolence as key attributes and Velasquez et al. (2005) looked for integrity, honesty, self-control, courage, compassion, generosity. Many of these qualities point directly to the need for an ethical stance. An existential

*Table 8.1* Coaching Attributes and Existential Concerns

|  | Coaching Qualities | Existential Theme |
| --- | --- | --- |
| Beauchamp & Childress (1994) | Integrity | Authenticity |
|  | Compassion | Relatedness |
|  | Discernment | Values and beliefs |
|  | Trustworthiness | Authenticity/integrity |
| Meara et al. (1996) | Respectfulness | Relatedness |
|  | Integrity | Authenticity/integrity |
|  | Prudence | Authenticity |
|  | Benevolence | Relatedness |
| Velasquez et al. (2005) | Integrity | Authenticity/integrity |
|  | Honesty | Authenticity/integrity |
|  | Self-control | Freedom and responsibility |
|  | Courage | Authenticity |
|  | Compassion | Relatedness |
|  |  | Anxiety |
|  | Generosity | Relatedness |

coach would seek to be all of these. In addition, existential ethics holds the highest good for humans as 'becoming an individual' (Kierkegaard) and acting with 'authenticity' (Heidegger, Sartre). Although integrity and authenticity have some shared attributes, authenticity calls for knowledge not just of the codes to which one is working but also of self.

There is much congruence in considerations of what makes a good, ethical coach. Existential thought would see it as essential for coaches and supervisors to also demonstrate the skills and qualities to engage with time and temporality, and uncertainty. In a very practical way, each of the existential concerns, which I have already introduced, can face the coach and supervisor with a number of ethical issues.

## *Anxiety*

It is fairly common these days to hear of people suffering from 'existential anxiety' or experiencing an 'existential crisis'. This experience may be their reason for seeking coaching. Within the existential framework anxiety of an existential or ontological nature is considered to be a valid response to living in a meaningless and uncertain temporal world, within which we are each required to find our own meaning and learn to coexist with uncertainty. Kierkegaard (1844) reminded us that we should not be afraid of anxiety or rush to get rid of it. One of our ontological tasks is to find a way of being-with-anxiety and understanding that such anxiety is part of being a sentient entity. Van Deurzen & Young (2009:7) suggest that supervisees (and indeed everyone) must 'learn to be anxious in the right way; not so little that they live in illusion, not so much that they lose their footing in life'.

Sometimes this acute awareness can feel unbearable for some people and so they may term it as an existential crisis. For existentialists, such a 'crisis' is considered part of life's journey, an awareness, a necessary experience, and a complex phenomenon. It arises from an awareness of one's own freedoms, the essential meaninglessness of life, and the temporality of one's existence. All of these important aspects of being can throw people into what may be termed and authentically experienced as a 'crisis'.

One ethical dilemma which can face a coach working with someone who sees themselves as being in existential crisis is the extent to which they challenge the client's view that it is a 'crisis' at all, rather than a 'journey', or even an 'existential developmental requirement'. Exploring paradox plays an important role in existential work, and a coach working existentially with such a client is faced with the paradoxical dilemma of remaining true to working authentically, and existentially, entering the client's worldview and therefore their definition of their experience, or challenging it. Phenomenologically their unique experience and interpretation cannot be denied. However, some people may use the term 'existential crisis' in a loose way to merely indicate a high level of anxiety. The supervisor would encourage a supervisee not to accept any term the client may make to describe their mood or experience before first exploring what the client really means by the term and how they are experiencing it. This could present the coach with another challenge. Would they know where to refer a client, or what information to give, if they were concerned about the client's level of anxiety and mental health? A supervisor would hold an ethical duty to ensure that a supervisee was not working with client material which was beyond their competence. To allow that to happen would be failing both the supervisee and their client.

The difference between the existential understanding that an 'existential crisis' may in fact be a period of existential enlightenment, which can bring new understanding and may change priorities, and the client's embodied feelings of distress, can also raise ethical issues and present the coach with a paradox. To work phenomenologically they would need to accept the client's worldview as the starting point for discussion, whereas their existential belief might challenge the validity of the client's terminology and understanding. Not all supervisees would be equipped to work with their own inner tension through this exploration and the supervisor would need to support them in their ongoing work, or in the decision that the client's experience indicated a period of more profound psychological anxiety and distress and represented an area they were skilled to work with and instead required the client to work with a specialist in mental health.

The supervisor's role is never to answer a dilemma for the coach in order to relieve the coach's anxiety, but to ensure that the coach is aware that such dilemmas are in play. The supervisor would require the supervisee to explore what is causing their anxiety and to reflect on how they will work with this in a way which is respectful to their own beliefs and those of the client, including considering whether it may be necessary to facilitate the client working with a different professional.

When supervising inexperienced coaches, coaches working with challenging client material, or coaches who are experiencing external personal pressures which may impact on their ability to be present to the client, the supervisor must help the coach explore and manage the anxiety which is present. An inexperienced coach may feel anxious about all their client work and the supervisor should look to provide support and encouragement while ensuring the coach is not taking on work that is beyond their experience and competence. The supervisor is often called on to help a coach, even an experienced one, to work with anxiety created by the expectations of self and others or by what is happening in their personal life. For some supervisors this may raise a boundary issue: to what extent do they need to know anything about their supervisee's personal life and stresses? Some supervisors, including those working existentially, would see the coach as the main offering in the coaching relationship and as such would see it as a valid role in supervision to check that the supervisee is alright in their coaching role at any given time. This does not mean providing therapy for the supervisee but enabling them to reflect on whether they are able to work to full capacity. If a supervisor does not feel a supervisee is fit to work, they have an ethical duty to speak with the supervisee about this. This may be a difficult conversation but one the supervisor must raise and then agree a plan of action with the supervisee. The supervisor may have the necessary skills to provide the required support throughout this period or may not feel comfortable with the supervisee's decision to continue to work. The supervisor must hold in mind that they have a responsibility to their supervisee but also to their coaching client.

## *Authenticity/integrity*

An existential supervisor places great importance on the authenticity of their relationship with the supervisee and would look to the supervisee to demonstrate the same integrity and openness with their client. To do so, it becomes ethically essential for the supervisor and supervisee to each be aware of their own biases and the ways in which they may influence the relationship. Our worldview influences our responses to others and so in order to behave ethically, we must constantly work to be self-reflective. The professional relationship with an existential coaching supervisor can help ensure that this is a regular part of the work.

To live life authentically is a goal of all those working from an existential framework. Authenticity requires us to live according to our own ethical code and to proceed with integrity in relation to ourselves and others, working to what may be termed 'ethical truths'. Such 'ethical truths' take us beyond truth based on objective and scientific understanding or defined metaphysically. Instead, we are called to live and work with the concept of what Somerville

(2006:82) terms 'temporal truth'. This means remaining open to challenging our own truths and when appropriate to changing our understanding. Approaching truth in this way means that we clarify 'previously inadequate or mistaken articulation of truth' (2006:82). This fits authentically with our existential understanding of the uncertainty of all things.

The ability to be authentic is very closely aligned to the level of truth we invest in another person. Although the behaviour of current political figures may challenge this we place less 'blind trust' in authority figures than we may have done in the past. 'Blind trust' is based on power and status. We now tend to look more towards 'earned trust' which is based on the level of trustworthiness we see and experience in individual and organisational behaviour.

The existential supervisor will not present as an 'expert' but as a fellow traveller and lifelong student who can walk alongside the supervisee, bringing in their own embodied experience as a coach in addition to any relevant theoretical knowledge they may hold. They would discourage the supervisee developing a 'blind faith' in them and would always try to act authentically, being clear if they are out of their comfort zone or have less knowledge of something than the supervisee may assume. They would seek to develop the attitude of 'not knowing' and not assuming in the supervisee, fine-tuning their ability to bracket assumptions and prejudices and so to work phenomenologically and authentically. This means checking that the supervisee is fully listening to their client in an open and active way. Being authentic requires courage, and one role of the supervisor is to develop that courage in the supervisee and to call on their own bravery in their relationship with the supervisee.

As a coach or supervisor, one aspect of being authentic is being clear about our competence and our boundaries both personal and professional. The coach must know what they understand as the role of coaching and be clear with the client what they are offering.

Weiner (2007) gives space in her small book on ethics in coaching to exploring the differences between psychotherapy and coaching, believing it to be an ethical requirement to be clear with the client regarding these differences. She points out that often coaching is (incorrectly) understood by an unknowing public to be a version of therapy. She draws on David Matthew Prior's work (2003) on coaching integrity to look closely at the different language which she considers should be used by a coach rather than a psychotherapist. Interestingly she calls on coaches to emphasise the client-initiated action and accountability of the coaching encounter, seeing the coach as the facilitator of the process by clients can fully empower themselves. Although I applaud the importance she places on the difference between coaching and therapy, she seems to be speaking of a more psychodynamic rather than existential psychotherapy model, going on to quote Fairley & Stout (2004:32), 'In counselling, the person is seen as broken, bruised and in need of healing. In coaching, people are viewed as creative, resourceful, and whole'. Neither existential therapists or coaches see clients as 'broken' so it is important for existentially trained coaches and therapists to have clear ethical boundaries regarding these differences when working with vulnerable clients.

Remaining authentically true to the role of supervisor, may in some cases, be even more challenging. Just as the coach must be aware of rescuing tendencies in relation to their client, the supervisor must consider this in relation to their supervisee. The relationship a supervisor has with their supervisee is often a lot longer than a coach may have with a client. Supervisees often choose their supervisors because they feel them to be a good fit. This means that the two are perhaps more likely to share many of the same beliefs and interests and the relationship holds a potentiality to develop into a friendship. If this happens then supervisor and supervisee must consider whether it is still possible to authentically challenge in a way which makes the supervision meaningful and professional.

## Freedom and responsibility

Kierkegaard and Sartre both express the ethical belief that if one has faith one must act accordingly and authentically. An existential ethical code is not a passive one. It requires us to take responsibility for our action with an understanding of potential consequences as an essential ethical issue. We must do so in an open and authentic way. The existential supervisor and coach see their role as facilitative and empowering and place emphasis on the existential importance of individual responsibility.

Peltier (2010) in his ten existential guidelines for an executive coach ends with 'clients must figure out their own way', taking the existential starting point as the belief that the client is resourceful and creative, with the task of the coach being to work to facilitate the use of those creative resources. To hold to this may present an ethical dilemma to some coaches who may feel they hold the answer to a client's dilemma and that all they have to do is tell them what to do. This viewpoint is inauthentic as we do not hold the answer to how someone else should live their life, or the steps they should take to make that life meaningful. It also challenges the existential requirement that each of us must take responsibility for own actions and for everything which results from our decisions.

This does not mean that existentialism does not recognise that contextually each individual has different obstacles to overcome in coming to any decision. We are thrown into certain aspects of our existence: the place, time, and nature of our birth; our family; race; culture; birth-given gender are thrust upon us. Heidegger (1927:135) uses the term 'thrownness' to describe this: 'The expression thrownness is meant to suggest the facticity of its being delivered over'. Rollo May (1981) also uses the term to describe that which influences us that we are unable to control. Destiny is a mixture of 'thrownness' and the impact of existential givens. Destiny, in existential terms. must always be understood in the context of freedom and our ability (and responsibility) to live in relation to our destiny. Destiny does not deny freedom but acknowledges that we are not **absolutely** free. Jaspers (1955) also recognised the same limits to freedom and the need for bravery in encountering them. He spoke of 'limit situations' (*Grenzsituationen*), which are moments, often accompanied by dread, guilt, or anxiety, in which we confront our restrictions and abandon the securities of its limitedness to enter new realms of self-consciousness. Jaspers argued that the freedom of consciousness to overcome its limits can only be achieved through intensely engaged communication with other persons aimed at challenging prejudices and sedimented attitudes. This can be seen as the core requirement of the coaching relationship. The coach and client must explore and understand thrownness and the limit situations which prevail, whilst holding on to Sartre's mantra (1943: from his note on the jacket cover for his play *Les Mouches*): 'no excuses'. An existential coach understands and works with the dread and guilt which the client may experience in discussing their situation and the challenges they encounter when determining their decisions. It is an area in which Beauchamp & Childress's (1994) call for showing compassion may be required. What may seem an easy decision for one person may raise many questions for another.

However, it would be all too easy to see 'thrownness' where it does not exist, and to claim that we do not have freedom in areas where we do. To accept the challenge of freedom means that we may choose to stay in a difficult position, but we cannot say we have not chosen to do so. This is an important area for the existential coach and supervisor to explore. To collude with a denial of freedom would be unethical.

The existential coach and supervisor approach their work with the belief that all human beings have free will and that all actions, expressions, and thoughts are the result of a decision. It is acknowledged that all decisions have losses and gains attached to them and are set within the limiting contexts of the client's psychological, physiological, and material needs.

Indeed, Yalom (1980) reminds us that the root of the word 'decide' means 'slay' as in to kill, so whenever we make a decision we exclude or 'kill off' another possibility. The making of a decision is an act of renunciation; for every yes there must be a no, this is one reason why decision-making is often such a struggle.

Although we have the freedom to make choices based on our needs, we cannot authentically do so without taking account of the fact that we are 'beings-in-the-world-with-others' and therefore must take account of how our decisions may impact on the free will and freedom of others, including the companies or organisations to which we may belong. It is part of the ethical duty of an existential coach or supervisor to ensure that this is considered in decision-making. This may differ from some modalities where there is a strong encouragement for the client to focus almost exclusively on what decision works best for them individually.

It can feel lonely and scary to take full responsibility for our decisions. We will often search for external direction. Some will look to utilitarianism for the answer, with its onus on everyone being obligated to do whatever will achieve the greatest good for the greatest number. Others may look to Kantian ethics by which everyone is obligated to act only in ways that respect the human dignity and moral rights of all persons. If we rely solely on professional ethical codes or the opinions of others, we may be in danger of ignoring the fact that ethical decisions are influenced by character and worldview with the propensity towards virtue ethics, our professional identity, and ethical training. In 'virtue ethics' there are certain ideals, such as excellence or dedication to the common good, toward which we should strive, and which allow the full development of our humanity. These ideals are discovered through thoughtful reflection on what we as human beings have the potential to become.

It is worth a coach and supervisor considering not focusing on what people should do or how people should act, although this is exactly what the client may ask for, as the 'moral principles approach' neglects the more important issue: what people should be. The need to engage with 'being' rather than 'doing' is a core component of the existential approach and demands the belief in freedom and responsibility.

## *Relatedness*

Most coaches and supervisors when thinking about relational ethics may focus on the personal and professional relationship between themselves and their supervisee or client. Existential supervisors would consider relatedness in connection with all the existential dimensions; Binswanger spoke of a relatedness between the environment (*Umwelt*), the world of social being and its signals (*Mitwelt*), and the world of actions (*Aliticwelt*). We encounter all of these within our coaching relationship. He argued that we are 'thrown' into a world we do not choose but we are obliged to be in and find authentic ways of relating within and to it. In the coaching experience coaches and supervisors are 'thrown' into the world of those commissioning them and bring their thrownness related to their own familial or institutional world of experience into supervisory and coaching relationships. In the wider world and the coaching ad supervisory contexts we must recognise the 'thrownness', accept it, and derive meaning from it. Out of thrownness and the awareness of a relation that is 'with-the-world' (*Mitwelt*), the world of the supervisee, client, and the organisations and groups in which they function, we can gain understanding of our relationships with a world that is 'social' and which focuses on our common humanity, but also on what differentiates us from each other. Both supervisor and coach must acknowledge the existence of thrownness but not use it as an excuse and must challenge themselves whenever they may be tempted to do so.

Returning to a consideration of the issues of relatedness within the supervisor/supervisee dyad and the coach/client dyad, Kemp (2008) stressed that the quality of the coach–client relationship, rather than any specific coaching methodology or model per se, may serve as the core catalyst for facilitating successful change. This is supported by evidence-based literature (Bordin 1979; Connor-Greene 1993; Greenson 1967; Rogers 1951; Horvath 2006; Horvath & Greensberg 1989; Kivlighan 2007; Lilliengren & Werbart 2005). Further support is provided by meta-analytical studies such as the one reported by Horvath & Symonds (1991). I consider this to be equally true in the supervisory relationship and thus allows for coaching supervisors to come from very different modalities to their supervisees. Supervision and coaching are relationships whose success is reliant on the strength of the connection and trust established between the individuals. An acknowledgement of the importance of the personal 'chemistry' between the two people is reflected in the practice used by many coaching organisations of starting a coaching or supervision contract with what is termed a 'chemistry session'. This session should go beyond sorting the practicalities of the proposed coaching contract, fees, venue, approach, etc., but also allow for the client to 'get a feel' for the coach, to experience their humanity and to see it they feel they 'click', i.e. whether the chemistry is good enough to be creative.

Such close trusting relationships can provide boundary questions for those concerned. These holds true within the existential perspective, where issues of respect and power must be openly and authentically addressed.

When considering the environmental (*Umwelt*) aspects of relatedness an existential coach or supervisor would need to consider the appropriateness of any venue for the sessions. It is not unheard of for coaching sessions to be conducted in fairly public places such as cafés. A supervisor would need to be certain that such as space was 'safe' for any discussion of confidential matters. Even if one party felt comfortable, the other may not. Whether we like to acknowledge it or not, there is always a power differential in the supervisor/supervisee dyad and the coach/client dyad. The power can rest in either party, or may move fluidly, but it is there. This may make it more likely that one party would agree to something the 'more powerful' party might suggest, such as where and when to meet. In a good phenomenological way, no assumptions must be made, and care must be taken that those types of decisions are freely made, and not resulting from a need to please.

There may be other parties who are also important within the circle of the supervisory relationship, such as commissioning organisations. The supervisor may encounter tensions between their own relationship with that organisation and the relationship their supervisee may have with the same people. A parallel process within the coach/client relationship would also need to be explored.

## Time and temporality

It is hard for any of us to understand or come to terms with the inevitability of our own death. We know it will happen, but it feels unreal to think of our end and of there being a time when everything will continue without us. For some people the temporality of life is terrifying, and in some cases, it is disabling, for others – why live at all when it will inevitably end and there is no universal meaning we can cling to? Let us not forget that for other people the knowledge that there is an end provides a stimulating challenge to be creative and meaningful in how we spend our limited time.

It is the ethical duty of a coach to be aware of the inevitability of endings and not collude with any client's desire to act as though this were not the case. Their life will end, their work will end, the coaching session will end, and the coaching relationship will end. To ignore this is unethical. This does not mean that the coach must continually cry out 'the end is in sight' but must consciously work with the knowledge that this is the case. Many of us can remember feeling, or indeed being told, that if we failed in our exams all potentiality would end; we would 'come to nothing'. As we journey through life, we have discovered this to be an untruth. We move through phases in our lives and must seek to find as much meaning as we can within each of these periods. To ignore time, be it external 'objective' time or internal 'subjective' time, would be unethical.

This understanding of the cultural and contextual nature of time and its fluidity and inevitability of endings is an important focus of existential coaching and supervision. The client may bring issues around ending to the coaching, e.g. endings of relationships, contracts, etc. If is ethically important that the coach does not collude with any unspoken fantasy that the coaching relationship will continue forever and does not seek to play down the psychological distress and sometimes accompanying pain which any ending can bring. An existential supervisor has a duty to ensure that such issues are not downplayed or overlooked all together in the supervisee's work.

Given the importance of time there are some very practical ways for the supervisee and supervisor to honour its importance. In contracting about timings and length of supervision sessions the supervisor is actively working with time, as is the coach in relation to their client. This is not to say that in the contracting there needs to be rigid time boundaries; this rigidity may not fit with the worldview of either supervisee or supervisor. However, what is important is that space is given to discussing what meaning time will be play in the supervisory relationship and in the supervisee's work with their client.

## Uncertainty

We have noted the importance in existential thinking of truly acknowledging the uncertainty of life. Somerville (2006:81) believes that complexity and uncertainty go hand in hand, and she points out that we are still a long way from developing an ethics of complexity. She sees 'learning to live comfortably with uncertainty is a fundamental requirement for "doing ethics"' and calls on us 'to hold certainty and uncertainty in creative tension'. Coaching should, in my view, be a creative activity. If we cling to certainty, then why would we risk, or desire change? To change we have to feel a little uncomfortable, or why move beyond the status quo? Uncertainty presents us with a blank canvas on which our creativity can play. We do not know what we will end up with and if we did why would there be any point in the journey.

Indeed, Adorno (1973) suggests that the highest form of morality is to never feel at home in one's own home; this challenges us never to be certain even in the most familiar of circumstances, but always to question. This is as true for ethics as for anything else. There is a danger that we can become complacent and believe we are acting ethically if we never stop to question ourselves. As Somerville (2006:81–82) puts it, 'we must always be questioning our ethics if we are to remain ethical; we must always be uncertain and listen to that uncertainty'.

In many contexts it may feel very unsafe to question what a group, community, or individual feel certain about; however, within coaching and within existential supervision there must be a safe place for such considerations. It would be existentially unethical to collude with a client's desire to see something as certain, when this was not the case. It may help the client to feel 'better' or more 'comfortable' but is ignoring the need to develop the 'courage to be' within an uncertain world.

## Values and beliefs

It is always a challenge to work with those people whose values and beliefs radically differ from your own. In our personal lives we have the right to challenge different beliefs and a duty to openly engage with the views of others with a willingness to have our own values challenged. When a coach contracts to work with a new client or organisation they may find that the ethical ethos of the commissioning organisation or individual differs from our own. We are immediately faced with the concept of 'thrownness' and limitations and must find a way to reconcile the ethical context we are thrown into, and our own individual set of existential values and beliefs, or we must refuse the work. This is a common ethical dilemma which a supervisee may bring to supervision.

Some coaching commissions challenge us to work with clients who are ambitious and wish to progress their careers within their organisation, despite there being a tension between their values and practices and those of the organisation. This may lead to a conscious state of living in bad faith, with the anxiety this brings. This may also be felt by the supervisor and coach who are being paid by the organisation often with a view to pulling the client more firmly into the organisation's ethos, values, and beliefs.

Many clients are faced with the dilemma of working in a job which pays well, gives status, and offers career development whilst at the same time draws the client further from the values and beliefs which led them to the work in the first place. Often coaches work with excellent and talented coaching clients who were happy in their work until they were promoted. They can gradually become more focused on individual career prospects than on their belief in the essential purpose of the work and as they enter the leadership circle, they may experience more closely a disconnect between what is stated as the company's beliefs and how they are lived out in the day-to-day reality of work.

This understanding that a person may be living in bad faith can heighten, or perhaps introduce for the first time, a deep sense of frustration and confusion which may be expressed in the coaching or in supervision. Sartre emphasises the existential view that we are entirely responsible for what we are and also what we will be. Neither, as supervisee or supervisor, can we blame the company, deeming it to be the architect of our choices, whilst choosing to stay within it. It takes moral courage to be honest with oneself and to lead our own life and to identify and pursue our own projects.

It has to be accepted that leaders of a company or a nation have more opportunity than most to affect more individuals by their decisions. For many existentialists the idea of politically superior individuals may be an anathema, yet it is a reality that some individuals are treated in this way and given power. Their position may mean that their actions take on more importance whether they wish this to be the case or not. An ethical dilemma can occur when personal responsibility and authenticity run in opposition to the responsibility to others and the potential power of the individual's position. Coaching a chief executive presents the coach with ethical dilemmas which cascade through the hierarchy of the company. Decisions which seem positive and ethical at one level may present issues for others. For a supervisor supporting a supervisee there is a need to recognise the ethical issue involved in challenging or not challenging an individual or organisation who are responsible for one's livelihood.

An existential supervisor will encourage their supervisee to work with the client to identify their authentic beliefs and values through the coaching discourse with its defined limit situations. The challenge is to identify one's values and beliefs and to authentically acknowledge within supervision one's thoughts and opinions, to express, not suppress them, and to act authentically in relation to those thoughts. Just as the coach will encourage their client to think, express, and act, so the supervisor will encourage the supervisee to do the same.

'Some of the most difficult conflicts to deal with ethically arise when the values that should govern at one level of doing ethics conflict with those of another level' (Somerville 2006:84). She goes on to identify four levels: micro/individual; meso/institutional; macro/societal; and mega/global. This is a particular ethical tension for coaches who are not directly commissioned by their client but through an organisation. It is not unusual for coaching clients to suffer from a tension between their personal values and beliefs and those of the organisation they are employed by.

Overlaid on the beliefs or values of the client and the organisation, are the values of the coach and the coach's supervisor. The supervisor has to be aware of any unconscious biases the supervisee may be bringing into their work, and if necessary, to identify and challenge them. Indeed, the supervisor has to do the same exercise for themselves in relation to their work with the supervisee. There is no requirement to change beliefs or values but there is an ethical requirement to reflect on them and authentically explore any paradoxes within the circles the supervisee is required to operate within.

If the values and beliefs of anyone within the coaching dynamic (client, coach, supervisor, or organisation) are in conflict then there is an ethical dilemma for all concerned, but the responsibility for identifying this will sit with the supervisee and supervisor. A coach has an ethical duty to consider how authentically and usefully they can work with someone if their values are in opposition at any of Somerville's levels: micro, meso, macro, or mega. In most cases it is possible to do so without becoming inauthentic; one may acknowledge that one's views and those of another differ, but an exploration of those difficulties may provide a positive creative tension which has the potential to enrich the work as long as ethical issues are not brushed under the carpet but instead are acknowledged and discussed with any action being transparent to all.

As we can see, ethical issues can arise in all the key existential concerns. Ethical issues are also found in all the existential dimensions – social, psychological, physical, and spiritual. The supervisor will alert the supervisee to any areas which seen to be absent in their work with the client and encourage awareness of the need to consider any potential ethical tensions.

# PART FOUR

- *Theory into action – four case examples demonstrating how a supervisor brings an existential approach into their supervision with four different supervisees*
- *The cases provide practical demonstrations*

# PART TWO

# INTRODUCTION TO CASE EXAMPLES

Having considered the main attributes of existential and phenomenological thought, and how these may be firstly used in existential coaching, and then in existential supervision, I felt it may be useful to ground some of this thinking in some practical examples taken from supervision sessions. These are not offered as examples of good practice but merely as real illustrations of existential supervision in action. I have tried to stay faithful to the content and flavour of the sessions whilst removing identifying factors in relation to people, places, or organisations.

Some of the supervisees were new to the existential approach and engaged with it in a spirit of openness, and sometimes of scepticism. Some were curious and just wanted to understand the theory behind the approach; others wanted to add something new to what they might offer clients. For others, they were seeking a more authentic way of working, feeling that they were not authentically attuned with the models and approaches they had originally trained in and were looking to move away from these and offer an approach centred on existential thought.

A third group of supervisees were already practising as existential coaches and used the regular supervision sessions as CPD and to continually check and challenge themselves as to what extent they were continuing to practice existentially.

I have tried to find examples which relate to specific existential givens. However, it is always the case that there will be more than one given in play, as these examples illustrate. I have placed the examples under the heading of the givens which were in the foreground of the client's narrative.

Any interventions or suggestions from the supervisor are tentative. It is intended that the supervisee, whilst accepting that comments are put forward in good faith as a starting point for debate, should feel free to challenge and interrogate the supervisor's vision rather than passively accepting the supervisor's comments which can inevitably only flow from their own experiences, knowledge, and expectations, and unfortunately assumptions, as no matter how hard we try we are unable to totally eliminate our presumptions. The supervisor's experience of the client can only ever be at two levels removed from the client's lived experience, as the client can only ever be presented as the supervisee's perception of their client, their existence, and worldview, and will have already been filtered through the client's own emphasis in presenting their narrative. Of course, the emphasis given by the client will tell the coach a lot about what the client deems to be most meaningful, or what the client believes to be the purpose of the coaching.

I have attempted to offer examples which cover different phases of the coaching project. For this reason, I am starting with an example which focuses on the very earliest part of the coaching relationship – 'the chemistry session' – in which the coach/supervisee hopes to be chosen by a potential client to work with them.

# 9

# CASE EXAMPLE 1

## The unsuccessful chemistry session

Sophie had recently begun working as an associate coach with a company who positioned coaches with corporate clients. The company would choose three of its associates to put forward to work with a potential individual client, sending their CV to the commissioning organisation. The commissioning organisation already held the code of ethics of the coaching company and their standard contract.

Each associate coach would then have a one-hour 'chemistry session' with the potential client. The associate was not paid for these sessions. As the name implies, a chemistry session provides an opportunity for the potential client to see whether they feel there is a good fit with the coach. It could be said that it also provides the opportunity for the coach to decide whether or not they wished to work with the client, but in reality, it is hard for a coach to say 'no' when they have been put forward by the company they are working for, as many feel it would reflect badly on them and may reduce the number of potential pieces of work they would be put forward for. When all the chemistry sessions with the different coaches have taken place, the client chooses which coach they wish to work with.

Sophie came to supervision very disheartened; although having only worked for the coaching company for two months, she had already been put forward for three chemistry sessions but had failed to convert any of them into a contract. She had felt very excited about the opportunities as they were with high-profile clients, and she had felt confident approaching the chemistry sessions. The previous coaching company she had been attached to had given their affiliates a structure for preparing and running these sessions. She liked using that structure and had a good record of converting chemistry sessions into a coaching contract. She had left the previous company as she was ambitious, and the company did 'not pay well or have access to the same calibre of clients to work with'. A colleague had recommended the new company, and Sophie had been very intrigued to read on its website that it prided itself on being innovative, creative, and progressive, 'drawing on ontological, existential and relational approaches'. Sophie had thought this sounded interesting but hadn't felt the need to learn more about what may be understood by 'ontological' or 'existential' as she considered them to be amongst a host of current buzzwords, merely used in an attempt by one coaching company to differentiate itself from another, whilst in reality offering very similar coaching experiences. This belief was reinforced when the new company provided no induction after the initial interview. Realising that the commissioning organisations may have specifically been drawn to her new company due to its existential and ontological approaches, and this may be a reason for her lack of success, she felt that she needed to know more about those approaches and so chose to find an existential supervisor.

The first part of the initial two-hour supervision session was rather like an 'existential chemistry session' in that the supervisor was focused more on who Sophie was as a person, what she valued and believed in, what she wanted in the supervisory experience, what she wanted for herself from her decision to be a coach, and what she desired for her future. From this early discourse it seemed that Sophie had become interested in coaching following the success of a friend who was now 'earning very good money as a coach'. Sophie had been surprised at the friend's success as she had not considered the friend 'to have any real experience or expertise in the business world to give her credibility with potential business clients'. This had allowed Sophie not to see her own lack of experience as a block in pursuing a coaching career for herself. She enjoyed a high-level lifestyle: good restaurants, exciting holidays, etc., and saw coaching as a way of funding this. She also mentioned *jokingly* that 'it might help me find a rich and successful husband as it would open doors to places where such potential partners may be found'. In later supervision sessions, Sophie spoke about how she had surprised herself by what she had said in that initial hour and how in the break before the first and second supervisions she had started questioning herself as to how true those statements might be.

In the second part of the first supervision the supervisor had asked Sophie if she prepared for all her chemistry sessions in the same way. Sophie explained that she drew on what she had learnt at her previous company as that had proved successful. She took the supervisor through the structure she had been introduced to there and which she had continued to use.

Her first step was to research the commissioning organisation, believing that this would allow her to show some knowledge early in the chemistry session and so allow her to have a view of the key challenges facing the organisation, and therefore she assumed, important to her potential client. When meeting the client for the first time, she took care to convey her professionalism by 'dressing in a professional way' and ensuring she had 'everything I may need tucked away in my coaching kitbag'.

She would start the session by speaking knowledgably and positively about the organisation the client worked for, believing this showed a respect for the client and what they had achieved. Sophie believed that it helped put the client at ease, so that they did not feel that coaching was in anyway remedial. She also used NLP (neuro linguistic programming) techniques, such as mirroring to help relax the client and build rapport.

In order to show she was well prepared she drew on the notes she had been given by her company with regard to the focus of the future work with the client. This meant she would start by explaining to the client what she understood about the nature of their dilemma, e.g. 'I understand that you are looking for coaching in order to rise to the next level in the organisation'; 'I believe that there were certain areas highlighted for development in your last appraisal'; 'You are looking for support and guidance during this period of rapid change in your organisation'.

She would also use the chemistry session to explain to the client how she liked to work and may even use some initial exercises to demonstrate this. If she had identified any relevant articles which she believed the client may be interested in she would also take these along and may choose to refer to them during the session or leave printed versions with the potential client at the close of the session. Finally, she would offer the client some case examples of her work with other clients which she had written up and collated in a brochure which also contained some testimonials from those clients.

The supervisor commented on the very thorough and structured preparation that Sophie put into preparing for each chemistry session and asked Sophie why she felt this had been unsuccessful recently. Her previous employers were very confident that their cognitive behavioural-based coaching approach worked well with corporate clients and previously this had indeed proved to be the case.

At this point in the supervision session, Sophie became quite emotional and said she felt 'bewildered and at a loss to know what was going wrong'. Her approach had been successful in her previous company and she had been 'certain' it was the right way to do things. The supervisor asked about the fears, assumptions, hopes, values, and beliefs that were informing her preparation. Sophie explained that it was important for her to present herself well, as a polished professional who knew what she was doing, and to bring expertise, and ultimately also experience, to the client's problem, with the hope of providing them with a correct and lasting solution. She wanted to impress her clients and eventually establish her own coaching company. Before that, she wanted to establish herself as a competent, professional, and highly sought-after coach working with global leaders.

The supervisor enquired whether it felt difficult for Sophie to have the apparent certainty of the model she used challenged by the lack of success in the new company. Sophie explained that she did enjoy clarity and the use of tried and tested systems and techniques. The supervisor explored with Sophie how these 'wants' may be challenged if she were to work existentially with her clients.

Planning for a chemistry session would look very different when approached existentially. The belief that every human has a unique relationship to the universal human givens means that an existential coach would not 'plan' for the chemistry session in a way which made assumptions about how they may experience the client. Although it may be useful to know something of the company the client works for, it can potentially be unhelpful. To follow a phenomenological approach, as described in Chapter Four, the coach needs to bracket what they have learnt about the company and guard against making quick judgements as to whether they are good or bad employers, whether the client enjoys working there, or even whether the client wishes to remain in their employ. If the coach starts a session with assumptions, techniques, and a rigid structure, there is a danger that the client will not feel they are being experienced as a unique being, but just another client to be processed through a system.

The supervisor enquired how Sophie had felt when the supervisor had spent the first half of the supervision session merely asking Sophie just to tell her about herself, setting no boundaries on what Sophie may choose to talk about; Sophie confessed that initially it had felt strange, she was not sure how professional she considered the supervisor in that time. She had expected the supervisor to overtly direct and structure the session. However, having thought about the experience since, she felt that in sharing her motivations and hopes she had experienced the supervisor as genuinely interested and caring for her as a person, not just as a supervisee. She valued the experience of being treated as an individual, rather than 'another supervisee'. She believed that this increased her trust in the supervisor and had very quickly helped to build rapport.

Together, the supervisor and Sophie considered what it might be like for her to start a chemistry session with a client in the same very open and non-boundaried way. Sophie found it difficult to accept that to do so would not make her appear unprofessional to the client, who may want 'proof that I am up to the job and have something to offer'. The supervisor queried how a coach can know what the client wants if the coach does not spend some time at the beginning of the coaching relationship getting to understand the client's worldview and facilitating the client's exploration of what they are looking for from the coaching. In the supervisor's experience, just as Sophie had been surprised by what she heard herself say at the start of the supervision session, the client often reformulated what was important to them after reflection on their uncensored and unstructured words, and as a result may wish to focus the coaching work differently than they had originally intended. Using active listening enables the client to feel and know they have been heard and therefore respected not just by the coach but by themselves. Not setting initial content boundaries allows the client to think creatively and openly, and if the coach can hold the space, reframe from the desire to show their knowledge or prove their credentials, and to be tentative in any response they do make; this gives the client freedom to reflect and change and to ultimately take responsibility for the focus of the coaching. However, at this stage to consider starting the session with little idea of where it might lead, knowing that as a result the brief may end up very differently from the one her coaching company had described before she met the client, made Sophie feel very unsettled.

Sophie's need for structure and certainty does not fit particularly well with the existential focus on the creative potential and ultimate truth of uncertainty. A client cannot be offered a solution which is *certain* to work, or be the right one, as such certainty cannot exist. Instead, the existential coach would need to feel secure exploring insecurity and uncertainty: looking at all the potentialities open to the client together with their possible outcomes for the client and others. The coach cannot know what is best for the client. Any solution they may propose is what *they* believe is right, and flows from *their* own worldview, not that of the client.

To be *certain* about the success of a suggested solution, or to imply *certainty* may also deprive the client of their experience of existential freedom and an acceptance of the responsibility for exploring the impact the logical solution may have on themselves and others: their experience of being-in-the-world-with-others. Obviously, such uncertainty and responsibility does not necessarily make the client feel good, and it does not allow much room for the coach to demonstrate their factual and strategic knowledge. This may feel less satisfying for the coach's ego but leaves the power firmly with the client. For the coaching to be dynamic, the client needs to acknowledge their own agency in the present, and for the future, in order to move on as an empowered and responsible individual.

The need to present to the client as professional and knowledgeable also touches on another existential concern, that of authenticity. Any inexperienced coach may feel the need to present as more confident than they feel, but they must ask themselves to what extent they are consciously choosing to bring one of their emotions to the foreground (e.g. excitement about the opportunity) in order to not focus on another (fear of failure), rather than being inauthentic, and like Sartre's waiter, 'playing the part of a coach'. As part of this exploration the supervisor reflected on Sophie's expressed need to dress as a professional and to present as knowledgeable. Whilst we can all become more skilled and knowledgeable, and it is important to continue to test and develop ourselves, we do need to remain authentic. As a coach we do not have to be an expert in the client's profession or feel the need to show everything we have in our 'coaching kitbag' in order to justify our role. An existentially informed coach needs to be aware what it is that best facilitates the development of the individual they are working with, in a way which is respectful and meaningful to the client, rather than predetermine what exercises and techniques they will use. It may be that dressing in the 'house style' of the commissioning organisation facilitates trust, but it could equally be the case that someone who offers a respectful challenge to the 'organisational norm' will encourage the client to step outside that norm and dare to think more creatively about their experience of being within that organisation and the dilemmas which this may present.

In this first supervision session we see the supervisor using a phenomenological approach through which a number of existential concerns, predominantly those of uncertainty, freedom and responsibility, meaning, vales, and authenticity are touched on. Sophie's need for certainty, clarity, and structure was apparent from the very beginning and was explored further in subsequent supervision sessions. To work existentially Sophie needed to be able to sit with and explore uncertainty without being concerned that this reflected negatively on her professionalism. It was noted that the need for security and certainty may result in allowing the client to disregard their own freedom and accountability. Facilitating the client's awareness of their freedom and the implications of their decision-making is an important aspect of existential coaching. The supervision also helped to explore and validate Sophie's authentic emotional response to the 'failed' sessions and to allow Sophie to reflect on what was important and meaningful to her in her coaching work. This allowed Sophie to see what potential gains there may be in allowing the client the same space and freedom to reflect and explore before tying them down to a 'presenting issue' which could then be worked with in and a structured way.

This different existential way of approaching a chemistry session challenged Sophie and called for her to be courageous if she was to work existentially. This caused her to question whether she was with the right coaching company. Did she share its values and beliefs, and was an ontological and existential approach one that fitted with her own way of seeing and being in the world? In her next chemistry session Sophie tried to work in a more phenomenological, less structured, and existential way. She did find that she learnt a lot more about her potential client and the client did wish to continue working with her and to set up a coaching contract. However, Sophie had not enjoyed the experience of uncertainty she had felt during in the session and acknowledged that at times she lost connection with the client as she felt a strong urge to grab for her kitbag and show 'the range of skills and exercises I could offer'. Paradoxically, following discussions in supervision it seemed that in order to be more existential and authentic in her being, Sophie needed to listen to her own emotions, needs, and values, and return to working with her previous CBT-focused company. Interestingly, she valued what she had learned of the existential approach and continued to have supervision sessions with the existential supervisor in order to increase her understanding and tolerance of the approach. Although choosing not to work in an existential way with her coaching clients at that present time, she used the sessions to explore how the work with the client might have been different should she choose to use the approach in the future.

In the following case examples, I look at ways of working with some of the existential givens. Most of the cases involve more than one of the givens but I have focused the example on those which seemed to be prominent in the clients' material.

# 10

# CASE EXAMPLE 2

## Working with authenticity, meaning, and emotion

Malcolm brought his work with his client, Marcia, to supervision. Marcia had worked in the same large organisation for several years. She was passionate about their values and aims, and it was their powerful mission statement that had attracted her. She was considered to be excellent at her job, valued for her passion and commitment, her organisational and interpersonal skills, and had risen rapidly to a post which carried a high degree of status and responsibility. The organisation valued her highly and she was already a member of the leadership team and expected to rise to a very senior position within their structure.

Marcia had hoped that being part of the leadership team would give her the opportunity to influence the future direction of the organisation. When she had been in this post for a year, she sought coaching to work through some of the tensions she was experiencing and to help her to make a decision whether or not to stay within the organisation.

Malcolm had already clarified a number of things with Marcia and had looked at how she existed within her existential realms. In her social being, Marcia liked her own company and that of a small number of very close friends. Rather than active pastimes she preferred reading, painting, and quite deep conversations with friends. She was in a stable long-term relationship with a man she loved, and within which she felt cared for and stimulated. She had always assumed she would have children, and so far she had chosen to progress her career first. Now she was in her thirties she was unsure about how she felt about the possibility of future motherhood. This was beginning to create some tension in her relationship as her partner felt ready to become a father soon. Despite the tension, she felt the relationship was strong and able to withstand tensions and disagreements.

Her job took her abroad and until recently she had enjoyed these times away. She had loved exploring the countries she visited and spending time with people whose lives were very different from her own. More recently, the organisation had been discredited in some of the countries they worked in, and this had become a source of personal embarrassment to her. She felt uncomfortable representing an organisation in which some people had behaved badly. Some of the incidents had involved sexual exploitation of women, and this had made Marcia more aware of her own gender. Previously, being a woman in a very male-dominated organisation, she had tried to be 'one of the boys' and not be 'bullied or harassed' by her male colleagues. She had changed how she dressed in order to minimise the visibility of her gender, and so as not to draw attention to herself and her body. Outside of work she liked to wear fun, colourful clothes but worried about the possibility of unexpectedly encountering work colleagues, as she was concerned about what they would think and how if may affect how they perceived, and then worked with her. Following the recent scandal in the organisation she had begun to struggle with eating and saw her weight loss as another way of disguising her feminine body and ultimately of protecting herself.

She remained committed to the same values and beliefs she had held when entering the organisation. These centred on respect for others, valuing their opinions, consulting with others, working with diversity, and ensuring opportunities in the organisation were open to all regardless of class, gender, race, or culture. She passionately wanted to do good in the world. Increasingly she was drawn to doing more for women in countries where women were not treated equally or were abused.

She was considering looking for a new job in a different organisation and Malcolm had worked with her on drawing up an up-to-date CV and finding suitable recruitment agencies to help her find a new post with a similar renumeration package. He had facilitated her analysing her skills set and undertaken some psychometric tests to help clarify her strengths. Marcia had reported that she had found this interesting but had learnt nothing new from the process and indeed felt she was becoming somewhat depressed and confused. This feedback had upset Malcolm who until that point, had felt the coaching was going well. Malcolm was not primarily an existential coach but liked to use some existential ideas in amongst his more structured work with psychometrics. He asked for three supervision sessions with an existential supervisor so he could get a different take on his work with Marcia.

The supervisor asked whether Marcia had requested help with her CV and skills assessment. On reflection, Malcolm recognised that he had suggested doing this as he tended to do with all his business clients who were looking to make a career change. Malcolm and the supervisor spent a little time exploring some of the key elements of existential work including the value of uncertainty, the need for the coach to be a follower rather than a leader, and to listen carefully to the client in order to gain some understanding of their worldview, rather than racing ahead to look for solutions to their perceived problem.

The supervisor was interested to hear what Malcolm considered to be the key dilemmas he and Marcia had identified. He reported that he felt Marcia had grown bored with the current organisation and somewhat disillusioned and was looking for new challenges, whilst needing to find a new post of similar status and renumeration. When the supervisor enquired what Marcia had told him about her need for a high salary and status, Malcolm could not recall them having specifically discussed it, and recognised that this may just be an assumption on his part as 'most people do not want a new post which pays less and is lower down the hierarchy'. He also recognised that Marcia had never claimed to be bored or looking for new challenges but had expressed discomfort in being in her current position.

On further reflection Malcolm believed that in some way Marcia's discomfort was tied to her gender. The supervisor asked Malcolm to stay with that thought and consider what exactly Marcia had said about her gender. Malcolm listed the following:

- She was used to working in a male-dominated organisation and downplayed her gender in order to fit in
- She changed how she dressed for work, although Malcolm considered that to be true of many women

The supervisor explored whether this way of being was something Marcia had been and remained comfortable with. Malcolm recognised that it was something Marcia was giving more attention to recently, following the scandals which had beset the organisation. He hadn't wished to 'pry' into what happened in the organisation, feeling it may have been uncomfortable for Marcia, but he did know that it concerned some male members of staff being accused of serious sexual assaults against vulnerable women in the countries the organisation worked with. At this point in the discussion with the supervisor Malcolm questioned whether Marcia may be better served by a female coach. This led on to exploring Malcolm's discomfort in working with Marcia because he was aware that she was working with issues of male bullying and rape, and he felt she may see him as a male aggressor. The supervisor reminded Malcolm that Marcia had chosen him after chemistry sessions with two other coaches, both females. They explored whether Malcolm's sensitivity was getting in the way of him talking more openly and deeply about what Marcia was experiencing.

When asked to think about what it may be like for Marcia, as a woman, with a high position in the organisation, to go into these countries to work, Malcolm saw that Marcia may also feel she was faced with being 'loyal' to the organisation or being 'loyal' to herself, her values, and her gender, and that this was one of the major issues she was struggling with. How could she continue to follow her passion and beliefs which had originally led her to work for the organisation, when the actions of some members of the organisation were in opposition to those values? How could she be true to herself, her meaning set, values and beliefs, as well as to her gender knowing that her status and foreignness set her aside from other women and gave her a certain protection not offered to the women she was working with?

Malcolm thought again about the issues Marcia had raised and committed to ensure that Marcia knew that he had noted them and was not afraid to explore them. He acknowledged that if she had brought them up, it was important they were looked at, and this was very different from a coach being led by prurient curiosity. He saw that some of these issues he needed to hold in mind included:

- What did Marcia feel about motherhood in relation to her own future?
- What did it feel like for her, in her embodied state as a female?
- How had her sense of her own gender increased recently? How did that leave her?
- How might this affect her relationship with male colleagues, friends, and partner?
- What were the differences she now experienced between the organisation's stated values and their practice?
- To what extent did she feel she could be truly herself in her professional and personal lives?
- What were the obstacles she identified which stood in the way of her being authentic?
- Was she happy with the balance and appropriateness of what she disclosed of herself to others?
- Was her current level of authenticity causing her anxiety?
- How had the organisational 'scandal' affected her as a woman, and as a high- status representative of the organisation?
- Did she want to try to change the organisation?
- Did she want to leave the organisation?
- What would any new job have to contain to make it meaningful for her?
- Were her next actions governed by time imperatives?

Being aware of these areas made the next session a rich one.

Malcolm started the session by reminding Marcia they only had two sessions left to work together, and so he wanted to share with her a summary of what he had understood were the main issues so far, and those which he felt had not yet been explored, drawing on the bullet points above. He did not put any level of priority on one issue over another and made it very clear that Marcia had no need to discuss any of them if she did not feel they were relevant. Marcia expressed her relief that Malcolm now seemed to have picked up some of her main concerns. She explained that almost from the start she had begun to question whether the organisation 'practised what it preached'. She had been uncomfortable about the way male members of staff had behaved to, and spoken about, female colleagues. Initially, she decided that in order to succeed in the organisation, she would have to behave more like her male colleagues. She now found it hard to live with what she saw as her bad faith. She felt that she had betrayed herself and her gender in exchange for success. Her visit to the country where several young women had been assaulted, by people working for her organisation, had devasted her. She felt shame. She was there as a representative of an organisation which she felt she no longer trusted, yet she had 'done her job' and attended meetings, drawn up improvement and strategic plans, whilst others in the organisation interviewed those who claimed abuse. She was concerned at how she had been perceived by people in that country. Was she seen as a heartless bureaucrat? As a woman who did not support other women? As a betrayer of her gender, placing power above all else?

All of this had made Marcia reflect on how she was living her life and what she wanted in the future. This was not just in her professional life, but also her personal life. She had told her husband that she wanted children because he was very keen to have a big family, but she now doubted whether that had ever been the case, and what she had seen on her travels had made her think that it was irresponsible to bring children into 'a corrupt world'. She felt that on several levels she was living a lie. She dressed soberly for work and presented as an ambitious careerist, whilst in the rest of her life she loved fun, music, dancing, and wine. This knowledge of her inauthenticity lay heavily on her.

In the next supervision session Malcolm was feeling overwhelmed and time was given to this. He was concerned that as a man he had failed to pick up on a number of issues which were important to Marcia. In discussion he considered whether it was his desire to do a good job and give Marcia a clear solution within the limited sessions available that had resulted in him not listening well to what Marcia was saying. He also identified that he did not 'want her to become emotional as that would get in the way of the work he needed to do'. The supervisor reminded him that only the client can know what work needs to be done, and at times clients may protect the coach, and therefore themselves, by not disclosing real concerns if they do not fully trust the coach's ability and willingness to work with them. The supervisor also reminded Malcolm that engaging with emotions can provide a quicker and clearer pathway to the heart of the problem.

Through discussion Malcolm identified that the chief issue which seemed to be causing Marcia distress was her desire to remain true to herself and her values and to live authentically. It was important for her to believe in and find meaning in her work. This had been the case when she joined the organisation but things had changed and she now felt trapped.

In their final session, Marcia told Malcolm she had written a long report to the head of the organisation detailing what she believed needed to change and her ambivalence about remaining in their employ. The head had immediately set up a meeting as he was reluctant to lose her. It was agreed that she would work from home for six months and only focus on acting as a consultant in developing their change strategy. During that time, she also wanted to explore whether there were other positions and organisations she might be interested in working in. She knew she needed work that was compatible with her values and which was aimed at 'doing good in the world in some form'. She felt she may be better suited, and able to be more herself, if the work was charitable and focused on working with women. This would mean a reduction in status and pay, but Marcia believed she would be happier. Marcia had also spoken to her husband about her ambivalence about having children and been amazed at how he had taken it.

He was pleased she would be home more and suggested that over the months they should find more opportunities to discuss what was important to both of them.

For Marcia, the coaching was very successful. Malcolm was surprised at how the coaching had developed and saw the outcomes as very different from what he might have imagined when he started the work. Although still concerned about emotion in the coaching sessions he was determined to try not to close it down in the future. He was interested to see that exploring issues which the client raised, but which he had considered to be uncomfortable or irrelevant, had led Marcia to a positive and practical decision.

# 11

# CASE EXAMPLE 3

## Working with paradox, self-esteem, emotion, relatedness, and boundaries

Often, clients are faced with making a choice requiring them to choose one path, which in doing so, would necessitate them giving up something else they also believed to be important. Supervisee, James, brought his work with his client Craig to supervision, as Craig was faced with such paradoxes.

Craig had recently been promoted to his first management role. Craig's company had suggested coaching as they had received a number of complaints about Craig from members of the team he managed. Some people complained that he was bullying, and others that he could not be trusted, citing examples of him 'slagging off' others, including senior management. Craig believed everything was well. He had been very surprised when the company offered him coaching but understood it was 'to improve his managerial skills'.

In fact, the company had told James that they were beginning to question whether they had made a bad choice in placing Craig in a managerial role and were considering demoting him back to his previous position. They had not been fully honest with Craig about their reason for the coaching. Craig was only told of the complaints against him the day before the first coaching session and responded to management by claiming the team were just 'serial complainers' and should not be taken seriously.

The first coaching session had proved to be a difficult one, in which Craig had been very angry. He couldn't understand why 'they (his team) have taken against me' or 'why management believes them'. He felt hurt and betrayed. He spent the session defending his behaviour, saying that the team were poor performers, and he had 'needed to give them a much-needed kick up the backside'. As it was the first session, James decided just to listen and not challenge any of Craig's perceptions. James had liked Craig's energy, but had felt intimidated by his presence, as Craig was a large, athletic man and James could see how some people may feel bullied.

In supervision, the supervisor agreed with the need to build trust before making challenges but encouraged James to reflect on whether his decision not to challenge Craig was solely to do with the need to spend more time building trust or was more linked to his own desire not to become the focus of Craig's anger. The 'courage to be' when working with another person is a vital part of the existential approach and the supervisor encouraged James to explore any emotions which were displayed and not attempt to shut them down, as they could provide important information about the values of the client, their self-concept, and the meaning they were giving to a particular event.

By the second session Craig had calmed down, though remained tense and worried. James reported that at this point he had felt confused as he was expecting to meet the same angry Craig he had previously encountered. In reporting this in supervision he realised how we all carry assumptions, and that people may change their views and ways of being between coaching sessions. For this reason, the supervisor encouraged him not to refer back to the previous session at the start of each session but to give the client time to express anything which may have changed.

James opened the next session with a very open question inviting Craig to start the session how he wished. Craig said he was still angry, although calmer, but now felt afraid. James asked if Craig could identify what he was fearful of, and angry about. Craig spoke about how important his new role was to him and his fear that he may lose it. In his previous role he had been very critical of management and now wished he had been more understanding. In saying this he realised that he felt guilty about his past criticisms, and at the same time feared that his managerial colleagues may have heard what he had said, and so not trust or respect him, and as a result may believe that he should not be part of the managerial team.

Craig described how previously he had enjoyed being part of a team, considering himself to be a good team player, collaborative, knowledgeable, skilled, and well-liked. He was nostalgic about being with 'other working-class guys who enjoyed life and having a laugh', recalling the good social times they had shared outside work. He now 'felt betrayed and cast aside' by those who he had considered as friends.

He was intimidated by the management team he had joined, who reminded him of his confident wife and her colleagues. He now felt that through taking the promotion he had put himself outside his previous circle, whilst unable to join the new managerial group, describing it as 'a lonely place to be'. Craig was struggling to find an authentic place for himself. Craig told James that he had prided himself on 'being real' and authentic yet now he was struggling to find a place where he felt he could be true to who he was.

When James explored why Craig had chosen to apply for promotion, a very different picture of Craig emerged. Craig had a very successful partner who earned double his previous salary. Craig believed that it was his role as the man to provide financial security for his wife and family, and recently his wife had started saying she wished to take early retirement but was unable to do so because Craig did not earn enough. 'As a man', Craig felt he was expected to show ambition and seeing younger, less experienced people gaining promotion he felt he had to apply for a more senior post. He said he was confident he could do 'a better job than the managers I have worked to' and remained critical about management and leadership throughout the company.

In supervision James looked at Craig's paradoxical needs of wanting to belong, whilst at the same time wanting to be special and to stand out. Craig was seeking greater connection and intimacy with his wife and in pursuing this was feeling isolated from his past colleagues and alienated from the other managers. It seemed that Craig also held a fear of being emasculated by his wife, or in Sartrean and Laingian terms 'engulfed' and 'insubstantial'. This may have led to his desire to show his power over others, resulting in what was perceived as bullying behaviour. Although it was important for Craig to recognise the causes of his behaviour, the supervisor reminded James that he was offering coaching, not therapy, and must focus on the negative impacts these behaviours were having for Craig in the present situation and resist any temptation to delve deeper.

In their next session Craig and James agreed to explore some of the paradoxical and contradictory desires Craig was expressing. Craig acknowledged that he enjoyed being in the social company of lots of other men, although he noted that there was a part of him that he kept hidden from that group. He spoke passionately to James about his love of art and of the time he spent painting, when he felt most at peace. He believed the other guys would ridicule him for his painting and also noted that his wife considered it to be time-wasting and effeminate, believing he should be spending his time improving his skill set. At this point, he disclosed to James that he had been involved in an affair with a colleague who loved his art and with whom he had enjoyed many trips to art galleries. The affair had ended a few months before the promotion when his wife had found out about it. He felt indebted to his wife for her decision not to leave the marriage but also felt that the way she now treated him was a form of punishment which he must endure. Conscious of discussions in supervision, James held the boundaries between therapy and coaching, whilst noting that Craig was feeling controlled by his wife and in turn seemed to want to control his team. He took the opportunity of the disclosure to look with Craig about the decisions Craig was making, encouraging him to take responsibility for his own freedom and actions, and not to act as though he had little choice.

Although one of Craig's stated values was to be truthful (authentic), he realised that he was currently not being honest with most people. James pointed out a number of paradoxes that Craig was dealing with. Craig wished to belong, yet sought isolation in his art. He valued the security his wife's finances gave and which had felt very confident in his previous post. This contrasted to his risk-taking in applying for a post without previous management experience. He recognised that he had spent many years in his previous post but considered himself ambitious. He thought of himself as being an honest and straightforward guy yet prided himself on being able to control and manipulate his team, choosing to share parts of himself with different people.

James' supervisor had mentioned that it sometimes helped people to physically see their contradictions and paradoxes, and so recognise the complexity of their choices. Craig agreed to work with James to present this in a rough diagrammatical form (see below). James made no comment about what Craig entered on the diagram.

Craig was surprised to see how clear this made his dilemmas. To gain one thing he wanted, he may need to sacrifice another. He immediately saw that ambition and security were sitting at poles to one another. It seemed that in order to answer his desire to be ambitious and successful he may need to sacrifice his sense of safety and belonging and experience the isolation of the new. Strasser (1997) pointed out that the human engagement in a 'perennial search for safety and security in a world that is replete with uncertainties and unpredictability is one of the

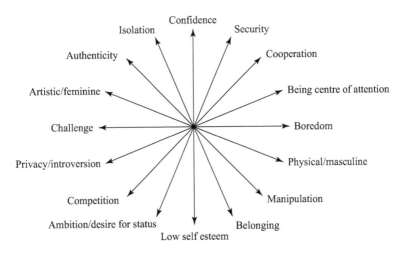

*Figure 11.1* Craig's paradoxes and contradictions

paradoxes of our existence'. Recently, Craig had chosen his ambitious polarity over belonging, moving from his group of peers where he had felt comfortable to moving into management and thus setting himself apart from them, whilst finding it very hard to integrate into the management group. In doing so he had given up a sense of certainty which he had previously held, to enter into an uncertain future. He recognised that the previous security had brought feelings of boredom and apathy.

Although Craig presented as confident, his self-esteem was low, particularly in relation to his relationship with his wife, but also now in relation to the other members of the management group, and the team he was managing. He realised that whilst previously he and others had considered him to be successful, he was now viewed as a failure. Craig had tried hard to cover his self-doubt by becoming officious and demanding, alternating between cooperation flowing from his desire to be liked, and competition to prove himself 'the better man'. He found it easier to acknowledge all of this when he saw it in black and white on his paradox diagram. He felt trapped, wanting to return to the security and belonging of his previous post but equally wanting to progress, and in so doing demonstrate his worth to his wife and earn the respect of colleagues.

At this point Craig talked more about his marriage and his feelings of emasculation leading to him fluctuating between submissive behaviour and trying to assert his superiority and masculinity. Having in supervision considered the boundaries between therapy and coaching, James took great care to feedback what he was hearing about the relationship and drawing out the parallels within the work situation but made it clear to Craig that therapy would be a more appropriate place to look in detail about the tensions within his relationship and how he might address them. Craig decided to suggest to his wife that they commit to some couple therapy.

Having understood more about the tensions Craig was feeling, James discussed in supervision how he should focus his final scheduled session with Craig. Returning to the existential givens, it was felt that Craig was now more aware of his paradoxes but still not fully connecting with his own power and his responsibility for his choices. Although he felt trapped in his current position, he could review and then change it if he wished but needed to acknowledge that all decisions brought both gains and losses.

James started the session by reminding Craig it was the last one the company had commissioned and asked what he wanted to focus the remaining time on. Craig expressed how much he had had valued the sessions, stating he had learnt a lot about himself, and now felt that he needed to make some more decisions. He reported that the decision to suggest therapy to his wife had 'gone down surprisingly well' and they were booked for a first session the following week. He felt that the biggest remaining position was about his professional life.

Craig did not feel he could be authentic in a managerial post, and yet was reluctant to step down from it, fearing that he would be considered a failure. He identified that relationships were very important to him. He was missing the sense of closeness he had felt with his colleagues in the previous post and did not feel this could ever be achieved in the management group. Since the previous session he had spoken to his wife about these concerns and she had expressed the view that she was hopeful that the therapy would bring them closer; she reminded him that they had met as penniless students and that she had loved him then and had loved him as the happy-go-lucky person he had been in his previous post. Although the increase in pay which his promotion had brought had been welcomed and set her thinking about early retirement, she had not enjoyed the longer hours and the emergence of what she saw as 'a miserable old get'. She told him that she would support whatever decision he made. Craig concluded that he would like to return to his old post (and endure any teasing from his old colleagues, knowing that they would really welcome him back). James asked him how he would deal with the ambitious part of himself and Craig said his ambition was now focused on his happiness. He did not want to become bored as before and so he and his wife had decided to take French classes together and were thinking of retiring to France in five years' time. He had hopes of having a painting studio there.

The organisation was delighted to move Craig back to his old post. They had valued his contribution at that level and although disappointed in his performance in a managerial role, they did not wish to lose him. Craig's self-esteem was no longer focused on career progression so he could embrace the return to people he knew well, and welcome being in a post where he was rightfully confident of his abilities.

James had not focused on paradoxes and contradictions so overtly in his previous work and felt it had unearthed a lot of material he may not have accessed otherwise. He was initially concerned that much of what was revealed was about Craig's personal rather than professional life. He had valued the supervisor 'keeping an eye open for the boundaries between therapy and coaching' and felt more confident about not closing down the personal as quickly as he would have done previously. His final boundary challenge had come when Craig had invited him for a drink after the final session. Knowing Craig's need for friendship and relatedness, he declined, although he told the supervisor he thought it would have been 'a fun night'.

# 12

# CASE EXAMPLE 4
## Working with existential dimensions

Even within the time-limited context of a coaching contract, an existential supervisor would be looking to a supervisee to gain a good understanding of the client's worldview. Without such understanding, any outcome from the coaching risks not being fully compatible with the client's values and meaning sets. This example shows how the supervisor introduces a supervisee to the idea of working with the existential dimensions as a way of checking their understanding of the client, and possibly of increasing the client's understanding of self.

Valerie, the supervisee, had taken a short module on existential coaching and was interested in learning more about the approach. She intended to incorporate elements of the approach into a holistic coaching offer.

Valerie's client, Joan, worked in university administration and for several years worked as a Personal Assistant to a Head of Department. She had loved the work. She felt it gave her independence and status and she felt valued by Thomas, her boss. She was shocked that in a recent restructure Thomas had decided to take early retirement and his department had been amalgamated with another. Joan had assumed that she would become the PA to the Head of this larger team and was shocked and disappointed when the new person brought his own PA across and Joan found herself in the pool of people looking for redeployment following the restructure.

Joan looked to Thomas to help her gain a new position, stating that she felt that he 'owed her at least that'. Thomas 'pulled strings' to get her a managerial post in the new structure. Joan was enthusiastic about her new post, but things were not going well; there had been complaints from some the people she was managing, and an accusation that the university had not used equal opportunity good practice in appointing her to a managerial post when she had no previous managerial experience. As a result, and with the hope of offsetting any industrial action or employment tribunals, the university had decided to commission a coach to work with Joan.

Valerie's first session with Joan had proved challenging. It is imperative that the coach pays attention to what is disclosed in the intial contact as it can often be, as it is in this case, a core aspect of the coaching material.

Joan was 'outraged' that the university felt she 'needed' coaching. She vented her rage at Valerie about the unfairness of it all. She felt disrespected, not cared for, isolated, picked on, and set up for failure. She told Valerie she did not need coaching and was a very good manager. She believed she had learnt all she needed through her work with Thomas and indeed believed that she was a better manager than he was. In her view, the team were not used to being well-managed and were 'refusing to do what they were told'. She was angry that the university were listening to the complaints against her and felt they should have supported her by telling the individuals who had complained that they should just get on with things and do as they were told. She was particularly vitriolic about one person, Fiona, who Joan believed was leading the 'campaign' against her. Valerie felt the first session served little purpose and that whenever she had tried to say anything Joan had spoken over her. She told her supervisor she felt deskilled and was not looking forward to the next session, questioning whether it would be better to acknowledge that the whole thing was 'doomed to fail' and pull out of the contract now. Valerie was particularly upset because this was her first opportunity to coach someone from the university and she believed that it could open up a lot of new opportunities for her.

Her supervisor spent a little time looking with Valerie at her ego needs and considering whether she had felt burdened by her desire to succeed to such an extent that she may have found it difficult to be truly present to the client, making it harder for her to feel empathetic and listen non-judgmentally. Valerie recognised that she had felt very tense at the beginning of the session and felt that she had failed to develop any connection or trust with Joan. In fact, she had found Joan intimidating and disliked her shouting and negativity. She had felt attacked and the supervisor noted that seemed to be the way Joan was feeling too. In discussion the supervisor reminded Valerie of the need for active listening, especially in these earlier stages where the client was looking to be understood. Instead of cutting across the client's negative monologue, the client needed to have what she was saying reflected back to her. On hearing herself she may recognise the continued pessimism and criticism of others. Although there was a danger that no intervention from the coach may reinforce her position, reflecting back rather than challenging at this early stage could enable her to hear the strong negative and defensive theme for herself, and allow her to silently and internally challenge herself. If this did not prove to be the case Valerie would be in a stronger position to challenge once trust was built.

The supervisor wondered if Valerie would find that she could work more effectively with Joan if she took some time exploring her wider worldview, gaining a more holistic picture of her. The supervisor took Valerie through the existential dimensions and suggested that after her

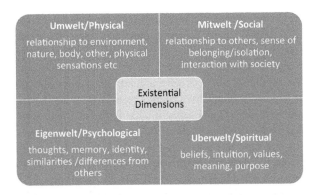

*Figure 12.1*  The existential dimensions

next session with Joan, Valerie may like to draw up her understanding of where Joan sat within each of her existential dimensions. Below is a reminder of what aspects of existence fit within a particular dimension.

Valerie requested specific questions she may use to gain knowledge of Joan's relationship to each dimension. The supervisor explained that as far as possible an existential coach would try to avoid closed or leading questions, particularly so early in the coaching contract and would listen out for information from the client which would help populate the coach's understanding of the client's dimensions. If a coach can identify a client's preferred way of being in each of the dimensions, they can approach them in a meaningful way and work with, not against their values. A client may not be very aware of their tendencies, and a better understanding of them can enable them to strengthen existing skills and begin working on developing skills that may be missing. Certain words and enquiries can help to form a more holistic understanding of the client.

The introduction, by the coach of words which are linked to each dimension can also help, e.g. asking the client what is meaningful and important to them can provide entry to the *überwelt* (spiritual). For some clients, meaning will be the most important aspect of their work and will be directly related to spiritual beliefs and moral values. In Joan's case, when Valerie asked about meaning she discovered that it sat more in the *mitwelt* (social) and *eigenwelt* (psychological). For Joan, the meaning of work lay in the status and position it gave her. In discussing this in the coaching, Joan expressed how she had often felt dismissed as just the secretary when working as Thomas' PA. This feeling of disrespect extended to her home life where she felt her husband, a very successful academic, behaved to her as though 'he thought her stupid' and had dismissed her previous post as 'something to keep her from getting bored'. She had hoped that her move into management would have changed his view and she had been too embarrassed to tell him about the difficulties she was encountering.

She recognised that she saw her colleagues as stupid and not ambitious and so had perhaps looked down on them in the way she felt others had dismissed her. Having recognised this she still reinforced to Valerie that they were not doing their jobs and should 'step up or ship out'. In this way they were acting as an obstacle to her own success. Valerie wondered whether to challenge this but as it was only the second session and they needed to build trust before any challenge could be effective, she let the remark go.

When meeting Joan at her desk Valerie had noticed that it was very tidy, impersonal, and sterile, whilst those around her were generally untidier, and most had photos of home and family and articles of interest put up on the screens behind their desks. In her previous coaching work Valerie would never have remarked on this but through discussion in supervision she could see that this may provide a way to gather more understanding about Valerie's relationship to her *umwelt* (physical world) as well as her relationship to her colleagues (*mitwelt*). When Valerie first mentioned the difference between Joan's workspace and others, Joan started by being critical of the untidiness and 'lack of organisation' of her colleagues but then rather poignantly said that she really didn't have photos to put up – 'not having children or even a pet, because my husband doesn't like mess'. Thinking further, Joan surprised herself when she remembered that as a secretarial student with her own flat her place had been a mess 'as I was too busy having fun'. She also noted that the flat had been full of personal things, photos, mementos from holidays, etc. Joan herself identified that her lack of openness about herself acted to emphasise her differences to her team. Although she had at first thought this was necessary to gain their respect, she recognised that this had not worked, and she was left just feeling isolated and lonely. This was a very emotional session for Joan, and Valerie was careful to hold the boundary between coaching and therapy, although she did feedback that Joan seemed lonely and did not seem to have much fun at the moment and that these may be areas for discussion.

The following supervision focused on maintaining the boundary between coaching and therapy, without filtering out important aspects of Joan's world which were impacting on her current work situation. Through the gentle exploration of her existential dimensions, it had become clear that Joan placed great emphasis on her professional life and had to some extent 'given up' on home as a place where she would receive affirmation and respect. Unfortunately, she had created an inauthentic self in work, built on a stereotypical image of what she thought a manager should be, rather than investing in building relationships with her team. The supervisor reminded Valerie that it was not the coach's role to change assumptions, but it was their role to point out that these existed and may have become sedimented. In Joan's case, they were not bringing her what she hoped for – respect and recognition.

Valerie started the next session with a review including the observations about sedimented values. Joan agreed that she needed respect and wanted to work with the coach to achieve this, recognising that her current authoritarian stance was not helping.

Joan was asked to think through her own time in employment to who had inspired her and quickly came up with her first boss who she said had been non-judgmental and whilst always supportive and there when she needed him, allowed her a great deal of autonomy. She felt there was mutual respect for each other as professionals and individuals. As she was speaking about this, she realised that what she had valued was the opposite of how she treated her staff and began to see how unproductive this was. She also saw that her team had no understanding of who she was as a person and that set her aside from the rest of the team who were often chatting about what happened in each other's lives. Joan requested training in a more transformative and collaborative management and leadership style. Valerie agreed that their remaining sessions could focus on this while Joan identified a suitable course.

In supervision Valerie identified a number of suitable courses she could let Joan know about and decided to use a questionnaire to identify Joan's current management style. The supervisor, whilst agreeing this may be interesting, expressed the view that Joan had probably already given Valerie a lot of information about her management style which was authoritarian and focused on outcomes. Valerie used her questionnaire in the next sessions which confirmed Joan's style. As a result, Joan decided to undertake some management training focusing on developing a more collaborative and transformational approach.

In supervision, Valerie noted the shifts in importance in Joan's existential dimensions.

At their final session Joan proudly showed Valerie her work area. She had added a photo of the exterior of her very attractive home and a number of her own still-life paintings. She was delighted that a number of her colleagues had commented favourably on them and one had asked if she would like to accompany her to a local exhibition. Joan had changed her opinion of her team, understanding that, like her, they had been thrown into new positions by the restructure and they too were finding their way. She had taken Fiona out for a coffee and listened to her belief that she was better suited to the management position and had more experience than Joan. Instead of feeling attacked and threatened she had agreed with Fiona that the restructure had been rushed and that they had all been placed in difficult positions, with lots to learn. She shared with Fiona that she was about to start a management course. Admitting that she had much to learn is something that not long ago would have felt dangerous. She also reminded

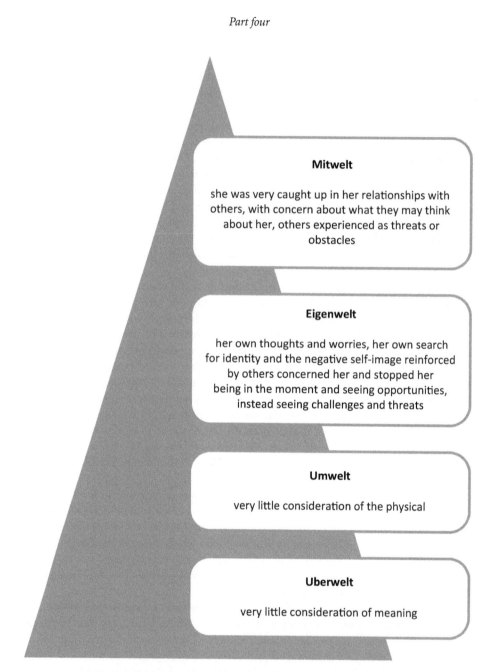

*Figure 12.2* Existential dimensions: Joan's priorities at the start of coaching

Fiona that she now had access to a training budget to help Fiona with her ambitions. Even in offering this, Joan had felt concerned as she believed that Fiona wanted her redeployed in order that Fiona could take over her management position. Joan was very surprised to learn that Fiona was not ambitious and now felt very grateful not to have been given the management post as she could see how challenging and stressful it was. Fiona's concern had been about the

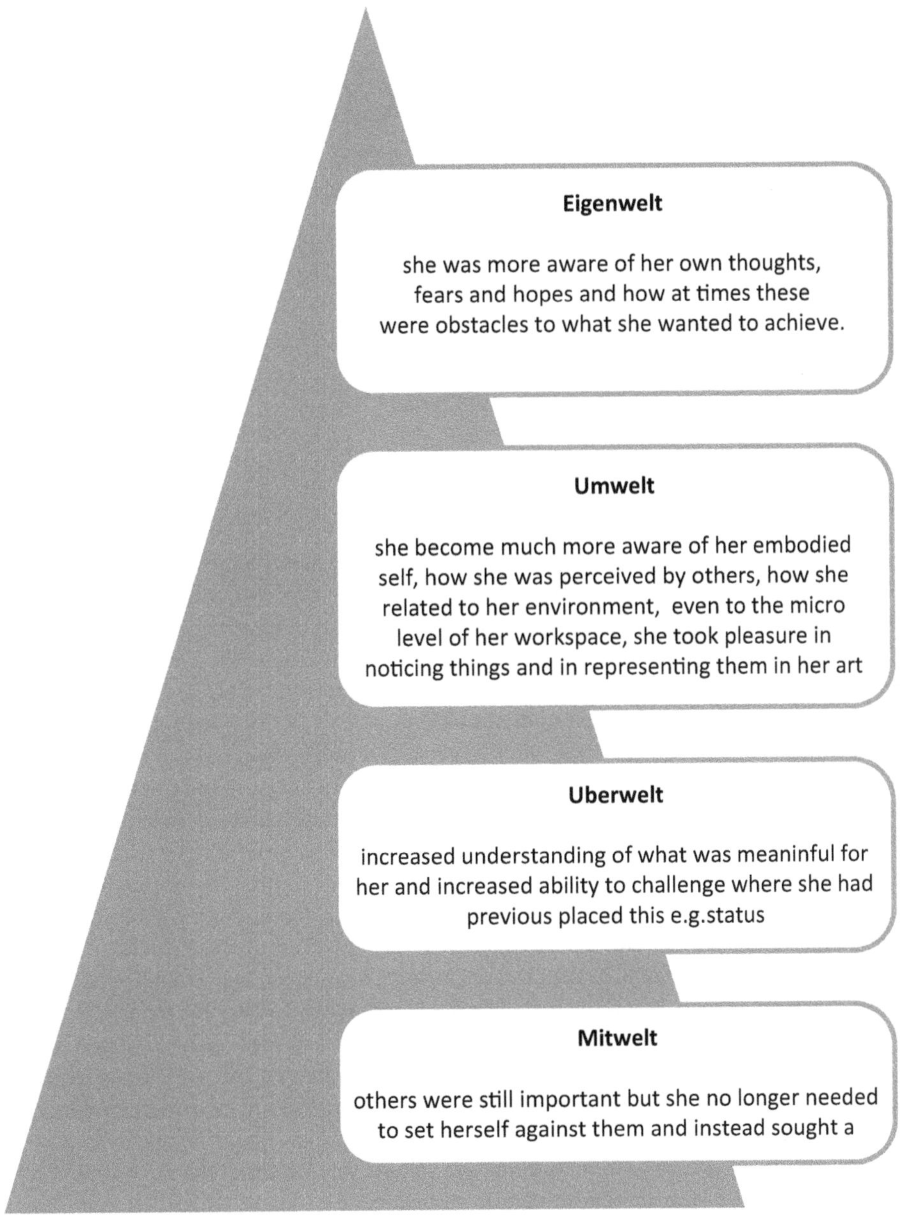

**Eigenwelt**

she was more aware of her own thoughts,
fears and hopes and how at times these
were obstacles to what she wanted to achieve.

**Umwelt**

she become much more aware of her embodied
self, how she was perceived by others, how she
related to her environment, even to the micro
level of her workspace, she took pleasure in
noticing things and in representing them in her art

**Uberwelt**

increased understanding of what was meaninful for
her and increased ability to challenge where she had
previous placed this e.g.status

**Mitwelt**

others were still important but she no longer needed
to set herself against them and instead sought a

*Figure 12.3*   Existential dimensions: Joan's priorities at the end of coaching

unfairness of the recruitment process rather than a desire to progress and she had disliked Joan's 'arrogant isolation' and 'authoritative style'. She valued that Joan was trying to change and that Joan seemed to be showing more respect for her team and building a more collaborative spirit.

Joan had taken the first steps towards a different management style which was already leaving her less isolated and more confident. In doing so her existential values had shifted.

# CASE EXAMPLES: CONCLUSION

Each of the previous examples are small segments of supervision sessions chosen to highlight one or more existential aspects of the work. Throughout the supervisory relationship the supervisor will also be working with the supervisee on any ethical or relational issues.

The supervisee is not required to hunt for existential aspects in the client's material, or to focus on them, but an existential supervisor would encourage the supervisee to be alert to their presence and to appropriately explore them. This may be challenging for supervisees who are used to a more solution-focused approach. They may fear losing time by wandering off in directions which they cannot immediately see as being relevant to the presenting issue. We have seen this fear in some of the case examples. For this reason, the existential approach does require a leap of faith, and a belief that all things are relevant and will in some way be related to the client's dilemma.

The client is aware of the time constraints of the coaching contract and will be as keen, if not more so, than the coach to find a meaningful way forward. Trust in the client is an important aspect of the approach. They hold the answer inside themselves but may need help accessing it.

Part of the supervisory role is to encourage the supervisee to develop the trust and bravery to venture down paths even when they have no idea where they are leading. Some supervisees will see this as liberating and will be keen to venture into the unknown and consciously experience uncertainty, and the potential creativity it brings to find a unique and meaningful resolution for their unique client.

However, the supervisee cannot continue to explore every path, and the supervisor will help the supervisee to develop the knowledge and confidence to know when they have enough material to gently call the client back from their worldview to re-engage with the presenting issue, this time through the prism of the client's worldview with a deeper knowledge of their values, beliefs, fears, and hopes. The fear that there is not enough time to work in this way when coaching contracts are usually limited in the number of sessions allowed, is not something I have found to be the case.

Hopefully the examples show that the existential supervisor is a follower rather than a leader, following a parallel process to that of coach and client. The supervisee is in an embodied relationship with the client which the supervisor cannot enter. Even watching videos of sessions is far removed from the experience of being with the client over a period of time and throughout a number of sessions. The supervisor must therefore follow what the supervisee brings and can

DOI: 10.4324/9781003130895-102

only tentatively draw on their own experience to suggest different ways of experiencing or working with the client. In some of the examples the supervisee was specifically requesting the supervisor to develop their understanding of the existential approach and so the supervisor offers more practical examples of ways of working than would be the case with more experienced existential coaches. When the supervisee already has an existential grounding, the role of the supervisor may be more akin to that of a prompter in the theatre, offering quiet reminders from the wings.

The supervisor would not be quiet when ethical or relational issues arise and would ensure these were not overlooked. The supervisor and supervisee would thoroughly take into consideration the ethical requirements of the world, the organisation, and the supervisee themselves.

The existential approach is not one that suits all supervisees as it offers little certainty and very little in the way of exercises and techniques. We have seen in the examples that the approach can feel destabilising to some supervisees who prefer to have clear plans of actions which they use with most clients.

# CONCLUSION

Although existential supervision concerns itself with the same elements as the majority of supervisory approaches, as we have seen, it places greater emphasis on the existential elements within the description of the client's narrative as told by the supervisee. Whilst many supervisees look to their supervisor to provide a level of certainty that what they are doing is 'correct', or to offer them tried and tested interventions, exercises, or tests which they hope will ensure a certain outcome for themselves and their client, I hope that this book will have shown that they will not get such reassurance from an existential supervisor. Indeed, such a supervisor will be encouraging the supervisee to embrace uncertainty and to recognise in it the opportunity for creative exploration and innovation. It is worth remembering that as Pierre in Tolstoy's *War and Peace* reminds us, 'All we know is that we know nothing. And that is the sum total of human wisdom' (1915:346). The ability to 'not know' or even to 'unknow' something is an approach which an existential coach needs to cultivate. This means that working existentially provides the coach with little certainty to hide behind and gives added emphasis to the supportive and encouraging nature of existential supervision paired with philosophical and practical challenging.

As I was nearing the end of writing this book, I discovered a newly published book by Dr Christian Busch (2020) exploring the place of serendipity in success. Although he was not overtly taking an existential approach, and is not writing about coaching, much of what he says is concerned with uncertainty and our need not to hide from it but to embrace it. He states that, 'the unexpected is often the critical factor, it is the force that makes the greatest difference to our lives and our futures' (2020:1) and he calls for us 'to recognize and leverage the value in unexpected encounters and information' (2020:26) through 'connecting two utterly unconnected ideas that were previously regarded as "strangers to each other"' (ibid). It is this attitude which an existential supervisor would hope to develop in a supervisee. What may appear unconnected to an observer may make sense to the client. My own career history is an example of this. I left school to pursue a degree in Fine Art, which took me into teaching, as there is little else one can do with a Fine Art degree. Teaching art allows one to intimately engage with the subconscious of others through their art, which led me to study psychology and started me on a different professional pathway. For me, there are clear threads in my professional journey, all of which stem from my values, beliefs, and interest (nosiness) about what makes others tick. I have stepped off successful and lucrative career ladders to take time working on the streets with the homeless, sex workers, and those misusing substances; I have chosen to

DOI: 10.4324/9781003130895-102

work as a coach with successful executives of global companies; and to operate a psychotherapy practice for clients from very diverse backgrounds, and to mediate all manner of disputes. I have followed my intuition and not a linear path. My path can appear confusing to observers but is meaningful to me. A supervisee will be encouraged to listen to a client's narrative and discover the meaning in it, which will inevitably reveal what is important to the client, their values, and beliefs. Busch warns us that we are conditioned to tell, and to look for a linear story, whereas we should be conscious of the more realistic and honest 'squiggle story' (2020:45) where chance encounters and thoughts take people into new places. In order to hear the client's 'squiggle story' it is necessary to work phenomenologically and to put aside one's assumptions about what the client's narrative will or should contain; it is important not to dismiss elements of what the client says because they are not related in some linear or chronological way to the dilemma they have brought to coaching. Indeed, all things are related in some way; if we cannot see the link, perhaps we are not working hard enough or paying sufficient attention.

People, be they supervisees, clients, or supervisors, can get stuck in what has worked in the past, and so fear moving into the unknown. They may filter out parts of the client's narrative which do not seem to fit or appear to make it harder to identify solutions. To work existentially, a coach has to value uncertainty and challenge any sense of certainty or any assumptions which they or their client may hold. If they fail to do so they miss the magic of the 'squiggle' and all that it will unveil about the client's worldview.

If a supervisee can learn to welcome the winding path and not attempt to straighten it out into something more recognisable, they will hear more of the client's truth, with all the hopes and paradoxes it will contain. It is only if the more difficult, challenging, and paradoxical elements of the client's narrative are not just heard but welcomed, that a solution which is meaningful to the client will be reached. A coach may believe that they can quickly identify a solution to the client's presenting issue; it may be very similar to what other clients have brought to them. Occasionally this may be true, but if the client has not seen such an obvious solution themselves then one must ask why.

Humans are complex beings and solutions have to work in all the existential dimensions to make them truly attractive. If the solution reached in coaching has taken heed of the client's complexity, and the coach understands how it fits with the client's values and beliefs then it will be meaningful to the client and they are more likely to commit to see through the required action. An existential coach will steer a supervisee away from focusing on the 'problem' as one that they have encountered before, leading them to use tried and tested ways of working with the client. Instead, the client not the issue must remain central and the client must be encountered in all their uniqueness, with the supervisee forming a trusting working alliance with them as someone who brings their emotional past experiences and future hopes into the coaching relationship.

An interest in uncertainty is growing in progressive professional organisations and in individuals. No doubt being faced with the coronavirus has helped us to see that we cannot plan for everything, the unexpected will happen, and we have to find ways of creatively living with the uncertainty it brings.

Of course, to sit and work with uncertainty requires both supervisee and their client to feel safe, and for a relationship built on trust to exist between the supervisee and their client, and between the supervisee and their supervisor. The existential supervisor will encourage and facilitate the development of approaches which will authentically work to create a trusting working alliance. These are not based on learned techniques but on sensitive awareness to the way each of us are with others, how we listen to others, and how we uncover and seek to understand the worldviews which are expressed verbally and non-verbally. Such approaches are centred on the authenticity of the supervisee, in the way they approach their own being-in-the-world and their relationships with clients and supervisor, and their sensitivity in exploring the worldview of their clients and its relevance to the presenting dilemma.

A coach is not a fount of all knowledge; neither is a supervisor. The role of coach/supervisee and supervisor is to engage on a journey with another, putting their energy into focusing on the dilemmas the other presents, in an open and honest way, not pretending to hold knowledge which they do not, or to offer solutions which promise to bring the supervisee what they desire. In this way existential supervision mirrors existential coaching. Busch warns us that 'both knowledge and expertise are a blessing and a curse' (2020:46), which can lead to 'functional fixedness' (ibid) which takes away openness to the novel, the innovative, and the creative. Existential supervision will aim to develop the supervisee's tolerance, and then love of the non-linear, non-structured approach, to challenge other people's theories and established techniques. This is not to say they will be encouraged to disregard them, or not to use any such methods, but to always analyse their relevance in relation to the unique individual they are working with, their narrative, and their worldview. It can be a challenge to a supervisee to trust the client to find the solution rather than to give them a solution which makes sense to the supervisee. The supervisee is acting as a midwife for the client, encouraging and supporting them in giving birth to the solution to their dilemma. If the birth becomes problematic the supervisee will draw on their past knowledge and experience, and that of their supervisor, whilst never stopping listening to and believing in the client.

I shall end with a quote from Busch who, when speaking about how to approach solving a problem, wrote:

> a great starting point is 'an open and curious mind, paired with the motivation to find and do something meaningful. Intellectual curiosity and uncertainty can be powerful ways to avoid overconfidence, to question preconceived ideas and to develop a healthy scepticism. If this is paired with hard work and motivation, often wonderful things emerge...
>
> *(2020:90).*

I believe that this sums up the approach to coaching which an existential supervisor would hope to encourage in a supervisee.

# BIBLIOGRAPHY

Achenbach G.B. (1984). *Philosophische Praxis*, Cologne: Verlag für Philosophie.

Adams D. & Carwardine M. (1990). *Last Chance to See*, New York City: Collins.

Adorno, Theodor W. (1973). *The Jargon of Authenticity*. Translated by Tarnowski Knut & Will Frederic, Evanston, IL: Northwestern University Press.

Arney E. (2006). Coaching the Coaches. *Training Journal*, November, 51–55.

Arendt H. (1994) *The Origins of Totalitarianism*, New York: Harcourt.

Arney E. (2007). Interviewed in feature focus coaching supervision. In *Where Are We Headed?* www.I-coachacademy.com, 04.03.2007

Arroyo C. (2009). The Role of Feelings in Husserl's Ethics, *Idealistic Studies*, vol 39, issue 1/3 Spring/Summer/Fall 11-22.

Arroyo B. J. & Gardner W. L. (2005). Authentic leadership development: Getting to the root of positive forms of leadership. *Leadership Quarterly*, 16(3).

Arthur N., & Achenbach K. (2002). Developing multicultural counseling competencies through experiential learning. *Counselor Education and Supervision*, 42(1), 2–14.

AskOxford Website Dictionary. http://www.askoxford.com/?view=uk. Accessed 2008, 2–4. www.i-coachacademy.com

Bachkirova T., Jackson P. & Clutterbuck D. (2011). *Coaching and Mentoring Supervision: Theory and Practice*, London: Open University Press.

Baltimore, M. L. (1998). Supervision ethics: Counseling the supervisee. *Family Journal*, 6, 312.

Barnes H. (1971). *An Existential Ethics*, New York: Vintage Books.

Barnet, J. (2007). In search of the effective supervisor. *Professional Psychology: Research and Practice* 38(3), 268–275.

Batthyany A. & Russo-Netzer P. (2016). *Meaning in Positive and Existential Psychology*, New York: Springer.

Beauchamp T. L. & Childress J. F. (1994). *Principles of bio-medical Ethics*. Oxford: Oxford University Press.

Beauvoir, Simone de. (1970) [1947]. *The Ethics of Ambiguity*, New York: The Citadel Press.

Becker E. (2011). *The Denial of Death*, London: Souvenir Press.

Berg M.E. (2006), *Coaching-a Hjelpe Ledere og Medarbeidere til a Lykkes*, Oslo: universitetsforlaget

Berlin I. (1969). *Four Essays on Liberty* (1st ed.), Oxford: Oxford Paperbacks.

Bernard J. M. (1979). Supervisor training: A discrimination model. *Counselor Education and Supervision*, 19, 60–68.

Bernard J. M. & Goodyear, R. K. (2009). *Fundamentals of Clinical Supervision* (4th ed.), Needham Heights, MA: Allyn & Bacon.

Binswanger L. (1946). The existential analysis school of thought. In May, R., Angel, E., & Ellenberger, H. F. (Eds.) (1958), *Existence*, New York: Basic Books.

Binswanger L. (1963). *Being-in-the-World*. Translated by Needleman J., New York: Basic Books.

Bion W. R. (1961). *Experience in Groups*, London: Tavistock.

Blocher D. H. (1983). Toward a cognitive developmental approach to counseling supervision. *Counseling Psychologist*, 11(1), 27–34.

Bluckert P. (2002). *Psychological Dimensions of Executive Coaching*, Maidenhead: Open University Press.

Bluckert P. (2006) *Psychological Dimensions of Executive Coaching*, London: Open University Press

Bond T. (1990). Counselling supervision: Ethical issues, *Counselling*, 43–45.

Bordin E. S. (1979).The generalizability of the psychoanalytic concept of the working alliance. *Psychotherapy: Theory, Research & Practice*, *16*(3), 252–260.

Brown L. S. (2018). *Feminist Therapy* (2nd ed.), Washington, DC: American Psychological Association.

Buber M. (1970). *I and Thou*, Virginia: T&T Clark.

Bugental J. F.T. (1992). *The Art of the Psychotherapist: How to Develop the Skills that Take Psychotherapy Beyond Science*, New York: Norton.

Busch C. (2020). *The Serendipity Mindset: The Art and Science of Creating Good Luck*, Milton Keynes: Penguin Life.

Butwell J. (2006). Group supervision for coaches: Is it worthwhile? A study of the process in a major professional organisation. *International Journal of Evidence Based Coaching and Mentoring*, *4*(2), 43–53.

Campbell P. & McMahon E. (1985). *Biospirituality*, Chicago: Loyola University Press.

Carrol M. (2006). Key issues in coaching psychology supervision. *The Coaching Psychologist*, *2*(1), 4–8.

Carrol M. & Tholstrup M. (2001). *Integrative Approaches to Supervision*, London: Jessica Kingsley.

Ciulla J. B., Martin C. & Soloman C. (2007). *Honest Work*, Oxford: Oxford University Press.

Clutterbuck D. & Hussain Z. (eds.). (2010). *Virtual Coach, Virtual Mentor*, Charlotte N.C.: Information Age Publishing.

Coffey A. & Atkinson P. (1996). *Making Sense of Qualitative Data: Complementary Research Strategies*. Thousand Oaks, CA: Sage.

Cohn H.W. (1997). *Existential Thought and Therapeutic Practice*, London: Sage.

Colaizzi P. (1978). Psychological research as the phenomenologist views it. In Walle R & Kings M (eds.), *Existential Phenomenological Alternatives for Psychology* (48–71), New York: Oxford University Press. Denzin, N.K.(1989).

Connor-Greene P. A. (1993). The therapeutic context: Preconditions for change in psychotherapy. *Psychotherapy: Theory, Research, Practice, Training*, *30*(3), 375–382

Crane A. & Matten D. (2004). *Business Ethics*, Oxford: Oxford University Press

Craven Nussbaum M. (1996). Aristotle on emotions and rational persuasion. In Rorty Amelie Okensberg (Ed.), *Essays on Aristotle's Rhetoric* (303–324), Berkely, CA: University of California Press.

Cremona K. (2009). *Coaching and Emotions: How do Coaches and Coaching Directors Engage and Think About Emotions*, Middles University Masters in Work based Kearning Studies (Professional Coaching).

De George R. T. (2006). *Business Ethics*, London: Pearson/Prentice Hall.

Du Plock S. (2007). A relational approach to supervision, *Journal of Existential Analysis* 18(1) 31–8.

Eagleton T. (1983). *Literary Theory; An Introduction*, Oxford: Blackwells

Echeveria R. (2013) *Ontologia Del Lenguaje*, Spain: Grancia Adelphi

Ehrenwald J. (1992). *From Medicine Man to Freud: An Anthology* New York: Dell

Ellis, M. (2001). Harmful supervision, a cause for alarm. *Journal of Counseling Psychology*. 48(4) 401–406

Erickson R. J. (1995). The importance of authenticity for self and society. *Symbolic Interaction*, 18(2), 121–144.

Fackenheim E.. (1961). *Metaphysics and Historicity*, Milwaukee: Marquette University Press.

Fairley S. G. & Stout E. (2004). *Getting Started in Personal and Executive Coaching*, Hoboken, NJ: Wiley.

Falender, C.A. (2009). Relationship and accountability: Tensions in feminist supervision. *Women & Therapy*, 33, 22–41.

Falender C.A. & Shafranske E. P. (2004). *Clinical Supervision: A Competency-Based approach*, Washington, DC: American Psychological Association.

Falender C., Shafranske A., & Edward P. (2007). *Professional Psychology: Research and Practice*, *38*(3), 232–240.

Ferrell O. C. & Fraedrich J. (2018). *Business Ethics: Ethical decision Making & Case*, Nashville, Tennessee: South Western College Publishing.

Fickling M. J. & Tangen J. L. (2017). A journey toward feminist supervision: A dual autoethnographic inquiry. *Journal of Counselor Preparation and Supervision*, *9*(2). http://dx.doi.org/10.7729/92.1219

Fisher C. & Lovell A. (2009). *Business Ethics and Values: Individual, Corporate and International Perspectives*, Harlow: Pearson Education Ltd.

Foster S. (2011). http://www.contemporarypsychotherapy.org/volume-3-no-2-winter-2011/integrative-supervision/

Frankl V. E. (1985). *Man's Search for Meaning*, New York: Pocket Books, Simon & Schuster.

Frankl V. E. (1997). *Man's Ultimate Search for Meaning*, New York: Basic Books.

Frawley-O'Dea M. G. & Sarnat J. E. (2001). *The Supervisory Relationship: A Contemporary Psychodynamic Approach*. New York City: Guilford Press.

Freud S. (1964). *New Introductory Lectures on Psycho-Analysis and Other Works*, London: Vintage.

Fromm E. (1995). *The Fear of Freedom*, London: Routledge.

Gallwey T. (1979). *The Inner Game of Golf*, London: Pan Books.

Gentile L., Ballous M., Roffman E., & Ritchie J. (2009). Supervision for social change: A feminist ecological perspective. *Women & Therapy, 33*, 140–151.

Goffee R. & Jones G. (2005). Managing authenticity: The paradox of great leadership. *Harvard Business Review, 85*, 86–94.

Greenson R. (1967). *The Technique and Practice of Psychoanalysis* (Vol. 1). New York: International Universities Press.

Greenwald M. & Young J. (1998). Schema-focused therapy: an integrative approach to psychotherapy supervision. *Journal of Cognitive Psychotherapy, 12*, 109–126.

Gurwitsch A. (1966). *Studies in Phenomenology and Psychology*, Evanston IL: North Western University Press.

Hammersley M. (2000). *Taking Sides in Social Research*, London: Routledge.

Hanaway M. (ed.) (2014). *Co-Mediation: Using a Paired Psychological Approach to Resolving Conflict*. Henley-on Thames: The CH Group.

Hanaway M. (2017). *Existential Leadership*, Henley-on Thames: The CH Group.

Hanaway M. (2018). *Being an Existential Leader*, Henley-on Thames: The CH Group.

Hanaway M. (2020a) *Handbook of Existential Coaching Practice*, Abingdon: Routledge.

Hanaway M. (2020b) *Psychologically Informed Mediation: Studies in Conflict and Resolution*, Abingdon: Routledge.

Hanaway M. & Reed J. (2014). *Existential Coaching Skills: The Handbook*. Henley-on Thames: The CH Group.

Handelsman M. M., Gottlieb M. C., & Knapp S. (2005). Training ethical psychologists: An acculturation model. *Professional Psychology: Research and Practice, 36*(1), 59–65 https//doi.org/10.1037/0735-7035-7028.36.1.59

Harris La'Wan (2019). *Diversity Beyond Lip Service: A Coaching Guide for Challenging Bias*, San Francisco, CA: Berrett-Koehler.

Harter S. (2002). Authenticity. In Snyder C. R. & Lopez S. J. (Eds.), *Handbook of Positive Psychology* (pP. 382–394), Oxford: Oxford University Press.

Harvey O. J., Hunt D. E., & Schroder H. M. (1961). *Conceptual Systems and Personality Organization*, Hoboken, NJ: Wiley.

Hawkins P. & Shohet R. (2016). *Supervision in the Helping Professions: An Organisational, Group and Organisational Approach*, Maidenhead: Open University Press.

Hawkins P. & Shohet R. (2020) *Supervision in the Helping Professions*, London: Open University

Hawkins P. & Smith N. (2006). *Coaching, Mentoring and Organizational Consultancy: Supervision and Development* (2nd ed. 2013), Maidenhead: Open University Press/McGraw Hill.

Hawkins P., & Smith N. (2007) *Coaching, Mentoring and Organizational Consultancy*, London: Open University Press.

Hay J. (2011). E-supervision: Application, benefits and consideration, in Bachkirova T., Jackson P. & Clutterbuck D. (Eds.), *Coaching and Mentoring Supervision: Theory and Practice* (239–248), Maidenhead: Open University Press.

Haynes R., Corey G., & Moulton P. (2003). *Clinical Supervision in the Helping Professions: A Practical Guide*. Pacific Grove, CA: Brooks/Cole.

Heidegger M. (1962). *Being and Time*. Translated by Macquarrie J. & Robinson E., Oxford: Blackwell.

Heidegger M. (2001). *Zollikon Seminars. Protocols-Conversations-Letters*. Edited by M. Boss. Translated by Askay R. & Mayr F., Evanston, Il: Northwestern University Press.

Holloway E. L. (1995). *Clinical Supervision: A Systems Approach*. London: Sage.

Hoogendijk A. (1991). *Spreekuur bij een Filosoof*, Ultrecht: Veen.

Horvath A. O. (2006). The alliance in context: Accomplishments, challenges, and future directions. *Psychotherapy: Theory, Research, Practice, Training, 43*(3), 258–263.

Horvath A. O. & Greenberg L. S. (1989). Development and validation of the Working Alliance Inventory. *Journal of Counseling Psychology, 36*, 223–233.

Horvath A. O. & Symonds, B. D. (1991). Relation between working alliance and outcome in psychotherapy: A meta-analysis. *Journal of Counseling Psychology, 38*(2), 139–149.

Hunt D. E. (1978). Theorists are persons, too: On preaching what you practice. In C. Parker (Ed.), *Encouraging Student Development in College*, Minneapolis: University of Minnesota Press.

Husserl E. (1970). *The Crisis of European Sciences and Transcendental Phenomenology*, Evanston: Northwestern University Press.

Husserl E. (1973). Phenomenology. In Zaner R. M. and Ihde D. (Eds.), *Phenomenology and Existentialism* (pp. 46–70), New York: G. P. Putnam's Sons.

Husserl E. (1982). *Ideas Pertaining to a Pure Phenomenology and to a Phenomenological Philosophy: First Book, General Introduction to a Pure Phenomenology*. (F. Kersten, Trans.), Boston: Kluwer Academic.

Husserl E. (2006). *The Basic Problems of Phenomenology: From the Lectures, Winter Semester, 1910–1911*. Translated by Farin Ingo & James G. Hart, Dordrecht: Springer.

Hycner R. H. (1999). Some guidelines for the phenomenological analysis of interview data. In Bryman, A. & Burgess, R. G. (Eds.), *Qualitative Research* (Vol. 3, pp. 143–164). London: Sage.

Inskipp F. & Proctor B. (1993). The Art, craft and tasks of Counselling supervision. In *Part 1: Making the Most of Supervision*, Cascade Publications.

Inskipp F. & Proctor B. (1995). *Part 2: Becoming a Supervisor*, Cascade Publications.

International Coach Federation (ICF). (n.d.). https://coachfederation.org/coaching-supervision. Accessed 5 December 2020.

Itzhaky H. & Itzhaky T. (1996). The therapy-supervision dialectic. *Clinical Social Work Journal, 24*, 77–88. https://doi.org/10.1007/BF02189943

Jacob Y. (2019). *An Introduction to Existential Coaching*, Abingdon: Routledge

Jaspers K. (1955). *Reason and Existenz*. Translated by W. Earle, New York: Noonday Press.

Johner P. Burgi D & Langle A. (2018). *Existential Leadership zum Erfolg, Philosophie und praxis der Transformation*, Freiberg: Haufe.

Jones A. (1998). Out of the sighs: An existential-phenomenological method of clinical supervision: the contribution to palliative care, *Journal of Advanced Nursing, 27*, 905–913.

Kaufmann W. (1956). *Existentialism from Dostoevsky to Sartre*, West Midlands: Meridian Books.

Kelle U. (1995). Introduction: An overview of computer-aided methods in qualitative research. In Kelle, U. (Ed.), *Computer-Aided Qualitative Data Analysis: Theory, Methods and Practices*, London: Sage.

Kelly G. (1963). *A Theory of Personality*, New York: Norton.

Kemp T. (2008). Self-management and the coaching relationship: Exploring coaching impact beyond models and methods. *International Coaching Psychology Review, 3*(1), 32–40.

Kierkegaard S. (1844). *The Concept of Anxiety*, Princeton, NJ: Princeton University Press.

Kierkegaard S. (1981). *Kierkegaard's Writings, VIII: Concept of Anxiety: A Simple Psychologically Orienting Deliberation on the Dogmatic Issue of Hereditary Sin* (New ed.), Princeton, NJ: Princeton University Press.

Kierkegaard S. (1985). *Fear and Trembling*, London: Penguin Classics.

Kierkegaard S. (1992). *Either/Or. A Fragment of Life*, London: Penguin.

Kierkegaard S. (2018). *The Sickness until Death*, Knutsford, Cheshire: A&D Publishing.

Kierkegaard S., Hong H.V. Hong E. H., & Malantscuk G. (1967). *Soren Kierkegaard's Journals and Papers, Part 1: Autobiographical, 1829--1848*, Bloomington: Indiana University Press.

Kivlighan D. M. Jr. (2007). Where is the relationship in research on the alliance? Two methods for analyzing dyadic data. *Journal of Counseling Psychology, 54*(4), 423–433.

Kohlberg L. (1969). 'Stage and sequence: The cognitive-developmental approach to socialization, in D. Goslin (ed) *Handbook of Socialization Theory and Research*, Chicago: Rand McNally 347–480.

Krug O. T. & Schneider K. J. (2016). *Supervision Essentials for Existential-Humanistic Therapy*, Washington, DC: American Psychological Association.

Kruger D. (1988). *An introduction to phenomenological psychology* (2nd ed.), Cape Town, South Africa: Juta.

Laing R. D. (1970). *Knots*, Tavistock Publications Limited

Laing R. D. (2010). *The Divided Self*, London: Penguin.

Lambers E. (2000). Supervision in person centered therapy: Facilitating congruence. In *Person-Centered Therapy Today: New Frontiers in Theory and Practice* (196–211).

Lane D. (2011). Ethics and Professional Standards in Supervision, in Bachkirova T., Jackson P. & Clutterbuck D. (Eds.), *Coaching and Mentoring Supervision: Theory and Practice* (91–106), Maidenhead: Open University Press,

Längle A. (2011). *Sinnvoll Leben: Eine Praktische Anleitung der Logotherapie*, Residenz: Auflage.

Längle A. & Bürgi D. (2014). *Existentielles Coaching: Theoretische Orientierung, Grundlagen und Praxis für Coaching, Organisationsberatung und Supervision*, Vienna: Facultative Universitätsverlag.

Lasch, C. (1979). *The Culture of Narcissism: American Life in an Age of Diminishing Expectations*, New York: Norton.

Lee, G. (2003). *Leadership Coaching*, London: CIPD.

Leviathan D. (2014). *The Lover's Dictionary*, New York: Farrar, Straus and Giroux

Lewin K. (1935). *A Dynamic Theory of Personality*, New York: McGraw-Hill.

Li C. & Bernoff J. (2008). *Groundswell: Winning in a World Transformed by Social Technologies*, Boston, MA: Harvard Business Press.

Liese B. S. & Alford, B. A. (1998). Recent advances in cognitive therapy supervision. *Journal of Cognitive Therapy: An International Quarterly*, *12*, 91–94.

Liese B. S. & Beck J. S. (1997). Cognitive therapy supervision. In C. E. Watkins (Ed.), *Handbook of Psychotherapy Supervision* (pp. 114–133), Hoboken, NJ: Wiley.

Liese B. S., Barber J. & Beck A. T. (1995). *The Cognitive Therapy Adherence and Competence Scale*. Unpublished instrument. University of Kansas Medical Centre. Kansas City.

Lilliengren P. & Werbart, A. (2005). A model of therapeutic action grounded in the patients' view of curative and hindering factors in psychoanalytic psychotherapy. *Psychotherapy: Theory, Research, Practice, Training*, *42*(3), 324–339.

Linger W. (2020). *Supervision Coaching Supervision and Reflection*, https://www.youtube.com/watch?v=VLr3kBP3XOM&feature=youtu.be. Accessed 16.07.20.

Littrell J. M., Lee-Borden N., & Lorenz J. (1979). A developmental framework for counseling supervision. *Counselor Education and Supervision*, *19*(2), 129–136. https://doi.org/10.1002/j.1556-6978.1976.tb02021.x

Loevinger J. (1976). *Ego Development: Conceptions and Theories*, San Francisco: Jossey-Bass.

Loganbill C., Hardy E., & Delworth U. (1982). Supervision: A Conceptual Model. *Counseling Psychologist*, 10(1), 3–42.

Madison G. (2008). Futurist therapy. http://www.goodtherapy.org/custom/blog/2008/01/05/futurist-therapy-what-role-willtherapy-have-in-a-post-human-future/ Good Therapy. Featured Contributors.

Madison G. (2011). Evocative Supervision. In van Deurzen E. & Young S. (Eds.), *Existential Perspectives on Supervision*, London: Palgrave.

Manen M. (2014) *Phenomenology of Practice: Meaning-Giving Methods in Phenomenological Research and Writing*, California: Left Coast Press

Mangione L., Mears G., Vincent W., & Hawes S. (2011). The supervisory relationship when women supervise women: An exploratory study of power, reflexivity, collaboration, and authenticity. *Clinical Supervisor, 30*.

Masters E. L. (1915). *Spoon River Anthology*, New York: Macmillan.

May R. (1950). *The Meaning of Anxiety*, New York City: Roland Press.

May R. (1999). *Freedom and Destiny*, New York: W. W. Norton & Company.

McConnell-Henry T., Chapman Y., & Francis K. (2009). Husserl and Heidegger: Exploring the disparity. *International Journal of Nursing Practice*, *15*(1), 7–15.

Meara N. M., Schmidt L. D., & Day J. D. (1996). Principles and virtues: A foundation for ethical decisions, policies, and character. *Counseling Psychologist, 24*(91), 4–77.

Merleau-Ponty M. (2002). *Phenomenology of Perception*, London: Routledge.

Milne D. (2009). *Evidence-based Clinical Supervision: Principles and Practice*, 2012, Oxford: Wiley-Blackwell.

Mitchell D. (2002). Is the concept of supervision at odds with existential thinking and clinical practice? *Journal of Existential Analysis 13*(1), 91–97.

Moja Strasser L. (2009). Deliberations on supervision. In van Deurzen, E., & Young, S. (Eds.), *Existential Perspectives on Supervision*, Basingstoke, Hampshire: Palgrave McMillan.

Monroig M. (2017). https://prezi.com/iu6452k-muz1/feminist-psychotherapy-model-of-supervision/ Accessed 27.04.2020

Moustakas C. (1994). *Phenomenological Research Methods*, Thousand Oaks, CA: Sage.

Mumford A. (1993). *How Managers Can Develop Managers*, Hampshire, England: Gower Publishing.

Murphy M. J. & Wright, D. W. (2005). Supervisees' perspectives of power use in supervision. *Journal of Marital and Family Therapy*, 31.

Nelson M. L., Gizara S., Hope A. C., Phelps R., Steward R., & Weitzman L. (2006). A feminist multicultural perspective on supervision. *Journal of Multicultural Counseling and Development*, 34.

Nietzsche F. (1960). *The Will to Power*. Translated by Walter Kaufmann & R. J. Hollingdale, New York: Vintage Books (Random House). Written 1883–1888 in notebooks.

Nietzsche F. (1974). *The Gay Science*, New York City: Knopf Doubleday.

Nietzsche F. (2012). *The Gay Science*, Mineloa, New York: Dover Philosophical Classics

Palmer S & Turner E. (2018). *The Heart of Coaching Supervision (Essential Coaching Skills and Knowledge)* Abingdon: Routledge.

Passmore J. & Mortimer L. (2011). Ethics in coaching. In L. Boyce & G. Hernez-Broome (ed.), *Advanced Executive Coaching,* (pp205–228). San Francisco, CA: Jossey-Bass.

Peltier B. (2010). *The Psychology of Executive Coaching: Theory and Application,* New York: Routledge.

Perris C. (1993). Stumbling blocks in the supervision of cognitive psychotherapy. *Journal of Clinical Psychology and Psychotherapy,* 1, 29–43.

Perry W. G. (1968). *Forms of Intellectual and Ethical Development in the College Years: A Scheme.* New York: Holt, Rinehart & Winston.

Pett J. (1995). A personal approach to existential supervision. *Existential Analysis* 6(2), 117–26.

Piaget J. & Inhelder B. (1969). *The Psychology of the Child,* New York: Basic Books.

Pinder K. (2011). Group supervision. In Bachkirova T., Jackson P. & Clutterbuck D. (Eds.), *Coaching and Mentoring Supervision: Theory and Practice* (196–204), Maidenhead: Open University Press.

Polt R. (1999). *Heidegger an Introduction,* London: UCL Press.

Prior D. M. (2003). *Professional Coaching Language for Greater Public Understanding,* www.joannapirie.com/ Professional Coaching Languagefor.pdf. Accessed 17 November 2019.

Purton C. (2004). *Person-Centred Therapy: The Focusing-Oriented Approach,* London: Palgrave Macmillan.

Proctor B. (2008) *Group Supervision: A Guide to Creative Supervision,* London: Sage

Rank O. (2003). *The Trauma of Birth,* London: Textbook Publishers.

Ray A. (2015). *Mindfulness: Living in the Moment, Living in the Breathe,* Atlanta: Inner Light Publishers.

Remley Jr., T P. & Herlihy B. P. (2000). *Ethical, Legal, and Professional Issues in Counseling,* London: Pearson.

Rest J. R. (1986). *Moral Development: Advances in Research and Theory,* New York: Prager.

Rogers, C. R. (1951). *Client Centered Therapy,* London: Constable and Company.

Ronnestad M. H. & Skovolt T. M. (1993). Supervision of beginning and advanced graduate students of counseling and psychotherapy. *Journal of Counseling and Development,* 71, 396–405.

Ronnestad M. H. & Skovholt T. M. (2003). The journey of the counselor and therapist: Research findings and perspectives on professional development. *Journal of Career Development, 30,* 5–44.

Sadala M. L. A. & de Adorno R. C. F. (2001). Phenomenology as a method to investigate the experiences lived: A perspective from Husserl and Merleau-Ponty's thought. *Journal of Advanced Nursing, 37*(3), 282–293.

Sartre J.-P. (1943). *Les Mouches,* Paris: Gallimard.

Sartre J.-P. (1948). *Anti-semite and Jew,* New York: Schocken Press.

Sartre J-P. (1958). *Being and Nothingness: An Essay on Phenomenological Ontology.* Translated by Hazel E. Barnes. London: Methuen.

Sartre J-P. (1963). *Search for a Method.* Translated from the French by Hazel E. Barnes, NY: Vintage Books (A Division of Random House).

Sartre J.-P. (1996) *Existential Psychoanalysis,* Washington: Gateway Editions

Sartre J.-P. (2004). *Sketch for a Theory of the Emotions,* London: Routledge.

Sartre J-P. (2007). *Existentialism is Humanism* (new ed.), Grantham, North Yorkshire: Methuen Publishing Ltd.

Scheler M. (1970). *The Nature of Sympathy.* Translated by Heath Peter, New York: Archon Books

Schunk D. H. & Zimmerman B. J. (2003). Self-regulation and learning. In Reynolds W. M. & Miller G. E. (Eds.), *Handbook of Psychology: Educational Psychology* (Vol. 7, pp. 59–78). London: Wiley.

Sherman G. L. (2009). Martin Heidegger's concept of authenticity: A philosophical contribution to student affairs theory. *Journal of College and Character, 10,* 7, DOI: 10.2202/1940-1639.1440

Skinner B. F. (1953). *Science and Human Behavior.* London: Macmillan.

Skovhot T. N. & Ronnestaf M. H. (1992). Themes in therapist and Counselor Development. *Journal of Counseling & Development 70,* 467–552.

Solomon R. C. (1993). *The Passions: Emotions and the Meaning of Life,* Indianapolis, IN: Hackett Publishing Co.

Solomon R.C. (1993) The Philosophy of Emotions. In Lewis M. and Haviland J.M. (eds.), *Handbook of Emotions,* New York: Guildford Press

Somerville M. (2006). *The Ethical Imagination,* Toronto, Canada: House of Anansi Press.

Spinelli E. (2005). *The Interpreted World: An Introduction to Phenomenological Psychology,* London: Sage.

Spinelli E. (2007). *Practicing Existential Psychotherapy,* London: Sage.

Spurgeon C. H. (2015). *The Complete Sermons of C.H. Spurgeon: Book 1 (Vol. 1-3),* Morrisville, NC: Lulu.com.

Stein E. (2008) [1917]. *Zum Problem der Einfühlung* (Gesamtausgabe Bd. 5), Freiburg: Verlag Herder.

Stoltenberg C. D. & Delworth, U. (1987). *Supervising Counselors and Therapists.* San Francisco, CA: Jossey-Bass.

Stoltenberg C. D. & McNeill B. W. (2009). *IDM Supervision: An Integrative Developmental Model for Supervising Counselors and Therapists,* London: Routledge.

Stoltenberg C. D., McNeill B. W., & Crethar H. C. (1994). Changes in supervision as counselors and therapists gain experience: A review. *Professional Psychology: Research & Practice,* 25, 416–449.

Stones C. R. (1988). Research: Toward a phenomenological praxis. In Kruger, D. (Ed.), *An Introduction to Phenomenological Psychology* (2nd ed., pp. 141–156). Cape Town, South Africa: Juta.

Strasser F. (2005). *Emotions: Experiences in Existential Psychotherapy and Life,* London: Duckworth.

Strasser F. & Strasser A. (1997). *Existential Time-Limited Therapy,* Chichester West Sussex: Wiley.

Szymanski D. M. (2003). The feminist supervision scale: A rational/theoretical approach. *Psychology of Women Quarterly,* 27, 221–232.

Szymanski D. M. (2005). Feminist identity and theories as correlates of feminist supervision practices. *Counseling Psychologist,* 33, 729–747.

Tillich P. (1952). *'The Courage to Be',* New Haven: Yale University Press

Tolstoy L. (1915). *War and Peace* (Vol. 1), London: Dent.

Trevino L. K. & Nelson K. A. (1999). *Managing Business Ethics,* London: Wiley.

Unger D. Core problems in clinical supervision: Factors related to outcomes. In Friedlander M. L. (Chair), *Psychotherapy Supervision: For Better or for Worse.* Symposium conducted at the 107th Annual Convention of the American Psychological Association, Boston, MA. (1999).

van Manen M. (1997). From meaning to method. *Qualitative Health Research,* 7(3), 345–369.

Velasquez M., Andre C., Shanks T. & Meyer M. S. J. (2005). *Can Ethics be Taught?* Linked from the Ethics Home Page, Santa Clara University, www.scu.edu/ethics/practicing/decision/canethicsbetaught.htl. Accessed 26 September 2020.

Vallack J. (2021). *Changing Art into Research: Soliloquy Methodology* Abingdon, Oxon: Routledge.

van Deurzen E. (1988). *Existential Counselling in Practice* (2nd ed. 2002), London: Sage.

van Deurzen E. (1998). *Paradox and Passion in Psychotherapy,* Chichester: Wiley.

van Deurzen E. (2001). *Existential Counselling and Psychotherapy in Practice* (2nd ed.), London: Sage.

van Deurzen E. & Arnold-Baker C. (2005). *Existential Perspectives on Human issues,* Basingstoke, Hampshire: Palgrave MacMillan.

van Deurzen E. & Hanaway M. (2012). *Existential Perspectives in Coaching,* Basingstoke, Hampshire: Palgrave MacMillan.

van Deurzen E. & Kenward K. (2005). *Dictionary of Existential Psychotherapy and Counselling,* London: Sage.

van Deurzen E. & Young S. (2009). *Existential Perspectives on Supervision,* Basingstoke, Hampshire: Palgrave McMillan.

van Deurzen-Smith E. (1987). *Everyday Mysteries,* London: Routledge.

van Deurzen-Smith E. (1997). *Everyday Mysteries: Existential Dimensions of Psychotherapy,* London: Routledge.

van Manen, M. (1990). *Researchig Lived Experience: Human Science for an Action Sensitive Pedagogy,* Albany, NY: SUNY.

van Manen, M. (2002). *Inquiry: The Evocative Turn: Nearness.* http://www.phenomenologyonline.com/inquiry/20.html. Accessed 15 April 2008

Vandenberg D. (1997). *Phenomenology and Education Discourse,* Johannesburg, SA: Heinemann.

Vasudevan S. (2015). *Multidisciplinary Management of Chronic Pain: A Practical Guide for Clinicians,* Milwaukee, WI: Springer.

De Villiers A. & de L'Isle-Adam V. (2000). *Tomorrow's Eve,* Champaign, IL: University of Illinois Press.

Vos J. (2018). *Meaning in Life,* London: McMillan.

Walsh R. A. & McElwain B. (2002). Existential psychotherapies, in Cain D. J. & Seeman J. (Eds.), *Humanistic Psychotherapies: Handbook of Research and Practice* (253–78), Washington, DC: American Psychological Association.

Watkins C. E. Jr. (2012). Psychotherapy supervision in the new millennium: Competency-based, evidence-based, particularized, and energized. *Contemporary Psychotherapy,* 42, 193–203 DOI 10.1007/s10879-011-9202-4

Watkins C. Jr. & Milne D. L. (Eds.). (2014). *The International Handbook of Clinical Supervision,* West Sussex, UK: Wiley Blackwell.

Weiner K. C. (2007). *The Little Book of Ethics for Coaches: Ethics, Risk Management and Professional Issues,* Bloomington, IN: Authorhouse.

Weixel-Dixon K. (2016). *Interpersonal Conflict,* Abingdon: Routledge.

Weixel-Dixon K. (2020). *Existential Group Counselling and Psychotherapy,* Abingdon: Routledge.

Welman J. C., & Kruger S. J. (1999). *Research Methodology for the Business and Administrative Sciences.* Johannesburg, South Africa: International Thompson

Werner, H. (1978). *Developmental Processes: Heinz Werner's Selected Writings.* Editef by S. S. Barlen & M. B. Franklin, New York: International Universities Press.

Whitmore J. (2003). *Coaching for Performance.* London: Nicholas Brearley.

Whybrow A. & Palmer S. (2006). 'Taking stock: A survey of Coaching Psychologists' practices and perspectives'. *International Coaching Psychology Review 1*(1), 56–70.

Williams H., Wright M., & Evans T. (1993). *A Reader in International Relations and Political Theory,* Vancouver, Canada: UBC Press.

Williams P. & Anderson S. K. (2006). *Law and Ethics in Coaching: How to Solve- and Avoid-Difficult Problems in | Your Practice.*, Hoboken, NJ: Wiley.

Wright R. (1996). Another approach to existential supervision. *Journal of Existential Analysis,* 7 (1), 149–158.

Yalom I. D. (1980). *Existential Psychotherapy* (1st ed.), New York: Basic Books.

Yalom I. (2003) *The Gift of Therapy,* London: Piatkus

Zahavi D. (2010). Empathy, embodiment, and interpersonal understanding: Empathy from Lipps to Schutz. *Inquiry 55*(3), 285–306.

# INDEX

Note: Page numbers in *italics* indicate figures, **bold** indicate tables and page numbers with "n" indicates the end notes in the text.

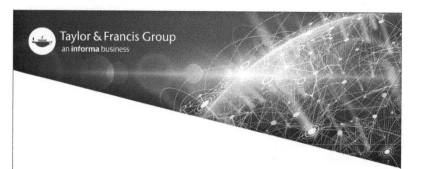